# THE TROUBLE WITH HER

## THE FORBIDDEN LOVE SERIES

### KAT T. MASEN

**Kat T. Masen**

**The Trouble With Her**

A Friends-to-Lovers Romance
**The Forbidden Love Series Book 4**

Copyright 2021 Kat T. Masen
All Rights Reserved

**Disclaimer:** The material in this book contains graphic language and sexual content and is intended for mature audiences, ages 18 and older.

**ISBN:** 979-8788264943

Editing by More Than Words Copyediting and Proofreading
Proofing by Nicki at Swish Design & Editing
Cover design by Outlined with Love Designs
Cover Image Copyright 2021
First Edition 2021
All Rights Reserved

*"She was wild. She was free.*
*Only a fool wouldn't love her." - Unknown*

# PROLOGUE

## ANDY

*Two years ago*

"Will you just stop and talk to me for a minute?" My hand is clutched around Jessa's bare arm, desperate for her to ease into my touch but instead, her muscles tense.

Inside my heated grip, she lowers her head to avoid my persistent stare while her chest rises and falls beneath the ivory laced dress she's wearing. Jessa's signature bronze curls fall to the side as she continues to remain silent. So much of me aches to reach out and tug on a strand, just as I have done a million times before. She hated it with a passion, even though I loved it.

But that was in the past when we were the best of friends, and when we couldn't go a day without talking to each other.

Then—it all changed between us.

I silently plead with her to look me in the eye, but the longer we stand here, the more she retreats. Almost as if she can't stand to be next to me.

"What would you like me to say?" Jessa questions in a dull tone.

I let go of her arm, running my hands through my hair in frustration. No matter how it plays in my mind, I don't understand how we got here. How two people who have been in each other's lives since they were kids can stand here unable to communicate maturely.

"How about you begin with the truth? Why you left home."

Around us, the music is blaring as Eric insists on going back to an era I don't care for. However, the oldies seem to enjoy it, laughing while drinking copious amounts of alcohol. My mother is the worst offender, singing out loud to then accidentally spilling her glass of red wine all over Eric's patent white leather shoes.

I wait for Eric's dramatic outburst, but he's so far gone even to notice.

If anyone was going to throw a party like this, of course, it had to be Ava. Given it's her wedding day, our families are having the time of their lives. Most of them are drunk or in a food coma from the banquet served at dinner.

As usual, the only one who appears to be in control is Uncle Lex. Somehow, he got babysitting duty, though it looks like he's enjoying his time with Ashton and Emmy.

Everyone is in the best of spirits, adding to the occasion of it being New Year's Eve.

All but the person with a massive chip on her shoulder.

"God, Andy." Jessa throws her hands up in the air. "Why do we have to go over this? I left because I wanted more. Believe it or not, there's more than just LA."

I cross my arms in defiance. "Yeah, I know, that's why I moved to Manhattan."

"Exactly, you moved away, so why is it a problem that I did too?"

How can I tell her the problem is how she left? We had a big fight, and the next minute, she packed her bags to rediscover herself supposedly. Jessa didn't care how I felt about her, despite trying to communicate my feelings. Instead, when I found the courage to say anything, she pushed me away before I could even get my words out like she sensed what I was going to say before I said it.

"God, Jessa!" I yell, then bite down to control my anger, cautious of our family overhearing. "You walked away from us like we were nothing. Then you don't talk to me for months, and suddenly, you're back? Oh, but let's not forget that I found out you were engaged to be married through Alexa, of all people."

Slowly, her gaze lifts until her eyes meet mine. For the longest time, the light hazel orbs brought me comfort, laughter, and a sense of security in a world full of uncertainty.

But now, they belong to a stranger.

"I wanted to tell you in person," she admits, her voice low. "But it didn't seem right to call you out of the blue and announce such a thing."

All this hurts more than I care to admit. The pain runs deep, but I suppress it like everything else I can't control— my biological father's death and the dreams which still plague me when I see his face even though I never knew him. According to Mom, we only had ten days together, and in those days, he managed to hold me only once. His fragile body was too far deteriorated even to cradle a newborn baby.

The only person I ever confided in about these dreams was the very person standing in front of me. The only person I trusted with these thoughts of mine.

There's no changing Jessa's mind. She ran away and fell in love with some British man who, according to Alexa, is the perfect prince charming—rich and handsome.

The same kind of guy Jessa and I would make fun of all the time.

"You're right," I tell her, still keeping my gaze fixed. "It would've been weird to call me out of nowhere. But what doesn't make sense is you getting married? We made fun of guys like this, and you, out of all people, thought marriage was a ridiculous notion."

"I'm not the same person you once knew, Andy..." she trails off.

"No, you're not, Jessa," I responded hastily. "Because the girl I knew wouldn't have run off on her own. She would've begged me to pack my bag and abandon my responsibilities, so we could chase cheese rolling down a hill in Gloucester."

She drops her gaze, unable to look at me any longer. My eyes gravitate toward the diamond ring sitting on her finger. It's big and no doubt an expensive piece of jewelry, all the things Jessa never cared for until Prince Charming rode his horse and carriage in.

Yet, it represents everything another man offers—a life together, marriage, a possible family—all the things I'll never be able to give her because the timing was never on our side.

Not when we're family.

And being romantically linked is something her father wouldn't approve of.

"Tell me, Jessa. What does Noah think of this?"

"My father is fine."

I cock my head, releasing a disturbing laugh with my gaze shifting to Noah on the dance floor with Rocky. "Really? He doesn't look fine since he's trashed tonight, and Kate is trying to get him to sober up."

Jessa crosses her arms beneath her chest. "What are you getting at? My father has no choice. I love Benedict and will fight for him if I have to."

My stomach hardens, the hurt rippling to every part of

me at her willingness to fight for another man—the words, sharp like a knife, cut deep into an already open wound.

Jessa will fight for a man she's known for five minutes.

But what we have built over a lifetime is over in a *heartbeat*.

"Well, I guess you've gotten everything you want," I say, ignoring the tightness inside my chest. "Happy New Year, Jessa."

I don't linger. Just standing beside her is too unbearable, needing anything to numb the pain. Anything at all.

With wide steps, I hit up the makeshift bar in Uncle Lex's patio. The bartender responsible for serving the liquor kindly asks what I'd like to drink.

"Fireballs, make it a tray."

Beside me, a body knocks into me. I turn briefly to see Millie as she rubs her pregnant stomach.

"Fireballs, uh oh," she mentions, then releases a sigh. "What happened, Andy?"

I shake my head as my lips curl. "Nothing, nothing at all. She's getting married to some British playboy, and that's it."

"I'm sorry, Andy. I don't know what she's thinking. Both me and Ava are surprised this happened. We had no idea she was even seeing someone."

"Well, now everyone knows."

I take the glass in my hand, then throw it back. The cinnamon-flavored liquor burns for just a moment, but I don't stop there.

"Andy, maybe you should slow down. If you want to go somewhere..."

I drown out Millie's words with another shot, this drink less potent.

"You know what I want?" I tell her with a rasp in my throat. "I want to get out of here."

"Sure, of course, but is it safe for you to drive? How much have you had to drink?"

"I'm fine."

"Look, Andy. I know you're angry but don't bullshit me. How much have you had to drink? Because I'm not allowing you to drive anywhere like this."

Again, I refuse to listen and throw back another drink. Then, just when I think Millie's silence means she'll leave me alone, I see her motion to Dad to come over.

*Great.*

I let out an annoyed huff, throwing back another as he places his hand on my shoulder. "I'll take you home, son."

"You want to take me somewhere? Fine. But not home. Take me to Melrose."

"Why Melrose?" Millie questions.

"Any club where I can find a woman to make me forget tonight ever happened."

Millie looks at Dad, but he doesn't say anything, and I don't expect him to. He doesn't involve himself unless he feels his opinion is of value, unlike Millie, who in many ways is just like my overbearing mother.

"If that's what you want, I'll take you," Dad informs me.

Across the patio, Jessa is dancing with Ava and Luna. Her body moves freely with a permanent smile and an occasional break into laughter.

But then, as if she senses me staring, her gaze shifts and the smile on her face disappears. I can work it in my head in so many ways and assume the furrowed brows and drooping shoulders express the hurt she feels. Maybe the downturned mouth and pained expression is the regret over how she handled us.

No matter how I break it down, it all comes down to this.

Jessa Bentley-Mason is marrying someone else.

And there's not a goddamn thing I can do about it.

# ONE

## JESSA

*Present*

My finger runs across the tips of the soft white petals.

The beautiful arrangement of flowers sits in the large gold vase, centered on the table in the middle of the foyer. It's a family heirloom, handed down to us on our wedding day by Benedict's great aunt. There's a story behind the vase, something about it being gifted by a great love on a birthday, only for tragedy to strike the next day. When it was given to us, I smiled and pretended it wasn't cursed, and we were honored to receive a beautiful antique on the day we became husband and wife.

A wedding day which feels like a lifetime ago.

In reality, it was just over a year ago when Benedict and I stood in the gardens of his parents' manor and said 'I do' in front of our family and friends.

The ceremony and reception were a grand affair with Benedict's family, friends, and business associates in attendance. Many of them reside here in England, but a few flew in from Spain and Germany.

As for me, I chose to keep my guest list small, especially because everyone lived in the States. Dad, Kate, Nash, and Sienna were the first to arrive, followed by Mom and my stepfather, Jack. My half-brother, Michael, and his wife came with their two kids, which I welcomed since it's been a while since I last saw him.

Despite my blended family, it worked without the drama. I think it has a lot to do with Kate. She's the glue holding us all together because Dad and Mom weren't exactly the best of friends. If anything, Kate and Mom were a lot closer.

Uncle Lex and his entire family also flew over, along with Rocky and Nikki. Eric and Tristan came, choosing to vacation on the Greek Islands afterward. Considering it was our honeymoon destination also, it was awkward when we ran into Eric wearing a gold thong.

Some things you'll *never* be able to unsee.

And lastly, the Baker family also attended. All but one person.

No one dared to bring up his name, and why should they? Andy and I were never an item. We'd kissed once, and even then, it was done out of anger the night of Austin and Ava's wedding.

A kiss I've long buried because I'm married to Benedict Banks.

"Mrs. Banks." Our nanny, Eliza, walks down the stairs with a relaxed baby in her arms. "Bentley is ready for his mother now."

My lips curve upward at the sight of my baby boy.

Bentley Benedict Banks is a surprise baby courtesy of our honeymoon. We talked about kids, but I wanted to pursue my career in journalism before taking on the responsibility of a child. So, just before our wedding, I lined up an interview with a reputable magazine in London.

But I guess life had other plans.

Two blue lines changed everything.

The moment we announced I was pregnant, Benedict's mother, Rosemarie, insisted I stay home and start preparing for my role. In ways, it made sense until I found out I wouldn't be alone.

Rosemarie hired Eliza to be Bentley's full-time nanny. At the time, he wasn't even born. Yet they planned out everything, despite my arguing I could raise my son without hired help. But according to Rosemarie, this isn't the Banks way. Nannies raised Benedict and his two brothers, and according to her, it's important for a wife to complete her role and not get caught up in tedious tasks like changing diapers.

I argued until I was blue in the face, causing a lot of tension between Benedict and me. On top of adjusting to being married, we were dealing with trying to figure out how to be parents. However, once again, his mother's word held weight, something which is happening more often of late.

Extending out my arms, I reach out for my son. "Come here, beautiful boy."

Bentley's deep hazel eyes light up with his curly hair brushed perfectly to the side. I run my hands over it, wishing to grow it out into ringlets so I can tie it in a man bun. Rosemarie would have a coronary.

"Are you ready to have lunch with Grandpa and Nanna Kate?"

His chubby little hand touches my face, and I grab it, then blow raspberry kisses to make him laugh. My heart does a joyous song and dance at the sound of his infectious laughter, a simple thing making life all the more beautiful.

With Bentley in my arms, dressed in his cute little sailor onesie, we walk through the main foyer to the back patio, where the housekeeper has set up a table for lunch. The spot has the most glorious view of the gardens and the rolling green hills in the distance. It's a picturesque view I've become fond of while sitting outside in solitude, enjoying a coffee.

The English countryside is beautiful, and although we reside in this home, we also have a flat in London which Benedict uses during the week to make the commute easier for work.

Above us, the blue sky weaves in and out of the hovering clouds. The air is cool as we begin the fall season, though the English prefer to call it autumn. I choose to wear a white blazer over the blush-colored tunic dress underneath, matching the outfit with stylish tan pumps.

Behind me, someone clears their throat. I turn around to see our housekeeper, Lucy.

"Mrs. Banks, your father and stepmother are here."

The word stepmother is so formal as I often introduce Kate as my mom, even though we're more like sisters at times.

"Please welcome them in," I tell her.

Moments later, Dad and Kate walk through the back patio doors. Kate extends her arms with a beaming smile, looking as beautiful as ever. Her blonde hair is cut into a short bob sitting just below her chin. My eyes are drawn to the white pantsuit with oversized gold buttons. Beneath the jacket, her royal blue blouse is barely visible, only her cleavage, which is full and perky considering she's not exactly twenty-one anymore.

"Jessa," she calls, then pulls me into an embrace. "Oh, how I've missed you."

Trying not to squash Bentley, I pull back for her to scoop him up in her arms and make all these cooing sounds. A smile falls upon my lips as I watch them, wishing we lived closer so they could spend more time together—the only drawback of living so far away.

Taking a deep breath, the air thickens as I turn to face Dad, who's keeping his distance.

Growing up with Noah Mason as your father wasn't as easy as some may think. Much like my cousins—Millie, Ava, Addy, and Alexa—an incredibly wealthy and supposedly handsome father came with challenges. People treated us differently because our fathers held power, and they were known to be ruthless in the corporate world, which is why they got to where they are.

But at home, surrounded by family, my father *was* a kind and loving man.

He supported my decisions for most of my life, and I've rarely felt trapped by his stubborn ways. Dad never questioned my college choice or my career. Instead, he encouraged me to spread my wings when it came to moving out. Overall, we had a great relationship until I met Benedict.

The thing is, I've had boyfriends, though nothing serious.

And the moment I announced my engagement to Benedict, Dad completely changed. He became cold and distanced himself. He wasn't happy, that much I knew, especially because I was moving to England permanently.

I'm surprised he walked me down the aisle because he had refused initially, and so Uncle Lex was asked, but at the last minute, Dad came around. I'm not sure whether it was Kate or Aunt Charlie's influence. Either way, it made the day complete.

Since then, our relationship has been strained.

Not wanting to feed into his stubborn persona, I stretch out my arms and go in for a quick hug in which he doesn't linger.

"Nice to see you, Dad," is all I say.

"And you, Jessa."

It's all too formal, but then again, Benedict's family is as formal as you can get, so I'm growing accustomed to this lifestyle. God forbid anyone is affectionate or shows their human side.

"Take a seat, please," I tell them both.

Kate sits beside Dad as he softens his expression when Bentley reaches out to him. I watch as Dad succumbs, taking Bentley in his arms with a smile on his face. Without drawing attention, I pretend to be admiring the view of the gardens but secretly watch Bentley with his grandpa. It's obvious Noah Mason still has a heart, just not when it comes to his eldest daughter.

"The gardens look amazing, Jessa. I miss the English countryside."

"It's beautiful," I say wistfully. "But so is your place in Malibu. I can't recall when I went to the beach last, aside from my honeymoon. I miss the sound of waves crashing against the shoreline."

Kate breaks out into laughter. "Oh, with Eric and the gold thong."

"Don't start. It still haunts me to this day," I complain while cringing. "So, tell me, how long are you here for?"

"It's a business trip, of course. Noah has meetings most of our time here, which is why this is the only time I could get him to take a break." Kate side-eyes Dad, looking overly annoyed. "About a week."

"And Sienna?"

"We left her in our flat in London. I'm pretty certain she's going to text any minute because she hit her credit card limit and needs money."

I smile, remembering the years of being a teenager. Sienna is a junior in college now, and her whole life revolves around fashion which is why she and Adriana get along so well. Back home, her wardrobe is massive but being the baby of the family, no one can say no to her.

Lucy brings out lunch and a bottle of wine to complement the meal. We talk about what's happening back home, but for most of the conversation, Dad is quiet, playing with Bentley and avoiding me. Bentley is giggling at Dad's sounds but becomes distracted when he notices the food. He reaches out for some fruit, so I pass him a small piece of banana.

"It sounds like it's all baby-making in LA. I can't believe both Millie and Ava are pregnant at the same time. Actually, I can't believe Millie fell pregnant again. Three kids under five, she must be crazy."

"She's Charlie." Kate grins. "It was hard enough being pregnant one time. I bow down to any woman who can go more than once."

"And Ava? I mean, I never thought she was the family type and wanted more kids after Emmy."

"Things change, and Austin is so great with Emmy."

I nod, thinking about my cousins. Despite both Will and Austin having demanding careers, they're both hands-on fathers, according to Kate. To be honest, I'd not expect any less from either of them—they adore their wives and are family-oriented. It makes me think about Benedict and how him being raised by hired help differs his views from mine.

With our family so big and the group chats out of control, I can barely keep up these days. Most of the time, I mute the conversations because they're nonstop over something random like the best sushi place in LA to gossip over who's sleeping with who. Occasionally, I'll make an appearance, but even then, I feel like an outsider being across the world.

Kate takes a sip of her wine with a pleased expression. "How is Benedict? He's not able to join us?"

"He's in Milan for work, back tomorrow."

"Benedict has been traveling a bit for work. How are you coping alone?" Kate questions, yet the second it escapes her lips, her eyebrows gather in with slight regret.

My eyes lift to Dad as he watches me with an unrelenting stare.

"I'm used to it now," I admit, distracting myself with drinking some wine. "I take Bentley for his daily walk, and I'm getting a lot of reading done."

My father clears his throat, but not in a good way. I wait for the judgmental comment, which will ruin our somewhat amicable lunch.

"And your writing?" he questions smugly.

"Well, I don't write since I don't have a job. I figured reading would be the next best thing."

I can see the judgment in his eyes, but is an argument even worth it? My eyes shift to Bentley, and for the sake of him, I bite my tongue.

"So, aside from that, is everything else okay?" Kate quickly intervenes, which is what she does best when things get heated between Dad and me.

"Yes, of course. Why wouldn't it be?"

"Just checking in," she concurs, then relaxes her shoulders. "When I first moved to France, it seemed like the most amazing thing, but the novelty soon wore off, although I was in denial at the time. Living my so-called best life with no one by my side."

"France is beautiful."

"It is, and you know you're welcome to use the chateau at any time."

"Thank you. It's hard to get away. I don't like leaving Bentley, and Benedict has a busy schedule. In addition, his company is launching some new buildings, so trying to get him to even sit down for dinner can be hard at times."

Bentley squirms in Dad's arms, fussing while rubbing his eyes.

I quickly check my phone. "He's due for his afternoon nap. I can call Eliza over to put him to sleep."

"Give the nanny a rest. I want to rock my grandbaby to sleep." Kate takes Bentley off Dad's lap, then stands up with him in her arms. They both walk away as Kate sings a song, leaving the tumbleweed to pass by as Dad and I sit alone in silence for what feels like an eternity.

"How's work?" I ask.

"Busy," he manages. "Lex and I have some projects in Singapore, so traveling too. Much like your *husband*."

And there it is—the judgment he just can't seem to hold back.

"Why did you say husband like that?" I ask, annoyed.

"Just pointing out what you mentioned."

I throw my napkin on the table, frustrated while I cross my arms beneath my chest.

"Just spit it out, whatever it is you want to say."

Dad purses his lips, keeping his expression at bay.

"I have nothing to say, Jessa. But, perhaps, you have a lot to say?"

"Yes, well, let me guess. You think I made the wrong decision by marrying Benedict. I don't know how you can even say that. Without him, you wouldn't have a grandson."

Dad wipes the corner of his mouth with his napkin. Then, places it gently on the table. His hazel eyes pierce into me, but behind them, I struggle to see the loving man who I once admired.

"You're a grown woman, and these choices you have made are your choices. My opinion may vary, but in the end, it's your life, just as you reminded me on your wedding day."

I shake my head, knowing exactly what he thinks.

"I'm happy, okay? So, I don't live in the States anymore, and so what if I don't have a job. I have a husband who loves me, a son I adore, and this beautiful house to call home. What more could I want?"

His merciless stare doesn't waver until Kate walks back outside without Bentley.

"That was quick. The poor little fella was asleep in my arms by the time I got to his room." Her glance darts between Dad and me. "I'm sorry, did I interrupt something?"

Dad rises from his chair. "No, in fact, your timing is perfect. I need to head into town."

We walk in silence to the front of the property. Dad nods goodbye, unable to even say the words, then enters the black Mercedes parked out front.

Kate places her hands on my arms, clutching them with assurance.

"We're still here for a few days. Can you come for lunch? Just us girls."

I nod, then smile back, ignoring the mixture of anger and guilt inside me.

Slowly, Kate raises her hand and touches a curl hanging near my cheek.

"Jessa, your father loves you. But he just misses you, okay? This distance thing is hard for him."

"It doesn't stop him from acting like a jerk."

"That's Noah, stubborn like the rest of the men in the family. I'll call you later, and we'll arrange something."

Kate kisses me goodbye, then enters the car. When the engine starts, she waves goodbye, but my father can't even look my way.

And then, before he takes off, he glances over.

No smile, no anger, just pity.

Turning my back, I enter the house, closing the door behind me. With my body resting against the large wooden door, I close my eyes for just a moment.

I can stand here and lie to myself, just like I lied straight to his face.

But the truth is—I'm miserable.

And the one person who can see right through my lies is the first man ever to own my heart.

I've always been a Daddy's girl.

Now, I'm his disappointment.

Maybe that's what bothers me the most. Everything he pointed out is exactly what I continue to bury.

I can paint this beautiful life I've built with Benedict, but in reality, most of the time is spent alone. Being alone isn't hard. It's the assumption no one cares about me.

But I wanted this life. I chose it.

So, there's no choice but to continue living this way because nothing in the world will change it.

No matter how much I can wish for things to be different.

# TWO

## JESSA

W hen I first traveled to London two years ago, I fell in love with the city.

London is breathtakingly beautiful, and there's something to be said about a place that can evoke so much emotion from you. It's one of those places with so much history. Wherever you visit, there's a story behind the old-time building or monument, and much like all the other tourists, I stood with wide eyes, absorbing the history in awe.

My fascination grew as the days carried on from taking a tour of Buckingham Palace, which took almost a day in itself, to walking down the streets and admiring the colored front doors of Notting Hill. As I took it all in, I realized how much I yearned to explore and fuel this part of me into my writing. Wherever I went, I carried the leather-bound journal my father gave me for Christmas the year before and jotted down my thoughts like diary entries to record the memorable moments.

Being alone for the first time in my life gave me ample time to do just that and discover what I wanted without the

"Oh, baby girl, you look like death." Kate frowns, rubbing her back. "Why don't you head back to the flat? Dad is in a meeting 'til late, so he won't interrupt you."

"Okay," is all Sienna can muster up.

Sienna grabs the keys off Kate, then waves goodbye without even the energy to say the words aloud. With our meals finished, Kate suggests heading over to a café that serves amazing coffee.

As soon we step into the quaint little place, the aroma is like heaven on earth. I've always had a fondness for caffeine, but nothing compares to European coffee.

"God, I miss this coffee. The stuff in the States tastes like ass compared to this," Kate complains while blowing the steam away from her cup.

"I don't want to ask how you know what ass tastes like, but I'll assume it has everything to do with Eric."

"Of course, if anyone knows, it's him, right?"

We both laugh softly, then drink our coffees in relaxation.

"I miss this place so much. London will never leave you," she says wistfully.

"But you've moved so much, right? Manchester, London, Manhattan..."

"Always for work and, of course, to be with Noah."

"Moving across the world for Dad couldn't have been easy."

Kate smiles with ease. "Believe it or not, it was easy. I had no commitment and a fantastic boss. Noah, on the other hand, had two children who needed him in LA. I was willing to sacrifice myself over you and Nash losing time with Noah. Children need parents, and although Noah and Morgan were struggling to co-parent at the time, I'd never have asked Noah to pick me over his children."

"True love." I grin, admiring her selfless act to give Nash

and me a good upbringing. "Dad is crazy in love with you, and it's always shown."

Laughter escapes Kate. "It helps that I feel the same way about him, even though he can be a stubborn man sometimes."

My fingers trace the edge of the cup, not wanting to bring up my strained relationship with Dad but suspect Kate will bring it up anyhow.

"Jess," Kate calls softly, a nickname she sometimes called me as did the rest of my family. "It's just us girls now. Tell me how you're really doing?"

My stare shifts toward a couple at the table beside us. The man and woman are laughing, but judging by how they're sitting spaced apart, the relationship is purely platonic. She appears to be teasing him over the cake on his plate, in which his response comes out cheeky and light-hearted.

"I'm fine." I clear my throat, turning my attention back to Kate. "I mean, it gets lonely with Benedict constantly traveling, but Bentley keeps me busy."

"And when Benedict is home, how are things between the two of you?"

I shrug my shoulders. "I guess the honeymoon is over, right?"

Kate watches me intently, but her expression is soft without judgment.

"Honeymoons don't last forever, but the spark does, Jessa. Never forget that."

Right, the spark. I'm lucky if Benedict will even look at me the way he did before I became a mother to his child. The only intimate time we have together is in the bedroom, and even then, he takes what he wants and claims to be too tired to spend more than five minutes inside me.

I'm ashamed even to admit I constantly resort to taking

matters into my own hands, going as far as to discreetly purchase a little pink vibrator that's supposed to get you off in less than a minute. I don't know whether the sales pitch stuck with me or I'm that sexually charged. Either way, a five-star review from me.

But it wasn't always this way.

When I ran into Benedict on Oxford Street during what happened to be a torrential storm, he evoked emotions in me I never knew existed. Six foot tall, mouse-brown colored hair, and a smile which became my weakness. The two of us collided with him in his drenched business suit and me in my t-shirt and jeans.

I remember the day fondly, feeling incredibly homesick and wanting so much to hop on a plane to head back home.

*"I'm sorry."* The man clutched onto my arms to stop me from falling. *"How rude of me not to see where I was heading."*

*I wiped the rain from my face, then lifted my eyes and met his deep brown ones. Caught off guard by how handsome this man was, I was lost for words with the rain falling heavily upon us.*

*"Um, no. I should've been looking. This rain is..."*

*"Awful," he interrupted "And very England."*

*I laughed, despite being uncomfortable as my wet clothes clung to my skin.*

*"It's rained every day of all the seven days I've been here. How I miss the Californian sun."*

*"C'mon, let's get you dried up."*

*I don't know why I followed a stranger to the building just down the street. Albeit grand and luxurious, it was still a stranger's home.*

*As soon as we were inside and took the elevator up to the*

*penthouse suite, I quietly welcomed the shelter from the pelting rain.*

*"How rude of me not to introduce myself, I'm Benedict Banks, but you can call me your knight in shining armor."*

*With a cheeky grin, my heart beat faster than normal.*

*"Jessa Bentley-Mason, and you can call me the girl who's somewhat impressed with how high you think of yourself."*

*He placed his hand on his heart. "Ouch, hit a man where it hurts."*

*I scanned the room in which we stood. It was very grand and made the shoebox apartment I was staying in look exactly like that, a shoebox. "Wow, this place is something."*

*Benedict looked around. "I guess so, just a place to crash while I'm in town."*

*"Oh, you're not from here?"*

*"I live in the country. Come here during the week." He then left the room and came back with a towel. "Here, to dry off. You're welcome to use the bathroom if you'd like."*

*I stared into his eyes, not knowing what came over me. I grabbed his shirt and slammed my lips onto his. He was slightly taken aback but didn't stop, kissing me deeply before I pulled away out of breath.*

*And then, his stare turned delicious as he glanced at my breasts. Without a second thought, he removed my shirt over my head to leave me in my bra. I threw my arms around him, kissing him once again as we stumbled to the bedroom, where he took me on his king-size bed in the middle of the day.*

A slight stir between my legs causes me to cross them to relieve the memory. In my entire life, I'd never done anything so risky and bold, despite the numerous times I had wanted to.

"Oh?"

I hand him the coffee as he nods thank you while I sit on the leather across from him.

"Actually, it's not just my business proposal. It's a joint venture with Noah. We've invested in a string of boutique hotels in Europe. All of them are currently undergoing renovations."

"Boutique hotels are very in. I've photographed a few in my time."

"I know, which is why Noah and I would like to hire you to capture the essence of our brand in Europe. We're looking for something unique, up the game on our competitors."

"Europe? Um, okay," I say, barely able to stay awake, let alone take this all in. "What exactly do you have in mind?"

The moment the words escape me, Naomi, I think her name is, walks out of my room wearing my black buttoned shirt from last night. Her legs are exposed, causing Lex to drop his head with a smirk playing on his lips.

"Oh...I didn't realize you had company?" she stammers, pulling my shirt down, but it proves pointless.

"My uncle, Lex Edwards," I mention, then clear my throat, praying I got her name right. "Naomi."

"Nina."

*Fuck.*

"I'm sorry, I had a lot to drink," is all I say.

"Lex Edwards?" Her eyes widen as if she just remembered something. "Oh, God, I had no idea. But, um, I have to use the bathroom, so please just forget you ever met me."

She disappears, looking totally mortified.

I rub the back of my neck. "Sorry about that."

"No apology necessary. Perhaps I should call next time rather than catch you off guard?"

"Honestly, I don't even remember last night. It's been a while since I drank that much," I admit, then finish the rest of my coffee and let out a rasp. "One thing led to another, and then we ended up here."

Lex places his cup down, keeping his gaze fixed.

"I remember those days. Adriana used to call me early on purpose to piss me off."

"Of course, Mom would do that. So, it's normal, right? I mean, I'm not even thirty yet. It's not like I'm tied down to one woman."

"Life is whatever you make of it. I went through a very destructive phase, but in ways, it forced me to focus on my career to numb the pain."

"The pain?"

Lex purses his lips. "Of regretting decisions made in which you lost the woman you loved."

*Aunt Charlie, of course.*

On a few occasions, Lex mentions bits from his past, but when it comes to anything before Charlie was his wife, he chooses to keep those parts to himself. Thanks to Ava and her snooping ways back when we were teens, it was brought to my attention that Dad and Charlie were engaged at one point. Of course, all of it was in the past, so what do I care? Mom and Dad are happily married as are Lex and Charlie. Things worked out the way they needed to.

Unfortunately, my cousins had a fascination with the past. Millie wasn't too bad, but Ava was like some FBI agent trying to solve a murder mystery. However, over the last few years, motherhood and being a wife have matured her. It's funny how quickly things change, and we don't even realize.

"I guess those are the choices we make," I mumble with a lowered stare.

Silence falls over the room, and unlike my mother, Lex knows when to change the conversation if things get uncomfortable.

"How about you come to my office this afternoon? Noah

THE TROUBLE WITH HER

and Kate are back from Europe. The two of them can join us."

"So, this is official business?" I almost laugh. "Suit and tie?"

"You're a creative genius. No need to impress us. It's more to discuss the finer details and show you a presentation of what exactly we're doing."

"Sure," I tell him the moment Nina walks out, prompting Lex to stand up.

"It was nice meeting you, Nina."

"Um, and you, Mr. Edwards," she stumbles out.

Lex leaves the apartment, and as soon as the door closes, Nina lets out a groan to then slap my arm, causing me to wince.

"You could've warned me! Let alone get my name right in front of him."

I shrug my shoulders. "My uncle doesn't care."

"I care!"

"Will you relax?" I rub my face, desperate to climb back into bed. Unfortunately, the caffeine has done nothing for me. "It's not like we're dating. It was one night."

Nina crosses her arms beneath her chest, eyes on fire. "So, all those things you said last night?"

"What things did I say?" I ask cautiously, swallowing the lump inside my throat.

"Just something about my hair, that it was beautiful and curly. You kept tugging on the ends and said we could really be something."

My memory is vague. Yet, the intent behind it refuses to leave me no matter how hard I try. A recurring nightmare I wish would go once and for all.

"I think you should go."

"Andy," she says in a high-pitched voice. "What the hell?"

I grit my teeth. "*I said go.*"

Nina storms out of my living room, returning a few minutes later dressed in her white dress from last night. Not wanting to show her any remorse, I glance sideways to notice just how short her dress is.

"You've got some shit you need to sort out."

"You don't know me," I tell her, my voice low.

"I'm glad I don't. You're a typical guy, just after the pussy because that's your escape. Thanks for last night," she responds sarcastically, storming toward the door, then slamming it behind her.

Nina's words have no effect on me. Yeah, so I'm a guy who drowned myself in pussy last night to escape. *So fucking what.*

My body immediately carries me straight to bed, where I fall headfirst into the pillow with a splitting headache from all the action this morning.

But as I'm finally surrounded by silence, and the voices in my head begin to speak.

I hate that she got to me.

The harder I close my eyes, the more her face appears. It's been almost two years since I spoke to Jessa, the night at Austin and Ava's wedding. We argued the same night, but just before I stormed out, she ran after me and called my name.

*"Andy, stop!"*

*My heart was thumping loud, filled with anger and hurt over Jessa's actions. Why should I give her anything when she couldn't even give me the respect of telling the truth? But my feet stopped before I could even finish my thought. Dad continued to walk to the car, purposely leaving me behind.*

*Slowly, I turned around with her only a few feet away.*

*Her expression was remorseful, and maybe Jessa finally realized what she'd done.*

*"Don't hate me because I chose someone else."*

*The words cut deep, a knife-edge which slew with only the tip but enough to cause the damage to inflict tremendous pain.*

*But then, something sparks inside me—an urge to fight for what I wanted.*

*Lost in this trance clouding any rational thought, I took long steps toward her until my hands cupped her chin, allowing me to smash my lips onto hers.*

*The moment my mouth touched hers, my whole body fell into an abyss, freefalling like nothing I could've ever imagined. Her taste was pure, sweet, and everything my body craved for the longest of time.*

*As my tongue softly caressed hers, I heard a moan, albeit faint, escape her lips. But with force, she pulled away, her breaths shallow as her chest rose and fell.*

*Shaking her head, she clutched her stomach. "Please don't make this harder than it already is."*

*"Harder? You're leaving me to go marry some man you barely fucking know!"*

*"Andy, please—"*

*"No, Jessa." I stopped her, fueled with anger. "You've made your bed. Now go lay in it with your fiancé."*

It was just a kiss.

I've done much worse than that, slept with dozens of women, sometimes multiple women at the same time. But how is it possible that nothing can compare to the kiss of a woman I'd once called my best friend?

I refuse to fall down this rabbit hole again. Closing my eyes, I force myself to sleep.

"Andy," Kate greets with a smile, extending her arms while I hug her for a quick moment. "It's been forever, and you're just as handsome as I remember you."

"Age does wonders for a man," I tease, glancing at Lex. "Look at this old fella. He can still pull in the ladies."

Kate laughs. "Say that in front of Charlie and see if you still have balls."

Beside Kate, Noah extends his hand, his eyes focusing on me, and the familiarity forces me to bury the memories once again. Despite what happened with Jessa, there's no bad blood with Noah. At least, I assume there isn't since I'm not the one who married his daughter and knocked her up.

Yeah, she's got a kid now, apparently playing happy families across the other side of the world.

"Andy, it's been a while. How have you been?" Noah asks politely.

"Busy, a lot of work here in Manhattan."

"Sit, please," Lex commands.

Inside the penthouse office, the views are amazing. I expect nothing less from Lex since he can afford the best of the best. However, upon sitting here with Lex on the opposite side of the table, I can see how intimidating it can be for people. Not me, though. Lex will forever be the man who annoys my mom and vice versa. They remind me a lot of Luna and me. We're exactly like them. My younger sister, Willow, is just like Dad—quiet with her head constantly buried in a book.

"Let's get right to it, shall we?"

Lex begins with a presentation showcasing 3D images of the hotels and the interiors. Each building is located in an iconic part of Europe. As I watch on, I can see their vision, the experience they want to create for guests, which many people will pay top dollar for.

In total, twenty new boutique hotels are expected to be launched in the next twelve months across various locations. The deadline appears tight, but if anyone can pull it off—it's these three people.

"This is quite some project," I voice openly.

"Yes, and if anyone can capture our essence for our marketing, it's you," Kate says with confidence.

"It's a big job, and as I see it, each location needs to be captured differently. For example, I see France being more sultrier, a romance destination versus London being more elegant and refined."

"Exactly," Lex concurs with a knowing smile. "This is why you're perfect for the job."

I nod, my mind conjuring up all these creative thoughts.

"When do you want me to start?"

"Immediately," Noah states firmly.

Kate glances at him as something passes between them. I assume it's husband and wife behavior since my parents do the same thing all the time.

"What Noah meant to say..." Kate intervenes with a fixed smile, "... is as soon as you're available. A sought-out photographer like yourself must have obligations you need to fulfill before traveling to Europe?"

"There's a fashion show next week. Then I have a job in Malibu. Can you give me three weeks?"

"That will work just fine," Lex assures me, though his gaze is fixated on Noah. "Now, let's talk money."

When it comes to paying someone for work, Lex isn't one to undermine talent where he sees it. He briefly goes through the contract, which most of it is standard for my freelance work. Regarding the payment, he's too generous, but it would be pointless for me to argue with him once his mind is set on something—he is rarely persuaded another way, especially when it comes to business.

Lex stands up, extending his hand. "So, do we have a deal?"

I follow in suit, shaking his hand with a slight smirk on my face. "How can I say no to the great Lex Edwards?"

Kate raises her hand with a cheeky grin. "Can I answer that question?"

Lex crosses his arms with a pinched expression. "If you must."

Beside Kate, Noah drops his head with a chuckle. "Leave the poor bastard alone. His ego was bruised this morning when a much younger billionaire went viral with a video saying he'll make Charlie his wife."

With my lips pressed flat, I try to suppress my amusement, but I fail miserably.

"Ouch."

"Do you need a wellness check, Lex?" Kate pouts.

"I'd rather we not discuss this." Lex fixes his cufflinks in annoyance. "Besides, it's being taken care of."

"Jesus Christ, Lex!" Kate groans while throwing her hands up in the air. "The guy's a kid. Leave him alone."

"He's not a kid. He's thirty. And if he wants to succeed, he needs to understand who you don't mess with."

"Here we go..." Noah drags.

Kate turns to look at him. "Like you're one to talk? Mister acts all jealous over nothing."

Noah shifts his body to face Kate. "Two young men are in your office. Then you make some joke about being in a sandwich?"

"Firstly, that joke was made in private. And secondly, I didn't make the joke, Adriana did. I just laughed and nodded."

"Okay, sounds like my cue to leave if you're bringing up Mom and her filthy mind."

Lex shakes his head. "I don't blame you. Now, how do we celebrate? I do have a flight back home in a few hours."

"How about when I'm back in LA next weekend? That way, your overbearing daughters can join us and pick my life apart about where I went wrong with women and how I should settle down."

A small chuckle escapes Lex. "Don't forget about all the friends they'll have lined up to match you with."

"I forgot," I mumble, then force a smile. "Such a loving family."

Lex's phone rings only seconds from Kate's. The two of them excuse themselves to take the call, leaving me with Noah.

It would be immature of me not to ask him how Jessa is doing. I bite the bullet despite my guard being up because chances are I won't like what I'm going to hear.

"So, how is Jessa doing?"

Noah lowers his head, focusing his gaze on his tailored suit pants.

"That depends on who's opinion you're after."

His answer stumps me, but judging by his somber mood, something seems amiss.

"Your opinion?" I tread carefully with my words.

"Well, let's see. In my opinion, although my wife may argue, I think my daughter is miserable."

The word *miserable* sends shockwaves through me. An answer I wasn't prepared for. My body stills with mixed feelings of surprise but also empathy. I may not be talking to Jessa, but I'd hate to see her in any pain.

"I'm sorry to hear that."

"Are you?"

"Yes, of course. Jessa will always be someone who was a

part of my life. She was my best friend. That feeling doesn't just go away," I inform him.

"She's changed, you know. Nothing like the bright and happy girl who admired her father like I was her world."

"Marriage and a child can change you," I lower my voice, pained even to admit that.

Noah angles his body, so his stern gaze fixates on me. I have no clue what's going on, but something warns me that things aren't as picture-perfect as I envisioned in my head.

"There's only one person who can get through to her, and that's you."

I shake my head with my lips flat.

"Not anymore, Noah. If I had any pull, she would've stayed here two years ago."

"It was timing. It was off. Just like Kate and me."

I tilt my head in confusion. "I'm sorry, I don't understand what you're saying?"

"The right timing, Andy, isn't always our timing." Noah stands up with his phone in his hand. His tall stature dominates the room. "And life is all about timing."

"She chose someone else," I barely mumble.

Noah places his hand on my shoulder as I keep my head low.

"And if I didn't choose someone else, Jessa wouldn't be here. Life has a funny way of working out. It's those second chances which count for everything."

He lifts his hand and leaves the office as I continue to sit here in silence, remembering the moment I realized I was in love with my best friend, and everything was about to change.

# FOUR

## ANDY

### *Three years ago*

"You know I hate shopping with a passion."

Jessa grabs my hand while ignoring my complaining, weaving me in and out of the crowds. Visiting shopping malls is one of my least favorite things to do. The trauma stems from my cousins doing the same thing when we were teens. If I need something, I buy it online. It's easy and less chaotic. We've already walked past several mothers with screaming children, one even throwing himself onto the ground demanding he go back to the toy shop.

"Will you just relax?" Jessa chides over the noise. "We need to find the perfect first birthday present for Ashton."

"Can't we just get him a ball? He loves balls."

Jessa stops mid-step. Turning around, her expression shows she's less than pleased with my suggestion. "A ball for a first birthday? How memorable is that?"

"It will be memorable since he loves them."

Her eyes roll backward with arms crossed beneath her

chest. Then, like a lightbulb moment, Jessa's eyes dance with delight. "You've just made the gift I was thinking extra special. Now, we just need to find it."

I let out a groan. "That sounds painful. Can't we just buy it online?"

"No, now put on your big boy pants and stop being a baby."

Jessa is relentless in her pursuit of the perfect gift. The stores we enter are posh, the sales assistants looking down on Jessa's cut-off denim shorts and midriff tank top. She has a killer body, but little do they know appearance has nothing to do with her wealth. After all, she's the eldest daughter of Noah and Kate Mason. Combined, their fortune is very lucrative.

But Jessa doesn't care. In fact, she rarely cares about other people's opinions. Her confidence is refreshing compared to some other women I know.

"This is it," she mumbles to herself when her eyes fixate on the gold piece of jewelry sitting inside the glass enclosure.

There are so many pieces inside, not making it easy to decipher which one she's looking at.

The sales assistant, an older woman with completely gray hair, greets us with a contrived smile. Her gaze wanders down to Jessa's exposed stomach with her barbell piercing sitting inside her belly button. But Jessa brushes it off, requesting to see the gold chain together with the small soccer ball pendant.

"My mom told me that on my first birthday, Adriana bought me this beautiful pendant with a butterfly because, at the time, I used to giggle every time I'd see one." Jessa's voice is soft, almost as if she's remembering the moment. "When my parents helped me open the gift, she said my eyes lit up, and I tried to say the word. But, of course, it came out as baby babble. And you know, I still have it in my jewelry box in my room."

Unable to hide my smile, I understand now why Jessa is so hung up on giving Ashton something with sentimental value.

"It sounds like something Mom would do. She's good with gifts like that. Always trying to think of something special."

"I know people give toys or even money, but I think something like this is special."

I scratch my chin. "Okay, if you insist. Now, can we get out of here? I'm paying for lunch if that will make it quicker."

Jessa laughs, knocking into my side. "Taco Bell?"

My body shudders at the thought. "You know how I feel about Taco Bell. It's designed to burn assholes. You're the only person I know who can stomach it."

She shakes her head. "Nash can too."

"It must run in the Mason genes then," I mumble, taking my credit card out so we can get out of here. "I'll pick up some Pepto-Bismol too."

"You're such a wuss, Andy." She grins before thanking the sales lady and dragging me out of the store.

---

Millie went all out for Ashton's first birthday. Clusters of balloons everywhere you look, tables full of food, and, of course, the trusty bouncy castle.

I guess, however, it isn't like I can compare it to other first birthdays since they're not exactly my scene. Will and Millie are the only people my age I know with a child. Everyone else is still partying their way through life.

The party is being held at their house with all our family in attendance and some of their friends who also have small kids. When Jessa and I arrive, Ava is standing behind us with a sour look on her face.

"I shouldn't have worn white. I see face paint."

Jessa hugs Ava with sympathy. "Cheer up. It's your nephew's birthday. Soon this might be you, and boy, will that be entertaining to watch."

"Are you kidding me, Jess? I can't think of anything worse than having kids," Ava complains. "Besides, I need a man first."

"Aren't you dating that Oliver guy?" I ask, confused.

"*It's Olivier,*" Ava annunciates. "He's of French descent."

I try my best not to roll my eyes at my cousin. Even when it comes to men, her standards are high, and God forbid he's not of French descent.

"Very romantic," Jessa says with a grin. "I wish I could be whisked away by someone exotic."

Beside her, my lips press flat, trying to hide my annoyance. Jessa jokes about this whole sweeping-away thing, which we always fight over, only for her to calm me down. The anger brews inside, but she pinches my arm to break me from my thoughts as if she knows.

"Maybe he has a cousin or something I can set you up with," Ava jokes.

"Hmm, don't think *Andrew* wants to become the third wheel." Jessa laughs.

These two always know how to crawl under my skin to annoy me. Being surrounded by women is frustrating. Hence, I often call upon Nash to hang out with or even Lex.

"You know I hate being called that."

Jessa turns to face me, now squeezing my cheek. "Stop being a sourpuss, and let's get your face painted!"

I let out a groan as she holds my hand and drags me into the backyard. Will is the first to greet us, but his attention is directed to Ashton, who attempts to put something in his mouth which he shouldn't.

"Why does this kid think it's okay to eat bugs?" Will asks while sticking his finger into Ashton's mouth.

Ava wrinkles her nose to then shudder. "Oh, God, I just had all these flashbacks to when Millie would dare me to watch her do the same thing."

I shake my head with a slight chuckle. "Hmm, me too. Although, if we're being honest, I may have swallowed a bug or two, not wanting to look like a pussy in front of you girls."

"Why does that sound like something my wife had done?" Will mumbles as Millie walks out with a tray of food.

"You guys made it," she says, eying all of us dubiously. "Okay, what happened?"

"Your son is eating bugs," I tell her.

"Again? He'll be fine." She shrugs.

Will glances at her with annoyance. "Um, do you know how poisonous insects can be?"

"Okay, helicopter parent," she mumbles.

The two of them have a stare-off, but Millie being Millie, doesn't back down to Will. She didn't when we were kids, and to this day, she still knows how to get what she wants with him.

"Okay, while the two of you argue over your son's safety, I'm going to go say hello to everyone else."

Jessa uses the escape to say hello to Noah and Kate as I make my way over to the grill where Rocky and Lex are standing. Only a few steps away from them, Eric stops me.

"Andy, darling." Eric pats down my shirt, pretending to pick lint off the fabric. "You're as gorgeous as I remember."

"You saw me yesterday. What do you want?"

"It's not what I want, but perhaps what I need." I brace myself for something ridiculous because, after all, it's Eric.

"There's this client of mine, and they have a daughter who has an important function to attend tonight but needs a date."

"C'mon, I don't do blind dates."

"You might want to when you see the rack on her," Eric informs me, then pulls back, tilting his head. "Wait, are you a tits or ass man?"

"He's a pussy man," Rocky yells while raising his beer. "Just like the rest of us."

"Rockford Romano, this is your grandson's birthday party," Nikki complains. "Have some respect."

"Well, you didn't have respect when you—"

Nikki's eyes widen, enough for Rocky to shut up.

"Please finish that sentence," Eric coerces. "Nikki's got her blow job hairstyle which she argues there's no such thing."

"I think," Rocky says with a smug look on his face. "I'll keep my lips sealed. I value my life, also my blow jobs."

Will walks toward us, catching only the end of the sentence. With a disappointed head shake, he then walks in the opposite direction mumbling something to himself.

"You're tormenting your son," Lex informs Rocky. "How is he not in therapy yet?"

"Maybe because he has someone who satisfies him every night," Rocky retorts.

Lex presses his lips together with a tight expression. "I really hope Nikki does rip your balls off one day."

"Okay, enough about Rocky's balls and back to this date," Eric interrupts with a desperate plea in his tone. "Please, I'm begging you. I'll even show you a pic."

Eric removes his phone from his pocket, flicking through before showing me the picture. Both Rocky and Lex move in to catch a look.

"Young," is all Lex says.

"But that rack...damn, boy, you'll be busy." Rocky nods

with approval. "The key to motorboating is all in your depth. Get in there, deep, which allows the sound to amplify."

Lex bows his head, trying not to laugh while Eric stands still in confusion.

"Wait, I thought the whole thing behind motorboating is to mimic a motorboat's engine, you know, the propeller-type thing?"

"Yeah." Rocky raises his brows with a sneer. "It should sound something like this..."

Rocky does an impression that's hard to keep a straight face over. To end this crazy conversation and also the unwanted attention from the sounds he makes, I blurt out, "Fine, what do I need to do?"

Eric claps his hands, rambling details about some Hollywood red carpet event, exactly where I need to go, and what to wear. When it comes to events like this, Eric doesn't skip a beat. Finally, he catches a breath, then abandons us to join Mom and Kate.

"What pushed you to decide?" Rocky nudges me. "The tits or mouth? Because fuck me what she could do with those li—"

He's cut off when Jessa appears, eyeing us like we'd been caught doing something wrong.

"Why are you all looking at me weird?" she asks, furrowing her brows. "Actually, why are you all looking at me like you've done something wrong?"

"Nothing wrong," Rocky says with an overbearing smile. "Eric just set up Andy on a date."

The minute he says it, I want to punch him in the face.

"A date? Like, with a person?"

"With this chick with a huge rack—"

Now I cut him off. "It's a favor to Eric. She needed a date to an event, that's all."

Jessa keeps her eyes fixated on me, her stare almost blank

until she nods with a forced smile. "Sounds like fun. Anyway, I just came over here because Millie is looking for you."

I should ask her if she's mad, since the last time I went out with a girl, we got into a fight over something ridiculous that I can't even remember. But I choose to leave well enough alone, for now, and go search for Millie.

Inside the kitchen, Charlie kisses me hello but has her hands full with platters in which I offer to help. My sister, Luna, comes to the rescue, leaving Millie and me alone.

My hands reach for a carrot stick while I watch Millie chop some fruit.

"What's happening?"

"Are you going on a date with a chick with a big rack?"

I stop mid-bite. "Did you call me in here to ask that? How did the news even travel in here?"

"Eric, plus I saw the photo."

"Jesus Christ, I'm just doing him a favor."

"No, you're not. You're selfish and want to get laid. And as your sane cousin, I'm telling you it isn't a good idea."

I observe Millie using a cutting shape thing that cuts the watermelon into the shape of a bunny.

"You're cutting watermelon into bunnies. You really think you're sane?"

She places the cutter down. "What about Jessa?"

"What about Jessa?"

"How does she feel about this?"

"I don't know, and besides, what does it matter? We're just friends, you know."

"You're best friends, Andy," Millie reiterates. "And we all know there's something more to it."

"We?"

"Yes, we, your family."

"You mean you and Ava?"

Ava walks into the kitchen, her timing impeccable.

"Are we talking about the big rack chick?"

I bury my face in my hands, wondering what I did to deserve this when my intent was to help Eric out with a favor. A favor I'm regretting on all accounts.

"Go on, what is it you need to say?" I question Ava as she turns to look at Millie and something passes between them. "I'll wait here so eagerly waiting for my opinionated cousins to have their say."

"You're in love with Jessa," they say in unison.

I shake my head with a hard smile, staring at both of them despite neither of them backing down. Their matching emerald eyes try to intimidate me, but I've spent my whole life around these two to not even bat an eye at their overbearing behavior and opinions.

"And I'm leaving," is all I tell them, ignoring the conversation and heading back outside.

Jessa avoids me for the rest of the party, purposely distancing herself with all the girls. I wait around for the cake to be brought out, then the singing which makes Ashton cry in Millie's arms. Poor fella, too much attention for the bug-eating birthday boy.

Eric corners me again, more details which get lost in my thoughts. I watch Jessa across the yard, and on occasion, her eyes fall upon me, but they quickly glance elsewhere when she catches me looking.

It's Millie's and Ava's fault. They're putting thoughts into my head that shouldn't be there.

Jessa is my best friend—that's it.

And family since we share the same cousins although not technically related to each other. When we were growing up, Jessa hung out with us a fair bit being only a few years younger than Millie, Ava, and me.

I shake my head, grab a drink, then check the time. We've been here for hours, with most of the little kids hitting their nap time and losing their shit on the way out. A few calmed down to receive their party favor, but the meltdowns were next level. One boy hid in the corner of the bouncy castle, refusing to leave. The poor single mom dressed in her nice blouse and jeans with heels was at a loss of what to do.

Of course, Rocky saved the day, pulled the kid out, and then whipped out his charm. You could almost see the steam coming out of Nikki's ears.

It's my cue to leave if I have any chance of getting to this red carpet on time. Eric informs me we need to go to his place for the suit, so I say goodbye to everyone, but I'm unable see Jessa anywhere as I search around.

Then, as I exit the gate, she's standing outside texting on her phone.

"Hey." I reach out to touch her arm. "I was looking for you. I need to go but just wanted to say bye."

Her gaze is fixated on the screen, and then a small smile appears. I want to know who she's texting but realize now isn't the time to interrogate her unless it's some guy. The thought sends a wave of anger throughout me. *For fuck's sake, Andy, just focus.*

"Oh cool, I'll see you later."

"Are we good? You seem upset."

She places her phone in her pocket. "I'm fine. You go on your date, and I'll talk to you tomorrow."

Jessa doesn't give me a chance to say anything else, walking away and back into the yard.

Eric yells for me to hurry up, then drives us to his place like a speed demon while all the way he bitches about all the movie stars who would be in attendance tonight.

Upon arriving at Eric's, I head straight to the shower then change into the suit. I don't even have a moment to text Jessa about something Eric says because he rushes me out the door and into a limo where I finally meet Chloe.

Her photos were an accurate depiction of what she looks like in person. She's beautiful and sexy—just not my type. The dress she's wearing—gold with thin straps and a plunging neckline—catch the attention of every man we walk past.

Chloe places her arm in mine as we snap pictures for the red carpet. For someone who's always behind the camera, I know which way you should pose to capture the best angle.

Inside the event space, we're seated at our table. There are a few actors seated with us, all of who Chloe knows of. I chat, keeping it friendly but can't help the urge to send Jessa a picture of this woman wearing a dress in the shape of a swan. Since Jessa has a fear of swans, I find it all so amusing. I decide to hold back, preferring to show her in person so I can watch her dry heave and poke fun at her.

My focus shifts back to Chloe. There's this awkward silence between us, so I try to come up with something worth discussing.

"Nice place," is all I say.

"It's so Hollywood, though."

I look around, followed by a soft chuckle. "Yeah, my best friend would love this."

"He would?"

"She would."

"Oh, right. I mean, it's tacky, but I guess the fairy lights make it romantic."

"Exactly," I say, thinking Jessa would've said the same.

Chloe begins to tell me a story, then the conversation drifts to her modeling career. I hear things being said, but my mind wanders elsewhere.

"Andy, are you even listening?"

"Yes, you mentioned something about Malibu and a bikini photoshoot."

The waiter serves us cocktails, distracting us from this

mundane topic we converse over. Chloe enjoys talking about herself, so the drinks being served are a nice way to hopefully switch subjects, except most of the glasses are filled with a pink liquor.

"I love a good pink drink," she says with a grin.

"There was one time, in Manhattan, my best friend and I went to this club. They served pink drinks exactly like this. I made some joke about how many would it take to drink and puke up a rainbow. We got so drunk, and she did exactly that. Not so great for me because I spent the night back at the hotel holding her hair back in the toilet."

Chloe plays with the rim of her glass, bowing her head. "Some best friend you must have."

"Yeah, she has her moments."

"It sounds like you're in love with her?"

I purse my lips, wondering why a stranger would say this based on what I just said. So what if I have a female best friend? People have this odd perception that a man and woman can't just be friends.

"I'm not in love with her."

"Are you sure about that? You speak a lot about her, and when you do, your face lights up. Considering you're on a date with me, with the potential to get laid tonight, it speaks volumes, does it not?"

I glance at Chloe as she watches me with a knowing look, surprised she would come to such a conclusion. It's only minutes later I realize she mentioned getting laid.

But it didn't matter. I'm not in the mood to climb into bed with another woman who wants me to worship her so she can brag about it to her friends.

I'm not in love with Jessa. I can't be. Sure, I have feelings for her, of protection. After all, I've known her my entire life. I'd lose my shit if anyone hurt her.

The event kicks off with awards and various speeches,

but the longer I sit amongst these people, the more I realize how much I don't want to be here. Not to look like a dick, I stick it out until Chloe finds another guy to latch onto, which is my cue to leave. I don't even say goodbye since I'll never see her again.

As I exit the event, wandering Sunset Boulevard, I need to see for myself if there's any truth to what everyone else can supposedly see besides me.

Surely, I can't be that blind when it comes to my feelings.

I drive over to Jessa's condo and knock on the door. It's past midnight, so chances are she's asleep, but this isn't the first time I've turned up at some godawful hour.

She opens the door, dressed in my Lakers tee she won from me in a bet and bed shorts. They're short, exposing all her tanned legs. I pull my gaze away from her legs and onto her flushed face. Her hair is out, the curls falling down her arms. I ache to reach out and run my hands through them as I've done many times before, but her face looks less than pleased I'm standing in front of her.

"Were you sleeping?"

"No, reading."

"Romance again?"

"Maybe...anyway, what are you doing here?" She crosses her arms beneath her chest, yet I try my best to ignore how tattered the fabric is of my favorite shirt and how her tits are bare without a bra. Jessa is all natural, nothing at all like the plastic women I'd been surrounded by tonight. "Aren't you supposed to be on some date and motorboating right now?"

"You didn't learn that term by yourself and need to stop talking to Eric."

I walk inside the apartment without an invite but pace the living room as she closes the door. She walks to the bedroom, ignoring me, and climbs into bed with her book. Only the small bedside light is on, illuminating the room.

When it comes to reading, Jessa loves paperbacks with a whole room full of them. But, of course, being a writer is something she loves, so naturally, she loves reading, though she's doing some freelance writing for a local magazine. It's why she spent so much time at my place growing up since Dad is a writer, and the two of them could talk for hours.

Removing my shoes and suit jacket, I climb into bed beside her as she picks up her book and ignores me. The cover has some guy in a suit, probably some billionaire story which makes me want to roll my eyes.

"What's with you and billionaires?" I yawn.

"What's with you and big tits?"

"That was Eric and Rocky. I never said I liked them."

"Every guy likes them," she drags.

"Hmm..." I murmur. "That's not true. I like yours, maybe if you show me..."

"Fat chance," she grumbles, then ignores me for her book again.

My eyelids begin to fall, the smell of her on the pillows always puts me to sleep like it's some drug. As my dreams begin to shift, I see his face.

The color of his skin is pale, but there's a glow, not sickly or anything.

His bright blond hair and deep blue eyes watch over me. I'm lying inside a crib, aware that I am, but he looks down with a loving smile. I can't help but smile back, but then Lex comes and is wearing blue scrubs. Lex places his hand on my father's shoulder, and then his skin turns ghostly white.

In the background, there's the sound of sobbing. Then a high-pitched scream echoes down a sterile corridor.

I wake up in a panic, sitting up with my eyes wide, sweat covering my forehead.

Jessa places her hand on my arm, a sympathetic expression all over her face. "Andy, are you okay?"

I'm perfectly still, my body not moving except for my heart beating at a rapid rate.

"Was it your dad again?"

I nod without a word.

Jessa places her book down, then turns the lamp off. There's the light of the moon coming through the window, enough to see the shadows of the room. She places her hand on my shoulder and pulls me into her. With her hands wrapped around me, my head lays against her chest, listening to the calm beat of her heart.

It's a beautiful tune. A soft melody I've known my entire life.

And as always, she's the calm in my raging storm.

But as we lay in the dark, I don't know which is the biggest nightmare. The recurring visions of my sick father or the fact that everyone was right...

I'm in love with my best friend.

# FIVE

### *Three years ago*

Ashton's birthday completely drained me.

Who would've thought a first birthday could be so exhausting? And I wasn't the one running around chasing bubbles or kicking balls, let alone jumping on the bouncy castle for what felt like an eternity.

If I was this tired from sitting around and eating copious amounts of food, I can't even imagine how exhausted Millie must be. Occasionally, she stops to have a quick bite to eat and chat, never appearing to be breaking a sweat. Some women are born to be mothers, and Millie reminds me so much of Aunt Charlie.

Millie is the most gracious host, attending to all the guests while keeping a smile on her face. Will spends most of the party making sure Ashton plays nice with his little friends since there were a few questionable moments with a stolen ball, resulting in tears.

Everything is perfect, except for Andy.

When I walk into the conversation with Eric and Rocky

talking so animatedly, it should've been the red flags of something unpleasant ahead. I never expected it would be Andy going on some date with breasts larger than Mount Rushmore.

Rocky mouthing off is normal. I expect nothing less. Uncle Lex keeping quiet is usual for him. He is very respectful when it comes to women. Eric, well, he's a mixed bag.

But never did I expect Andy to be so... shallow.

That's not even the word.

Asshole.

Jerk.

Insensitive dick.

It's not like Andy is a virgin, but he isn't like the other men I know. At least, I didn't think he was until today.

Perhaps, in hindsight, my anger shouldn't have resulted in venting to Ava, who then went ahead and told Millie. But if anyone can knock some sense into him, it's *our* cousins.

When I stroll outside to clear my head, I happen to get a text from this guy I stayed in contact with after college. He's in town next week and wants to catch up for coffee. Of course, there's no reason not to meet him, but just as he is about to respond, Andy comes to say goodbye.

I do my best to hide my disappointment in him, pretending everything is fine, but the truth is, I'm far from fine. The moment he leaves, I know the anger and jealousy inside me needs something or someone to calm it down. So, I text Christian back, expressing just how much I'm looking forward to seeing him.

Since Andy left, it was my cue to leave. I could've stayed with my cousins, but I'm not in the mood. I'm desperate to bury my head in a book and live vicariously through a fictional boyfriend sweeping me off my feet.

I promise Mom I'll drop by her place quickly before they

leave for Europe. Her husband, Jack, and she are traveling for a much-needed getaway. In addition, my aunt Scarlett, who Mom works for, just won an Oscar for a movie role which means Mom is busy scheduling all her press tours.

"Hey, Mom," I yell through the house.

I pass the living room where Jack is watching a game, waving to him. He acknowledges but is too busy yelling at the television.

Jack has two grown daughters of his own and has been divorced for several years before he and Mom married. They've been married for close to ten years now, and honestly—they're so perfect for each other. Jack is a movie director, and he and Mom have so much in common since her life revolves around movie sets too.

After me, Mom never had any more kids. My half-brother, Michael, is still in Mom's life. She treats him like her own, and now that he just had his first baby with his wife, Mom is always talking about more grandkids.

God forbid it's from me.

I still want to enjoy my freedom, not to mention move up in my career. I've got all these plans, goals written down, all the things I want to achieve before I hit thirty. My journals are full of dreams and bucket lists, many of which involve my best friend, who I'm angry with right now.

We sit inside the kitchen as Mom has her laptop open, trying to reschedule a shoot for Aunt Scarlett. I can see she's getting annoyed as she releases small huffs while talking to herself. The word 'incompetent' is vocalized several times.

"Okay, done, now we don't have two photoshoots sched-uled at the same time all because the brand manager wants to fly to Cabo to hang out with his eighteen-year-old girlfriend."

I scrunch my nose. "How old is he?"

Mom presses her lips flat with a hard smile. "Old enough to be your father."

A groan escapes me. "Pleasant."

"Anyway, how are you doing, and how was the birthday party?"

"It was loud and tiring. Lots of kids, and I think I can still hear ringing in my ears."

Mom laughs. "I remember your first birthday. It was the size of a wedding. Noah wanted only the best for you. Bouncy castles, ponies, and performers who did something with balloons which freaked you out."

"When I have a kid, it's going to be intimate with one smash cake. The end."

A glass jar with Oreos strategically stacked in circles sits on the counter. I open the lid and retrieve one and split the Oreo apart so I can lick the inside. Why I'm even snacking on this is beyond me, especially after everything I've eaten today.

"And Andy?" Mom asks while taking an Oreo for herself and doing the exact same thing. "I thought you'd bring him over. I wanted to ask his opinion on some shots sent over which Scarlett wants to use for a new campaign."

I lower my head. "He has, um, a date."

"Oh."

"Eric, actually set him up on a blind date while we were at the party. It was a last-minute favor, something about big titties."

"Big titties?" Mom tilts her head. "That doesn't sound like Andy at all."

"No," I drag, still trying to stomach the situation. "That was Rocky and Eric making a fuss over it."

"Sounds more accurate," Mom says, only to meet my gaze to observe my expression better. "I can see it's upsetting you."

"Me? No, Andy is free to do whoever he wants."

Slowly, Mom places her hand on mine. "It's okay to have these feelings, Jessa. The two of you are best friends. But, sometimes, you need to question why you feel a certain way?

You're right. Andy is free to do whoever he wants. But if there's more to this, perhaps the truth will set you free."

"The truth?"

"Maybe your feelings have extended beyond friendship."

"I'm not in love with him."

"I never said that. All I'm saying is when feelings begin to stir, what lies ahead may turn into something greater."

"Is that what happened with you and Dad?" I question, trying to understand where she's coming from.

"In some ways, yes. We loathed each other, and resentment was because of our underlying attraction to each other at the same time."

I bury my head in my hands. "Life is too hard."

"You're young and beautiful. It will work out, sweetheart."

Maybe, but it all became too much. Why is our friendship so complicated all of a sudden? And why are my emotions running rampant? This is Andy, not some new guy I'm crushing on.

I say goodbye to Mom and head home to what will be a miserable Saturday night. I order my favorite Uber Eats meal, then soak in my bath, resulting in my skin turning into a prune.

Then, I indulge in my favorite pastime—reading. There's no greater feeling than climbing into bed with fresh sheets and a new book. The blurb is promising—a woman engaged to some man until she runs into her ex. I'm a sucker for love triangles, and my eyes can't read this book fast enough.

Somewhere in the middle of what's going to be a steamy scene, my thighs press together, willing the urge to take care of myself to subside, but suddenly, there's a knock on my door.

And there is only one person who knocks that way —Andy.

The walk to the door is like a splash of cold water. Upon opening the door, Andy is standing outside, still dressed in his black tuxedo. Why he looks so sexy is beyond me, but I blame the book, and that's it. All this reading with men in suits and tuxedos has brainwashed me.

Our conversation is short as I ignore him and climb into bed. He follows me into the room, removing his jacket and shoes, then lays beside me.

When he questions my book and billionaires, I can't help but bite back. The conversation shifts to big breasts, all of which I think is ludicrous. Andy is a man with needs, and despite him wanting to prove me wrong by asking to see my own, I shut him down but wonder what would happen if I did it, just to shock him.

*Maybe next time.*

Within minutes, he falls asleep, so typical of him. Of late, I struggle and lay awake for hours with stupid flashbacks of my childhood. Every embarrassing thing to ever happen to me comes roaring back to life at three in the morning, only to keep me awake longer.

As Andy sleeps beside me, I continue to read my book until his moans filter inside the room. He's having one of those dreams, one which turns into a nightmare.

I place my book down, waiting for him to wake up because I know not to wake him up myself. Suddenly, he jolts up, out of breath, eyes wide open. I wish I could take his pain away, never understanding how hard it is to never meet your own father.

Julian is fantastic, and he's always been Andy's father, but it doesn't erase these unknown feelings. And despite Andy's reluctance to get professional help, I genuinely believe there's a message behind this, googling it myself in the hope he'll at least talk to Adriana about the dreams.

But right now, I see his torment. I turn the light off, but

this time, I hold onto him. My fingers run through Andy's hair while his face rests against my chest. When his body begins to relax, I continue to stroke his hair to help him fall asleep.

Somewhere, listening to his soft breathing, I fall asleep as well.

When the morning light filters in the room, it's unusually gray. It follows with the pitter-patter of rain, very uncommon for Southern California but refreshing all the same.

I move slowly, then Andy shuffles until he opens his eyes and stares right at me. Something in his stare runs deep, filling my mind with unknown thoughts and scenarios which women fantasize about. Just not with your best friend.

Slowly, he moves his fingers toward a loose curl and pushes it away from my face. It's a simple gesture that makes my heart beat erratically, then something panics within me. I sit up to break my thoughts.

This is Andy.

You can't feel anything for him.

He is off-limits.

Best friends.

As I try to move off the bed, he grabs my arm to stop me. If I turn around, this is it. I might not be able to say no, and the worst-case scenario—what if we ruin what we have?

"I have to use the bathroom," I barely choke. "Then I have to catch up with a friend for coffee."

"A friend? Who?"

"Just a friend from college."

"What's her name?"

"His name..." I clear my throat, "... is Christian."

Andy's breathing becomes noisy inside the quiet room. "You're going on a date with a guy today?"

"It's not a date, Andy. It's a catch-up."

An exaggerated sigh escapes him. "I don't get you. Why are you so obsessed with this whole finding the love of your life?"

"Excuse me?" I question while crossing my arms. "Me catching up with a male friend isn't searching for the love of my life. I take offense to you saying I'm obsessed. You make me sound like one of those girls."

"Well..." he trails off.

My teeth bare down as an unwanted growling sound leaves my mouth. His behavior is uncalled for and so beyond his normal jealousy.

"You know what? I haven't dated anyone in forever. I haven't even slept with a guy for God knows how long, certain I've been revirginized if that's even possible," I blurt out with my heart racing. "And you know why? Because every time I do, we get into a stupid fight."

Andy closes his eyes, throwing his head back against the pillow, but I can see him straining. We've had arguments before, but something warns me this will be our biggest yet.

"I know you want to say something?" I allege, reading him like an open book. "Just say what you need to say."

He jumps out of my bed, unable to look at me, grabbing his jacket and shoes in a rush.

"Why does my opinion matter?"

"You're my best friend, so your opinion matters."

Andy throws his hands up in the air. "Then don't go out with this guy, okay? God, Jessa, can't you see it?"

The words are like a giant wrecking ball, designed to knock me out until I'm left numb and speechless. And that's exactly what it's done. My emotions are fighting for attention, all of which becomes a blur of nonsense. Both of us are angry, and for different reasons, so this isn't the time to admit my feelings have shifted, not when too much is at stake.

"I don't know what you're talking about," I lower my voice.

"Of course not," he responds with malice. "It's all in my head, I guess."

It wasn't in his head, and as much as I want to tell him that, my fear cripples my ability to admit the truth. Pushing him away is easier than telling my best friend I feel something more for him. He's my world, a world with the air I breathe. Losing him because we take a risk on something more is too great. I've seen relationships end because of this and losing him entirely isn't an option.

So, I continue to lie to protect us.

"I have to start getting ready."

"Right, well, don't let me stop you," he barks before leaving the room without a goodbye.

And just like that, I hear the front door of my apartment slam.

I half wait for him to return, to lecture me on staying protected or some bullshit like that. But it never comes, and neither does a text or phone call.

The hardest thing to swallow isn't his absence. It's what his absence does to me. It makes me realize my feelings are more than I've been willing to admit, and this fight between us has brought everything to the surface.

I don't want to lose what we have, and even if he feels anything for me, taking it a step further can destroy everything.

And nothing means more to me than our friendship.

So, there's no choice but to protect it at all costs, even if it means I need to step away for a while to forget Andy is the man I can't seem to get out of my head. Create distance between us.

My phone pings with a notification from *Pinterest* of cool places to visit. I open it up to pictures of London.

It's a sign—it has to be.

A few weeks away, traveling around London and Europe. A break between us is just what we both need. Andy can stop worrying about me, and I can return with a stress-free attitude, and all will go back to normal.

I bet my life on it.

# SIX

## NOAH

### *Present*

"I need to make a call."

Kate simply nods as I step onto the terrace of our flat in London, closing the glass door behind me while moving close to the edge.

The gray clouds hover as the call connects, and Lex's voice is on the line. Our conversation begins with business, of course, but it isn't the purpose of my call.

"How is Jessa?" Lex asks, which isn't unusual since he has always treated her like his own daughter. "Charlotte has been trying to get in touch with her."

A heavy sigh escapes me. "She's not happy, Lex."

"She told you this?"

"No, I see it on her face," I strain, trying to control my anger over the whole situation. "The way she talks. Do you know she's not even writing anymore?"

"C'mon, Noah..." Lex tries to calm me down. "She's adjusting to motherhood."

I shake my head even though he can't see me. "No, it's

not that. She's not herself. Benedict is never home, according to her. She's given up everything to be all alone in a country so far away from her family."

"What are you trying to say?"

"It should've been Andy."

It's Lex's turn to sigh, a sound so prominent over the speaker, almost as if he's here in person.

"Yes, well. We can't change that."

"No..." I begin with, then continue, "... but if Andy is to go to London, say on a work assignment."

"You're playing with fire. You know what your opinionated cousin will say to this?"

"Jessa is my daughter. I can no longer sit back and watch her destroy her life. She deserves more, goddammit," I raise my voice, then remember Kate is inside. "Andy is the only one who can bring her back to life."

"How do you know that, Noah?"

"Because you and Charlie did the same for me. You knew I needed Kate, and you made it happen."

Silence falls between us because Lex knows it's true. I was in a bad place, not knowing what was missing in my life or even how to fix the mess I found myself in. If it wasn't for Charlie insisting I join them on that business trip to France, I wouldn't have reconnected with my best friend, made her my wife, and watched her bring our daughter into this world.

Timing is everything.

If anyone understands what I'm going through, it's Lex. He went through this with Will and Amelia too. He understands the need to protect your children.

"I'll call you tonight. I have an idea," is all he says.

During our trip here, I occupied myself with work and meetings with our design team over the new hotels launching across Europe. Kate joined me for a few of them but wanted to spend time with Jessa and Bentley.

The night before our flight back, we have dinner in London. Benedict joins Jessa and Bentley, despite his displeasure of his son being in attendance. The talk over dinner is mainly from Kate, as I chose to keep quiet and only converse when I need to, using the time to spend with my grandson.

Bentley is the only good thing to come from this union, and I loathe my so-called son-in-law, barely able to sit near him.

It all began two years ago when my bright and talented daughter took a solo adventure to Europe to experience life. I thought it was a great idea. She was young, finished college, and given her desire to follow her creative mind and write, experiencing life would fuel her career choice. Kate couldn't have been any more excited, demanding Jessa visit all the places my wife was homesick for.

Then, my little girl came back with news shocking us all —she was getting married. It was a whirlwind romance to some English guy she's known for two seconds. Not only was she to wed, but she was also to move permanently to the UK.

It was like one explosion after another.

And I didn't take well to any of this.

You don't fall in love after two-fucking-seconds and give up your entire life. But no matter what I said, Jessa was no longer listening to me. Instead, she was adamant about leaving her life behind.

None of this made sense. Everything is so rushed, and when the wedding was planned, we got into a heated fight in which I refused to walk her down the aisle. My decision caused conflict between Kate and me. Morgan, however, chose to keep quiet on the matter despite Kate pushing her to get me to see the bigger picture.

Lex, in the end, was the one to convince me since he had been asked to replace me.

My daughter was choosing this life, and regret was something I didn't want to live with. Walking Jessa down the aisle evoked more emotion than I care to admit. I have no fucking idea how Lex has done this twice, given the symbolic meaning behind letting your daughter go.

In the short time Jessa had known Benedict, there wasn't much to him to raise concern despite my reluctance to accept the relationship. He's an English man with polite manners from a wealthy and prestigious background.

And though none of this made sense, overhearing my nieces made the picture come to full view. I still remember the conversation word for word, the day of Jessa's wedding.

*"Did you speak to Andy?" Ava asked.*

*Millie nodded. "Yeah, he's not doing well. I heard crackling and some women's voices in the background."*

*"Of course, he's not doing well. The love of his life is marrying another man. A man she met to forget about how she's in love with her best friend."*

*"C'mon, Ava. She wouldn't just marry Benedict to get over Andy. Jessa is the romantic one of us. You know she must genuinely love Benedict to marry him."*

*"There's deep, core-shaking love, and then there's this," Ava continued. "Just admit it, Millie. She's not over Andy. This is temporary."*

*"Marriage isn't temporary. This will work out," Amelia stated.*

*"Right, just like it did for Mom and Uncle Julian?"*

*"Oh, don't start that again. If Dad hears you."*

*"Or even Uncle Noah and Morgan?"*

*"Look, what Noah and Kate have is strong. Their friendship—"*

*"Exactly. This is Noah and Kate all over again."*

"*This isn't the same as them. There's no baby involved. I mean, she's not pregnant.*"

"*How do we know?*"

"*Ava, look at her? She's just downed three champagnes in a row.*"

"*Fair call. But also, is she getting that wasted because she realizes she walked down the aisle with the wrong man?*"

"*Look, she made this decision, and we need to respect that.*"

"*So, you're admitting Andy plays a part in this?*" *Ava continued to push.*

"*If I admit it, will you drop this subject? This is the first kid-free event I've had in... I can't even think. I want to get wasted too and then fuck my husband into oblivion in our fancy hotel room.*"

"*Such a mouth on you.*" *Ava laughed.* "*And you're supposed to be my role model.*"

*The two of them broke out into laughter before Amelia spoke again.* "*Poor Daddy. What happened to his angels?*"

"*We discovered all about the di—*"

I shake my head, remembering how I chose to leave the conversation then and there. Poor Lex has no clue just how wild his daughters are despite them both being married.

And then I remember Austin and Ava's wedding. How Jessa and Andy barely spoke a word to each other. They've been best friends for as long as I can think back, and yet the tension was palpable.

The first stop when we arrive back in the States is a meeting with Lex and Andy. Lex informed me yesterday of offering Andy a job. It made sense. We need a photographer, and Andy is the best person we all know.

During our meeting, we all get straight to the point despite me coming off eager when Andy asks when we want him to start. Kate shoots me an annoyed glance, but I ignore her.

And then, when Andy and I are alone in the room—I say what needs to be said. At least part of it. It wasn't the moment to tell him it should've been him. It was always meant to be him.

Yet as I sit here inside Lex's office, with Andy having just left, Kate is still on a call as Lex sits back in his chair with a deep sigh.

"I don't like seeing my nephew like this," Lex begins, tapping his fingers against the desk. "I didn't want to mention anything in front of Kate, but when I saw him this morning, he wasn't himself."

"How so?"

"Late night partying, hungover, some unknown woman in his bed. Jesus, he couldn't even remember her name."

"We've all been there."

"Right? And remember why we went through that phase? Random women and meaningless sex in our beds for just one night?"

I bow my head, my own time less than pleasant. It was a way to forget, bury ourselves inside some stranger's pussy to forget a certain woman ever existed. I did it during my separation with Morgan and ended up with Nash. A blessing in disguise.

"Before I saw Charlotte again in the restaurant, I was destructive. Then, it all made sense, exactly what was missing."

"Sure, but she wasn't married nor had a son," I remind him. "This complicates matters with Jessa."

"You're right. Eliminating Julian at the time was easier since they weren't legally bound, nor did they have children.

Noah, I'd never break up a family, but you're telling me she's not happy?"

"I know my daughter, Lex. She's miserable."

Kate walks in, interrupting our conversation. She's intuitive and knows what we're discussing but changes the topic to work for the rest of the afternoon.

———

Back in LA, it begins to eat away at me, and if anyone can give me more insight into this, it's Morgan, Jessa's mother.

"Noah?"

I stand outside Morgan's office until she welcomes me in. She's changed offices a few times as I haven't been here before.

"Morgan, I need to discuss something with you."

"Okay..."

"It's about Jessa."

Morgan draws her eyebrows together. "What about her?"

"Is she happy? With Benedict."

Releasing a sigh, Morgan's shoulders relax as she leans back into her white leather chair. Jessa looks so much like her —beautiful, of course. Despite our divorce and our turbulent past, Morgan is still an attractive woman.

"Unless my daughter expresses concerns, I don't get involved. Noah, she's not a little girl anymore, and you need to stop treating her that way."

"I know she's not a little girl, but she's not fucking happy, okay? I saw her only last week. She's not herself, and she's given up her writing. I mean, the girl we knew who loved and only talked about writing has given it up."

"Noah, she's just had a child," she reiterates, which seems to be everyone's answer. "This is her first time being a mother."

"Morgan, don't bullshit with me. Something's not right."

"What does Kate have to say?"

"I need to respect her decisions."

"Sounds like good advice."

I stare into my ex-wife's eyes and know she understands her daughter, maybe better than I do. They have a mother-daughter bond, and Jessa has always remained close with Morgan even after the move.

"Noah, this is Jessa's life. While I may not agree with every decision she's made, she made them. She has the right to live her life how she sees fit."

"She's made a mistake."

"Her son isn't a mistake," Morgan states adamantly.

"But letting go of Andy is."

Morgan purses her lips. "You know, both you and Kate had a friendship just like theirs. In the end, it prevailed."

"It's not the same."

I nearly say it's not the same because there was a moment when I saw a future with only Morgan, when I blocked out any memory of Kate. But we were never meant to be, too different people who just got caught up in the heat of the moment. We fell pregnant with Jessa and did what we thought was right at the time for our daughter.

She places her hand on mine. "Noah, if Andy is the one for her, let the universe do its thing. Don't force it."

With those words, I leave her office annoyed she's being so blasé about the whole thing. How can I let my daughter continue to make mistakes? I don't care how old she is. She's my daughter.

When I arrive home, Kate is sitting inside our home office wearing her glasses. I stare at my beautiful wife, thinking how, of late, our conflict over this matter has driven a wedge between us. But Morgan is right. Kate is more than my wife, she's my best friend, and our bond tightened well before we became intimate. In the end, the universe led us where we were always meant to be.

"You're home," is all she says, not looking at me.

"Is Sienna home?"

Kate shakes her head, then grabs her mug and heads toward the kitchen as I follow her. "She's staying at Ellie's house."

"I went to see Morgan."

Kate stills, removing her glasses with a sigh. "Don't force her to be part of your sick and twisted game. It's not fair on me, and it's not fair on Morgan."

"What game?"

"You think I haven't figured out that you insisting Andy take on this project is because of Jessa? You and Lex are both just as bad as each other."

"Andy is the best photographer I know. Both Lex and I believe he's the best of the best."

"I won't argue that, but our plan wasn't to hit this phase until the end of the year, and suddenly, it needs to be done now. Right after our visit to Jessa?"

I lower my head, the memories of my past crippling my emotions. "I know what it's like to lose my best friend."

"So do I, Noah."

"And here we are."

Kate sighs, closing her eyes momentarily. "Here we are. Married, business partners, and parents to three kids."

I move closer to her, wrapping my hand around Kate's waist to bring her closer to me. I've fucking missed her and hate when we get into fights because we're both as stubborn as each other.

"With how much we've fucked each other, how we didn't have more kids is beyond me."

She slaps my chest gently with a wide grin. "Uh, let's see?

You have an addiction to blow jobs and anal. Scientifically, you're choosing the wrong holes."

"Hmm." I lean in and kiss the base of her neck, then whisper, "So is that where I went wrong? I didn't fuck your sweet pussy enough?"

"I think so. Maybe you need to make up for it like right now and here," she teases.

I push her back against the countertop, sliding her skirt up. With my lips pressed against hers, I'm ready to bury myself inside because I fucking miss her.

A slam of the door interrupts our moment, forcing us apart. Both our eyes widen as we stare at each other with shock and annoyance.

"Mom, Dad? Are you home?"

*This kid is a goddamn cockblocker.*

Kate fixes her skirt, and I do my best to fucking control my dick. Kate turns me around, so it appears I'm washing up while she opens the refrigerator to cool down her face.

"In the kitchen, Sienna," Kate yells.

Sienna appears moments later, oblivious to our silence, and heads straight for the refrigerator to grab a drink and a bowl of fruit as Kate steps aside.

"I thought you were staying at Ellie's?"

"Yeah, I was until she snuck out to go see her boyfriend. So, I'm there in her room all like what the fuck?"

"Sienna," I growl. "Language."

"Sorry, Dad. So anyway, I'm like, I'm going home."

"Great." I smile through my teeth as Kate tries to hold in her laughter.

We hear the door open again, followed by a bunch of cuss words. How is it only minutes ago, I was ready to blow inside my wife to all the kids being home?

"Oi, is anyone home?"

Moments later, Nash walks in. He stops to grab food off Sienna's plate, much to her annoyance.

"Ew, grub. Don't touch my food. God knows where your hands have been."

"Oh, sister dearest, the stories I could tell," Nash murmurs with delight.

"You're a douche."

"Okay, enough, you two," Kate warns them playfully. "Nash, did we know you were coming home?"

"I told freckles over here."

Sienna scrunches her face. "Sorry, Mom, I forgot."

"Andy's flying in this weekend," Nash informs us. "So, boys' farewell."

"Argh, that's so crass. You'll find any excuse to make it a boys' weekend, so it justifies you being a player," Sienna drags.

The two of them have always butted heads, with Jessa being the mediator between them. There's never a dull moment when these two are in the same room.

"Why don't we go out for dinner?" Sienna suggests.

"I'm in," Nash responds with an overbearing grin. "Hooters?"

Kate purses her lips. "I don't hear a no from you, Noah?"

"Whatever my son wants." I smirk.

Nash has zero care in the world for settling down. Unlike Andy, who's quite private with his personal life, Nash is the more women, the merrier. The kid is lucky he's damn good-looking, working on modeling gigs and anything involving his social life. I don't question his choice to sleep around, knowing he's far from ready to fall in love and commit himself to one woman.

"I'm going to get changed," Kate informs us. "How about we leave in thirty minutes?"

I follow Kate, yet the kids don't notice because they're too busy arguing over some song. Their voices become louder. Neither one of them cares how vocal they are.

Inside our bedroom, I close the door and follow Kate to our wardrobe.

As I watch Kate slide her skirt off, revealing her garter, I can't hold back until tonight.

"I just need maybe thirty seconds."

"Our children are downstairs and could barge in here at any moment. Do you not remember the incident in which I nearly bit your cock while sucking you off?"

I cringe. "I've tried to forget."

My hands run along the groove of her ass while she attempts to hang her blazer.

"You know I don't take no for an answer."

I watch the way her nipples harden beneath her white lace bra. Despite all the worries and stress of late, it always leads back to my wife.

My best friend.

I don't ask anymore, removing my belt to unzip my suit pants and take my wife just the way she likes it...

Fast and hard and with a double orgasm to make it even more special.

# SEVEN

## ANDY

"Look who the cat dragged back to LA."

Ava bites into her apple with a smug expression on her face, forcing me to look at the clock on the oven. It's before nine. How is she even in my parents' house this early?

I grumble a hello as she squeezes me tight, then, rather annoyingly, she pinches my cheek only for me to slap her hand away.

There's a glaze over my eyes, obstructing my vision while yawns escape me as I attempt to work out Mom's fancy coffee machine. The buttons are confusing, knowing if I fuck this up, all hell will break loose. Trying to figure this, I scratch my head with frustration, close to giving up until Ava demands I move out of the way so she can make me a coffee.

Another late night, another club, but this time in LA. A childhood friend of mine, Masen Cooper, insisted we go out, and, of course, Nash came. We drank and danced with women who invited themselves to our table. No one caught my eye, and oddly so, Masen wasn't interested as well. He has quite the reputation, but something was off last night. I didn't ask, figuring if he wanted to talk, he would talk.

And even after stumbling home at some ungodly hour, the nightmares returned.

Same face.

Same lifeless body.

"What are you doing here this early?"

"What are you doing in LA?" she counters.

"Someone needs to make sure you stay out of trouble." My eyes fall upon the bump of her stomach. "But clearly, you managed to get yourself knocked up again."

"Correction, my sexy doctor husband managed to make this happen again."

It's too early for this, or shall I say too early for Ava.

"Can we not go with the sexy doctor stuff again? You do realize I'm your cousin with zero interest in how your husband looks?"

Ava grins with a nod. "It's good to have you back, cuz."

Mom walks into the kitchen, dressed in her workout clothes which is laughable since she loathes any exercise. In my entire life, she's never gained a pound, or so it seems.

"Uh-oh, why the face?" Mom questions as her eyes dart back and forth from Ava to me. "Who's in trouble?"

"I'm talking about my sexy doctor husband inseminating me."

I drop my head with a groan, burying my face in my hands.

Mom laughs. "That he did. Poor Andy. You've been sheltered from the girl talk for quite some time."

I purse my lips. "Oh no, it still finds a way into our group chats. But usually, Nash diffuses the convo by throwing in some chick on a motorcycle."

"The last photo he posted, you couldn't even see the motorcycle because her boobs were ginormous," Ava exaggerates. "I mean, really, Andy. Are you into watermelon-size breasts?"

"That big?" Mom asks.

"Dolly Parton on crack."

Mom nods knowingly while I chuckle softly at her uninterested expression. I'm not going to voice my opinion on this subject in front of my mother. Some things are better left unsaid.

"One day, some woman is going to tame that boy," Mom adds.

Ava shakes her head. "Nash, tamed? Please, that's like saying Masen will be tamed. Two player peas in a player pod, thank you very much."

"I don't know," I say with ease. "Something got to Masen last night. Not one single woman caught his attention."

"Masen 'manwhore' Cooper in love?"

"I never said in love," I drag.

"Same thing."

I tilt my head in confusion. "How is it the same thing?"

"Someone has crawled under his skin." Ava's eyes widen as if she has revealed some secret. "Oh, this is juicy. I wonder if Addy can ask Cruz if he knows who it is."

"Firstly, Cruz is Masen's younger brother, and the two of them aren't exactly tight."

"So? It's like me saying I don't know what's going on in Addy's life."

"I have no clue what's going on in Luna or Willow's life," I inform Ava.

"Well, I can get you all caught up with the goss—"

I raise my hand. "No, because you'll tell me something I don't need to know about my sisters. They're both virgins. End of story."

Mom chooses to keep quiet, her silence not helping my

cause. Of course, she's close with my sisters. If Dad was in the room, he would completely back me up.

"Dinner tonight at Lex and Charlie's house," Mom reminds me. "You're free, right?"

"Yeah, of course." I finally manage to drink my coffee, welcoming the steaming hot liquid as it slides down my throat. "I've got a few work things to do today, but I can meet you guys there."

I walk out of the kitchen with my cup in hand as Ava picks Mom's brain over a design for her new swimwear line. When the two of them talk fashion, the conversation can go on for hours.

As the sounds of their chatter begin to fade away, the smell of something familiar engulfs my senses. I've never quite figured it out, but whatever it is—it smells like home. Growing up in this house only brings back fond memories. Unlike Lex and Charlie's house, this house isn't a mansion but a decent size for our family of five. Everyone has their own rooms, and the common areas are large enough to entertain when all our family comes over.

The yard is open, looking into the canyons with luscious green grass. Dad and I would spend hours kicking the soccer ball around when I played in my younger years. He even installed soccer goals so I could practice properly.

I walk down the long glass hallway toward Dad's office, admiring the tall plants against the glass.

With a gentle knock, I open the door to find him sitting behind his desk. Not saying a word, I take a seat in the armchair across from him. I've always enjoyed spending time in here, the smell of leather-grained books lingering in the air. There are bookshelves all around the room from classic literature to non-fiction books. I enjoy reading, but of late, something about it triggers my inability to fall asleep.

My gaze shifts toward the window.

"They're back again," is all I say.

Dad stops typing, and then I hear his sigh before he removes his glasses and fixates on me.

"How bad?"

I shrug. "They're worse. I see Lex. Then I see him fade away into this..."

The memory of his face deteriorating is too raw for me to voice loudly. Instead, my glance falls toward the dark wood floors, struggling to comprehend it all. I wasn't there when my father passed away, so why these dreams plague me makes no sense. I have zero recollection of the man whose blood runs through my veins.

"Have you spoken to Mom about it?"

I shake my head. "It'll just worry her."

"Is that all that's troubling you?"

I can't lie to him. I've never been able to.

"This trip to London. Noah mentioned something..." I try to gather my thoughts, but part of me thinks I'm overthinking things. "I just get the feeling this is more than a business venture."

"Lex and Noah wouldn't have asked you unless they genuinely believed you could do the job. Neither one of them gives favors for the hell of it. That goes for Kate too."

"I guess," I murmur, then scratch my neck. "Noah alluded to Jessa being unhappy."

"Jessa, unhappy?"

"Miserable is the exact term he used."

"She's had a lot of changes. It's not easy to get married and have a child all within such a short time."

I purse my lips. "Right, of course."

"Unless you think it's something else?"

"I don't know what to think anymore," I tell him honestly. "She still crawls under my skin when I least expect it. Her name alone is a trigger."

Dad nods but leans forward with a thoughtful glance. He's never been one to judge nor give advice to sway me in one direction. He always makes me see both sides of the so-called coin.

"Grieving a relationship takes time. But eventually, a rainbow appears, and the world is bright again."

I smile softly. "If Mom heard you say that, she'd probably cry."

Dad laughs. "She's romantic like that."

"But what if you don't want to grieve? What if it's the biggest regret you have to this day?"

"As someone who has seen their fair share of heartache, I'll say this..." he says, stalling for a brief moment. "If she's the only woman you can think about, then maybe that's speaking the words you're not willing to say out loud."

It's all too much, and no matter how hard I've tried to bury these thoughts, they keep resurfacing like unfinished business.

"But how do you know?"

"You just have to look for the signs. They're everywhere."

The only sign is this trip to London, but in some ways, it wasn't a sign. It was Noah and Lex conveniently needing me to work for them.

"With you and Mom, were there signs?"

Dad smiles fondly. "There was, but we had so much trauma we needed to work through on ourselves. We had to learn to live life on our own before we could love someone else. Does that make sense?"

"Yeah, it does."

When it came to the past, my parents were an open book. Mom would tell Dad and me stories about my father, how when she met him in high school, she knew right away it was love. Dad never made her feel uncomfortable with her stories, allowing her to remember the past without the usual jealousy a man would have for past relationships. It's rather comical, though, that Lex is the exact opposite. Once Rocky brought up Dad and Charlie being engaged, Lex saw red.

"And as for these dreams, I really wish you would get some help. Maybe it's something you and Mom can do together?"

"I'll think about it."

----

Charlie is hands down the best cook in our family. Even Mom will say it, having little to no patience for cooking. If anything, Dad spends more time in the kitchen than she does.

The table is full of all my favorites, and once again, Charlie has gone all out.

Lex is seated at the head of the table with Ashton beside him and Emmy on his lap. His two grandkids fight for his attention, but he doesn't seem to mind, making it look so easy.

Will is on the other side of Ashton with their second son, Archer, who's already fussing in his highchair. It's been a few months since I've seen all the kids, each one of them growing at a rapid rate.

Of course, Millie and Ava are beside each other, arguing about something which is none of their business. Austin is beside Dad and Mom, then on my side is Charlie. Addy and Alexa are on campus studying for finals.

"How long are you back for?" Charlie asks.

"Two days left, then off to London."

Charlie smiles, then without even realizing it, her gaze darts to Lex with a hard stare.

"You'll love London," Will adds. "I mean, the weather is awful, but there's a great vibe if you're in the mood to get out."

Millie clears her throat, staring at her husband with a

pressed smile. "Did you have fun in London? Because according to your stories, you were miserable."

"Heartbroken," Ava points out with a mouthful of food.

Millie crosses her arms, waiting for a response.

"Your dear old father made my life hell." Will passes the blame onto Lex.

Lex is unimpressed, though distracted by Emmy begging him to pay attention to her. She places her hand on his cheek, calling his name.

I chuckle. "Nice, blame the patriarch so you can stay out of the doghouse."

"I'll take Lex over the wrath of a pregnant woman," Will grumbles.

Mom whistles. "Mr. Romano, you're landing yourself in hot water."

"Burn, Romano," Ava teases. "How about you try pushing a baby out of your vagina and see if you can handle that, huh?"

I shake my head. "Ava, I just want to eat."

"Why is Austin the only one who can handle me?"

"Because I'm a doctor, and I've seen far worse," he reminds her.

"Right, I forgot you're always looking at vaginas."

Lex lets out a huff. "Can we please eat now? Without all the talk?"

We eat in silence for not even a minute before the conversation shifts toward work, babies again, anything which gladly doesn't involve vaginas.

Absent from our family dinner are Noah and Kate. According to Charlie, they were in Phoenix for work. Nash had some function to go to, and Sienna went back to campus.

After dinner, I hang out in the living room while Ashton explains Pokemon to me, which, thankfully, I was clued in on from my childhood. The kid can talk nonstop about characters evolving. For an almost four-year-old, he's damn smart.

"Uncle Andy, why don't you live here?"

"I live in New York, you know, the place your parents take you to with the big buildings."

"The place that smells like wee?"

Unsure of what to say, I can't argue since some streets in the city are questionable.

"Sometimes, but it's home."

"Why don't you have a girlfriend?"

Will snickers beside me. "Uncle Andy likes lots of women and at different times."

I chuckle faintly. "Millie will kill you."

Charlie calls the kids for dessert as we head out to the patio where a fire is lit. Austin and Ava join us while we sit around admiring the burning flame.

"How do you really feel about London?" Ava asks. "Without the parentals around to judge your answer."

I lean back into the patio chair, staring at the flame.

"Not sure yet."

"Is it because a certain someone lives there, and you feel obliged to see her?" Millie asks.

"I don't know. Do I have to see her?"

"She's family," Ava reminds me. "I understand you don't talk, but family is family."

"Okay, you're giving it to me from a woman's perspective," I drag.

Ava turns to Austin. "What do you think?"

"I think if she's married with her own family and seeing her will raise unwarranted feelings, just stay away."

"Well, that's rude," Ava complains, then turns to Will. "What about you?"

Will lowers his gaze. "I agree. Nothing harder than seeing a woman you love with someone else."

It suddenly becomes quiet. It dawns on me the history between the four people sitting around me. I lose myself in thought, questioning why this has to be so damn hard.

"Yeah, but addressing the pink elephant in the room..." I begin with but choose my words carefully. "Everyone is where they're meant to be, right?"

"Yes," Millie admits first. "But Andy, sometimes we hurt people and make poor decisions. If you can avoid that, it will cause less heartache in the end. Maybe see where London takes you and go from there."

"It could take you into the pants of some English heiress," Ava muses. "You could be our only hope of being connected to the royal family."

"Too much Eric," Millie tells her as we all laugh.

As we sit here poking fun at Eric's obsession over the royal family, I can't help but admire the two couples in front of me. As corny as it may sound, all of them went through hell to find their great love.

But as for me, I don't know what I want.

All I know is being in London will be the ultimate test as to whether I face my demons or not. I've felt the pain of losing everything important to me, and experiencing the raw heartache all over again is my very reason for wanting to stay away from her.

Hurt me once, shame on you.

Hurt me twice, shame on *me*.

# EIGHT

## JESSA

We enter the grand ballroom as guests of the annual black and white gala held in London.

It's my first time in attendance. This time last year, I was in my third trimester, the size of an elephant, and ready to become a mother for the first time. Most of my pregnancy flew by, but the last few weeks dragged on, making it my least favorite part of the experience.

My arm is linked into Benedict's. The fabric of his designer tuxedo is soft against my bare arm. I wear an Oscar de la Renta gown, white with a strapless bodice and full skirt. The moment I laid eyes on the picture of it, I knew it was the perfect dress for the occasion.

Earlier in the evening, the stylist suggested my unruly hair be tied up into a classic bun. However, it was apparent when she gazed at my hair for what felt like minutes on end, she wasn't impressed with my untamed curls.

I didn't argue, trying to feed Bentley at the same time. Of course, it annoyed her, but I ignored the attitude. She was paid to do the job, and spending time with my son is important to me, especially since he's been fussy of late.

Benedict insisted I wear the diamond necklace he gave me on our first wedding anniversary. It's a beautiful piece, and the sentiment behind it isn't lost on me. Maybe, tonight is the night we can enjoy ourselves, and the Benedict I fell in love with will finally make an appearance again.

During our walk inside the ballroom, Benedict has stopped several times to introduce me to his acquaintances. Wherever he goes, someone knows of him or his family. The Banks are a very influential family, which is why Rosemarie insisted I be 'on show' at all times. Thank God she has been struck with the stomach flu as of this morning. I pretended it was awful, but secretly, relieved she wouldn't be here to criticize my every move.

My gaze moves around the room, admiring the high ornate ceilings with chandeliers hanging and the crystals reflecting across the room. The soft tones are inviting, and the décor enchanting. Organza drapes hang from the arch windows, matching the tablecloths with intricate gold candelabras centered on each table.

The detail is simply exquisite from the china positioned symmetrically on each table to the napkin holder circling the expensive linen—only the best of the best.

As my eyes dance around the room in admiration, the gowns and tuxedos are what make this all the more beguiling. Designer labels, ballgowns, sequins, and even satin—each person is looking beautiful in their own right.

All of it, combined with the band's soft music, is so romantic.

My heart skips a beat as I release a sigh, hoping Benedict will enjoy the night with me. But, as I turn to whisper something to him, his attention is elsewhere.

"Will you excuse me, Jessa? I must speak to Mr. Fairmont. He's been avoiding my calls, and I know he is trying to be difficult on purpose."

As I go to open my mouth, Benedict kisses my cheek and then walks away.

So much for *romance.*

I find myself wandering around, quietly admiring things that catch my eye. Finally, a friend of Rosemarie's stops to say hello, graciously introducing herself and reminding me she was a guest at our wedding. The day had been a blur, and despite me refusing to acknowledge it at the time, I drank way more than I should've to the point where Millie and Ava held back my hair while I repeatedly threw up in the toilet.

My stroll around the ballroom lands me right beside Benedict again, but unfortunately, he doesn't acknowledge my presence in the middle of a conversation with another friend of Rosemarie's.

The conversation is incredibly dull. My eyes are barely able to stay open. It didn't help Bentley was teething last night, keeping me up with his pain. I spent hours cradling him to sleep until we both fell asleep in the rocking chair. There's only so much talk you can take about the countryside before you want to poke your eyes out. The hills are green, the trees are swaying, and there's the smell in the air. Okay, I'm done.

"And the foliage," Mrs. Bruick comments as Benedict nods, only entertaining this because Mrs. Bruick is thinking of selling her land, which he wants in on. "Just stunning."

"Absolutely stunning," Benedict echoes.

My eyes wander around the room, mesmerized by a young woman dressed in a laced white mermaid dress. She's absolutely stunning, tall with what appears to be long, lean legs beneath her dress. Her chestnut brown hair rests against her olive skin in loose, soft curls.

A song plays with a mesmerizing beat, setting the mood, and just when I'm about to ask Benedict if he'd like to dance —the woman catches my attention again. She's across the room, but she is laughing as a man beside her leans in and whispers. Her partner must be saying something to make her eyes dance with such delight, and although it's rude of me to stare, I'm unsure why I can't seem to turn away.

Then, slowly, he pulls away from her ear with a delicious smile on his face. His hair color is oddly familiar, a mixture of golden brown with blond, styled to the side and away from his face.

His striking jawline is masculine, though from where I'm standing, it appears freshly shaven against the warm lighting inside the grand room. Inside my chest, my stilled breath makes no sense, not when my husband is beside me.

*So what if the man looks hot. There's nothing wrong with admiring a good-looking human being.*

And in a split second, the man's eyes meet with mine, drawing every last breath from within my lungs. Goosebumps spread across my skin from the baby blue eyes which are fixated on me, the same eyes I've tried my damned hardest to forget for the last two years.

*This can't be happening.*

My gaze falls to the ground, a hard swallow accompanying the sudden move. This is my imagination playing tricks on me. I blame it on all the romantic talk or maybe the music, certain when I raise my eyes, the man will be a stranger.

The exhaustion, it has to be why I'm delirious with thoughts.

At a slow and agonizing pace, I suck my stomach in, enlarge my chest to take the deepest of breaths, then lift my gaze across the room.

They're gone.

My shoulders fall slightly as my lips press tightly into a grimace. Beside me, Benedict is still talking but this time about history and war. I desperately need champagne and scan the room to see all servers busy with guests. Thankfully, one walks past as I manage to barely swipe a glass. I bring the glass to my lips, relishing in the bubbles which make my mouth tingle before enjoying the drink and allowing it to calm my nerves.

As I turn around, my heart stops like a car slamming its brakes at a red light, the momentary screech becomes a vacant sound so loud the noise inside the room drowns out. The familiar blue eyes are staring right at me, no longer a figment of my imagination.

"Well, hello there, old friend," he greets with a fixed smile.

"Andy?" I barely get out.

"In the flesh."

Benedict stops talking, suddenly appearing beside me, glancing at me, then Andy. It would've been the right moment to hug Andy, but the moment passes, and the only thing left is to introduce him.

Benedict extends his hand to Andy. "Benedict Banks, Jessa's husband. And you are?"

"Andrew Evans-Baker."

*Since when does he use the name Andrew?*

"And how do the two of you know each other?"

"Andy is family, my cousin," I blurt out. "He's Uncle Lex's nephew."

"Family? I don't recall seeing you at our wedding?"

I lower my eyes, trying to rack my brain to think of an excuse, but it's completely blank. Between my heart racing a mile a minute to the nerves crippling any rational thoughts I have, I can't seem to even string a proper sentence together.

Andy is calm and collected, appearing completely unaffected by meeting my husband. The man who ultimately drove a wedge between us.

"Jessa and I haven't seen each other for years, my fault

really," Andy says without emotion. "I travel quite a bit for work, so rarely get to see any of the family."

Benedict nods, appearing satisfied with the response. Someone walking past catches his attention, and quickly, he excuses himself.

As I stand across from Andy, my eyes scan his face, but everything is just how I remember—the two small creases near his left eye and the dimples in his cheeks when he smiles. The seven tiny freckles scattered across his nose, each one I'd named after the seven dwarfs—grumpy being my favorite—since that was Andy's mood after I'd torment him while touching his face.

Perhaps, he has aged, but it only makes him look more mature and devastatingly handsome.

"What are you doing here?" I ask, still trying to process this.

"No, how are you? How have you been?" he questions with the tilt of his head. "I'm in London for work. As for this ball, I was instructed to attend to meet some important contacts."

"You're in London for work? For how long?"

"For as long as I need to be," he discloses, staring deeply into my eyes. "It's a beautiful city."

The woman he was with earlier is walking toward us. Suddenly, a pang in my stomach comes out of nowhere. In closer proximity, she's even more beautiful than from across the room. I have no right to be jealous, so why am I suddenly trying to pick her flaws, of which I'm unable to find any.

"Andy, sweetheart, I'd love for you to meet Mrs. Davenport. She runs a high-profile modeling agency, and word is she just fired her top photographer."

Andy's eyes fall to where she touches his arms, then, slowly, his head lifts to meet my gaze.

"Work calls," is all he says. "I guess I'll see you around."

I stand in the same spot as they walk away, and whatever this woman is saying catches his attention for him not to even turn around to look at me, as if I'm a stranger.

Yet how can I blame him? I chose to move on and abandon the life I knew in the States. Leave my best friend behind without considering his feelings. All my actions were because I lived in fear, running away from everything that scared me.

It would be easy to blame being young, but all of this was only two years ago.

As a waiter walks past, I quickly down my champagne and request another. If I have to get through this night, chances are it won't be sober.

The MC requests all guests to take a seat. Even at the table, Benedict is busy talking to the person beside him. The night begins with speeches, then to dinner being served. I find myself without an appetite, staring at my plate in a daze.

My mind drifts to the blue eyes watching me from a few tables away. Then, suddenly, my skin breaks out into goose-bumps again as if I can feel his touch all over me. With a hard swallow, I shake my head to clear my focus and reach for the champagne rather than the food.

"You haven't touched your food?" Benedict mentions beside me. "Is something wrong with it?"

I force a smile. "It's fine. I'm just tired because Bentley kept me up last night."

"Oh, right."

His response sparks anger within me, especially since he's never woken up to take care of Bentley in the middle of the night. The one time I asked him to help me, he rolled over and said to call the nanny.

"I mean, it wouldn't hurt for you to help on occasion."

"Jessa, I have a stressful job and need to be in meetings all day long. I can't wake up and do what exactly? Mother hired

Eliza to help you," he insists, his tone cold and stern. "I think it's about time you accept her help full-time."

My blood boils, and no doubt, the several glasses of champagne are fueling this argument. Our differences on raising our son is creating a lot of tension between us, but for some reason, right now, I pick an argument.

"When my sister, Sienna, was born, my father would wake up and feed her so Kate could sleep." The memory is all too clear, all the times I'd come into the kitchen at some early hour, and Dad would be walking around with Sienna in his arms trying to put her to sleep again. "My Uncle Lex, he would take my cousins, Ava and Andy, and me to soccer practice twice a week. If you think your job is stressful, I'll argue and say Uncle Lex and my dad's jobs are ten times harder."

Benedict presses his lips flat. "Right, of course, I forgot how rich your family is. Billionaires."

"That has nothing to do with it. My point is all the men in my life have always put their children first."

I throw my napkin onto the table, grab my purse, and head to the restroom to splash cold water on my face. My skin feels red and heated, a mixture of the champagne and our spur-of-the-moment argument.

But I stand by what I said.

Never have I ever felt neglected by my father growing up, and the same goes for Uncle Lex. He treated me like his own daughter, just like he treated Andy like his son.

*Andy...*

I quickly exit the restroom and head back to the ballroom, my eyes scanning the room to see where he is. There are too many people, some of who are moving toward the dance floor. I slowly make my way back to the table, take a seat, and bite into the food. My appetite is less than par, the food cold and bland. Eventually, I give up and go back to the champagne.

The music is a familiar melody, soft with a tune my head hums along to. I find myself gazing at the couples, and then I see Andy dancing with the woman. They're having a conversation and laughing again, all of which rubs me the wrong way.

*You have no right to be jealous.*

I turn to face Benedict. "Let's dance."

Oddly so, he agrees, reaching out for my hand. We walk toward the dance floor, then he brings me in as I rest my hand on his shoulder. His scent invades the air around me, reminding me he's my husband, who I chose till death us do part.

"Jessa," he begins with, but this time his tone is soft. "Let's just enjoy tonight, okay?"

I nod, then force a smile only for my stare to be caught on Andy. His expression is blank, not at all readable. Perhaps, my feelings about how we ended are different from his. He doesn't appear bothered by seeing me with Benedict. Nothing at all like the Andy I remembered who would basically sabotage every date I went on, claiming the men weren't good enough for me, so why bother.

But then I remember that two years have passed. A lot can happen in that time, I mean, look at me—I got married and had a baby.

"I was thinking," Benedict says, moving his lips toward my ear. "How about a weekend away? Just you and me? Maybe in a few weeks once this deal I'm working on is complete. We can visit Spain and have dinner at that restaurant you love so much."

As Benedict's lips touch the base of my neck, my gaze flicks back to Andy, and everything I said earlier isn't the face staring back at me. His jaw is sharp, as if he's biting his tongue. Even from where I dance, his pupils appear wide with anger. I've seen this look several times before, and instinctively, I turn away.

"It sounds like a nice plan," I respond.

"Oh, Jessa, I must speak to Mr. Featherington. His son has a prize horse mother has been dying to get her hands on."

Benedict doesn't even wait for my answer, abandoning me for some prized horse? I stand alone on the dance floor, ready for the wave of humiliation, when my eyes fall upon the shiny black shoes standing near mine.

"Mind if I have this dance?" My gaze drifts up until I'm locked into Andy's deep stare. "I'm sure your husband wouldn't mind, you know, for old times' sake."

"Um, sure," I barely swallow.

Andy places his hand on my waist, and the second he touches me, this current runs through my entire body, leaving me breathless. I dare not look him in the face, scared he'll know what just happened. He brings me in close to him, so we can easily talk.

And there are so many things to be said.

Yet only one comes to mind.

"Won't your girlfriend get jealous you're dancing with someone else?"

"For starters, she's not my girlfriend. She's a business associate," he informs me. "But I guess the real question is won't your husband?"

"Benedict isn't like that."

"Sounds like a true gentleman."

"Just say what you need to say, Andy."

He pulls back slightly to create distance between us. "I have nothing to say, Jessa. I said everything I had to say two years ago. As for you, perhaps you have something you need to say?"

There were so many things to be said, but what did it all

matter anyway? We're both where we need to be in life, and nothing will change that.

"To quote you, Andy, I chose my bed, and now I need to lay in it," I answer back bitterly.

Silence falls between us until he softly whispers, "Jessa..."

But then, Benedict appears beside us. "My wife, can I have you back for another dance?"

I clear my throat, taking my hands off Andy with a smile. "Of course."

Andy shakes his head, then turns his back on me while Benedict grips onto my hand a little too tight.

"You're hurting me," I tell him.

"Well, I walk away for a few seconds, and you're dancing with another man. How does that look to everyone in this room?"

I try to pull back, but his grip is tight. "I don't care what other people think, Benedict. Andy is family. Someone I haven't seen for a long time. All these stuck-up people can go find something better to worry about."

"So, you don't care about shaming our family?"

This time, I force myself out of his grip. His words are the fuse to spark the bomb which just went off inside my head.

"Shaming our family?" I repeat with malice. "I have done nothing but bend over backward for *your* family. What Rosemarie wants, Rosemarie gets. We haven't even gone back to the States since Bentley was born to visit my family."

"Will you lower your voice," he commands.

The nerve of him to even think I'm selfish when all I have ever done is sacrifice myself for him and his family.

Every single part of who I am is no longer *me*.

I'm about to open my mouth to argue his condescending tone when my phone vibrates in my purse. Quickly retrieving it from my clutch, I see Eliza's name on the screen.

"Eliza?" I answer in a hurry. "What's wrong?"

"Mrs. Banks, Bentley is quite ill. His temperature is high, and he won't settle."

My gaze flits around the room as my neck stiffens. "I'm coming home."

I hang up the call with a dry mouth, clutching my stomach with worry.

"You're going home?" Benedict asks angrily.

"Bentley is running a fever. I need to be with him."

"Jessa," Benedict says sternly. "He has Eliza. You can't leave me here. How would that look?"

Deliberately raising my brows, I tilt my head in absolute disgust.

"You worry about everyone here, and I'll worry about our son."

I don't allow him to get another word in, disappointed once again at his inability to put our son first. My feet move fast, knowing it's an hour's drive home.

The moment I step outside, the cool night's air graces my face. I scan the area for our driver, but all the cars look the same and black in the dark.

"Jessa," my name is called.

Taking a deep breath, I choose not to turn around until Andy is by my side.

"Are you just leaving without even saying goodbye?"

"No, I'm leaving because my son is sick and needs me." I let out a long-winded sigh. "Our nanny just called. Bentley is running a high fever. And, of course, Benedict thinks it's more important to be here than with his son."

The moment I say it, I regret being honest. Despite Andy being my best friend for my entire life, I don't want him to see how unhappy I am in my marriage.

And there's the truth.

As bold as it gets.

"Where the hell is our driver?" I mutter beneath my breath.

"I'm taking you home."

"You can't take me home."

"Why?"

"Because you have a date inside, and I'm perfectly capable of dealing with this once my driver is here."

Andy grabs my hand without my permission, then fumbles for keys in his pocket until he extends the remote out and a black Range Rover's taillights flicker orange.

"Get in. I'm taking you home."

I'm too tired to fight, the champagne wearing off, and the stress of tonight all too much. As I sit inside the car on the tan leather seats, Andy asks for the address to type it into his GPS. The navigation tells us it will be just under an hour to get home.

I quickly call Eliza to get an update, hearing Bentley wail in the background. My heart is breaking, knowing my son is in pain. I try my best not to cry in front of Andy, needing to remain strong since that's what mothers are supposed to do.

Music plays on the radio. It's Andy's playlist, and, of course, his taste is so vast you don't know whether you're going to get something modern or a classic from the '70s. I recognize the song, a tune from Queen. We sang it often when drunk at some karaoke bar.

"Your taste in music hasn't changed, I see," I begin, then stall, unsure how to talk to him. "I remember singing this when Ava got so wasted on shots. You had to carry her out just as Uncle Lex called you."

A small smile plays on his lips. "My cousin sure knows how to have a good time. Thankfully, she's no longer a wild party girl."

"How is Ava?"

"Good, the same."

I nod quietly, my gaze drifting toward the window, but all I see is pitch black. Sitting beside Andy feels nostalgic, yet at the same time, parts of him feel like a complete stranger. Of all the times we would be in the car together, our conversations would be nonstop, several of them turning into heated debates. We argued over everything, but in the same breath, laughed at everything just as much.

"So, you said you're here for work?"

"Yes," is all he says.

I bite my tongue, but as always, restraining myself can only last so long.

"Look, I'm not good at small talk, and I think we're beyond that. Just answer my question like a normal human being, please."

"Demanding much?" he deadpans. "I'll be photographing and directing the filming of new luxury boutique hotels across Europe. Would you like to know more?"

"Why yes, please," I drag.

"Lex and Noah approached me to work on this as they want to launch as quickly as possible."

The moment I hear my dad's name, I flinch my head back in confusion.

"My dad wanted you to work in London?"

"Actually, Lex approached me. Noah and Kate were at the official meeting."

It's odd neither Dad nor Kate had said anything considering they know I live here. Dad, I can excuse since we barely said two words to each other, but I'm surprised Kate mentioned nothing.

The house appears on our right. "The house is just through those gates."

Andy drives through the gates to park the car out front. I expect him to leave, but he insists on making sure Bentley is okay, catching me by surprise that he even wants to see him.

We head inside, and Andy follows me toward Bentley's room. As my steps get closer, I hear Bentley's tired cry, which causes me to run inside, nearly tripping on my gown.

Eliza is sitting on the chair, trying to soothe him. She looks exhausted, and quickly, I take him from her to rock him in my arms.

"Mama's here, baby boy," I whisper.

I place my hand on his forehead, the skin heated from just a touch.

"Eliza, please bring me some pain reliever and a cold washcloth."

I continue to rock Bentley while Eliza disappears to return moments later. As I administer the medication, Bentley fusses but thankfully swallows. When he calms down, I dab his forehead with the washcloth knowing his teeth are incredibly sore, which is why he's in so much pain. I'd looked it up online, then called Mom and Kate for advice. They weren't the best of help since apparently Nash, Sienna, and I passed the teething stage with flying colors. However, Aunt Charlie's experience was different. We texted back and forth, and she gave me tips on how to manage it since apparently, all her daughters were a nightmare.

In my arms, Bentley's eyes begin to close, and his breathing becomes heavy.

"I've got it from here," I whisper to Eliza. "Go get some rest. You did amazing, and I can't thank you enough."

"Are you sure?" she asks, eyeing Andy.

"Yes." I smile. "Oh, Eliza, this is Andy, my cousin."

She nods to say hello but quickly leaves the room, looking relieved for the chance to rest. Eliza is in her early twenties with no children of her own. I feel terrible given this is her first child to take care of, and she must have been worried sick to have to call me.

My gaze falls upon my baby boy, grateful he's finally sleeping through the pain.

As I walk around the room, I stop near the window as Andy walks toward me.

"He's beautiful, Jessa," Andy murmurs, his eyes fixated on Bentley with a loving smile. "Motherhood suits you."

And then, the memories begin to play. How on occasion, I allowed my imagination to wander, and when I carried a child in my arms, the child belonged to Andy. They began as teenage dreams, but every time, I told myself it was wrong. We were family.

My lips part, the weight in my chest heavy as Andy lingers beside me. Slowly, my eyes lift until inside the dimly lit room, they're locked into his like a magnetic force I can't control.

"Thank you," I barely manage, the surrealness of him standing beside me coupled with exhaustion, toying with my emotions. "For taking me home."

"It doesn't have to be this way between us, Jessa."

I divert my gaze, scared of breaking down in front of the one person I don't want to see my flaws.

"Andy, I'm not the same person anymore."

"Neither am I," he tells me.

"I don't know what you want from me..." I trail off, willing the pounding inside my chest to even out to a normal pace. "I have nothing to offer you."

And then, Andy places his finger beneath my chin and raises my head, so our eyes meet again. His penetrating stare has always been ingrained in me, but if only our circumstances were different.

If only he wasn't raised to be my family.

If only he had been a boy next door or even a classmate in school.

If only I didn't run away and fall head over heels for a man to escape the person standing in front of me.

But then, I remember the little boy in my arms is why I'd never change anything, no matter how my heart thinks things could've been different.

"You're family, Jessa," he breathes. "We were family before best friends. Our branches may have grown elsewhere, but our roots remain as one."

I stare into his eyes, and just like that, a piece of the old Andy comes back to life.

"Family," I whisper while watching my son sleep. "When we have family, we have everything."

# NINE

## ANDY

"Andy, we need to be across town in an hour."

I pull my face away from the lens as Anastasia stands beside me, waiting for a response. She's typing away busily on her phone while I try to focus on the room in front of me. I tilt my head left, then right, not understanding why I'm unable to capture what my vision so desperately seeks.

And then, Jessa's face flashes in my thoughts.

The memory of last night is too raw. From the moment I laid eyes on her from across the room, I knew there was a reason for me being forced to attend an event I didn't care for.

Anastasia was telling me an anecdote, something about a similar event she attended once with a drunk MC. The story was humorous enough to lighten my mood, coupled with the wine served to us.

But then, one glance across the room, and my fate had been met.

The second our eyes connected, a warm rush spread across my entire body, stilling the beat inside my chest, if only for a moment. There has only ever been one person to make me feel this way, and she was standing across the room equally as shocked to see me.

My body stiffened even when Anastasia pulled me away to meet some English billionaire like I gave a goddamn fuck. I was introduced to a couple, names I can't even recall. The only thing I wanted was to find Jessa and talk to her, desperate to see her only inches away and feast upon her like my imagination had done over and over again since the moment she left home.

The talking continued, but I excused myself and walked around the room, remembering how Noah insisted I attend this ball to meet clients. He was adamant my work is beyond anything they've ever seen and the importance of making new contacts.

That was business-driven Noah Mason talking. I'm more inclined to think Noah's protective stance on his daughter was his true agenda for me attending.

The coincidence is all too much.

Jessa stood by herself, her back toward me, but her delicate skin was only an arm's length away. I tortured myself by standing this close to her, knowing my limits were being pushed. She's married, and nothing will change that.

But tormenting myself for a moment with her was my guilty pleasure.

When she turned around, the hazel eyes fixated on my face, her stare almost *killing* me on the spot.

*I still fucking loved her.*

And I got that all from one stare.

The rest of the night's memories come and go—our conversations, to how beautiful she was in her white gown. The brief, albeit introduction to her husband. A man I loathed with every fiber of my being. In a heartbeat, he'd offered Jessa everything I waited too long for. I blamed myself for the longest of times, but I wasn't the only one at fault. Jessa jumped into his arms like I was nothing.

The dance I dared to ask for, our small conversations, to the drive home to care for her sick son.

And while all of last night plays in my head, the vision of her cradling her son sticks with me the most. She'd never looked so perfect, destined to be a mother, of that, I'm sure. But it broke me at the same time, knowing there'll never be a chance for us, not when she has a family of her own.

The wounds and scars from her decision to walk away from us were raw and exposed, bleeding at the edges as I stood inside the home belonging to Jessa and her husband. The brick and mortar representing more than a house. It's a place they built a life together—a place to share memories and experience all the wondrous things as husband and wife.

All the things I could've offered her if she had just stayed.

If I'd had the guts to fight for her like I should have.

As I stood watching Jessa with a dullness inside my chest, the anguish on her face was enough to tell me Noah had been right. His daughter wasn't happy, and I hated seeing her struggle with her son alone.

Her husband should've been there instead of allowing her to go home with me. It made me think of all the times my dad or Lex made sure I was never without their support. From the earliest of memories, they were always around, and Mom always said she was grateful for the men in her life who loved me like their own.

When I drove away, I went straight to the hotel and nursed a bourbon beside the window until dawn. Then, at least the nightmares had no way of finding me if I didn't fall asleep.

"Andy, sweetheart. You look tired, more coffee?"

I shake my head to bring myself back to reality, then force a smile. I've lost track of how many I've drunk today, another reason why my concentration is close to non-existent.

"I might have to try this again tomorrow," I inform Anastasia, then remember this thing she needs us to go to. "How important is this meeting you need me for?"

Anastasia looks up at me with concern. "I can reschedule. Is everything okay?"

Again, I force a smile because speaking about my personal life isn't an option right now. My phone vibrates in the back pocket of my jeans, a welcome distraction as Anastasia steps away so I can take the call in private. I pull it out of my jeans, glancing at the screen to see the unknown number, yet answer it anyway.

"Hello, Andy speaking."

"Andy, this is Benedict Banks," he introduces himself formally, causing me to still my movements. "I hope you don't mind me calling you on this number? Kate was so kind to pass it onto me."

"No, it's fine."

"I'd like to invite you to lunch tomorrow if you're free. I know Jessa doesn't have family here, and with Bentley being a bit difficult of late, I thought it would be a nice surprise to have you over."

I hesitate, not knowing him at all. If the true intent behind this is for Jessa, then, of course, I want to see her, despite my brain telling me to back the hell away. Stepping back into their home will only torture the feelings I'm trying to bury.

But the pain is a reminder of the mistakes I made, and the only way to move on and let go of her as anything more than a friend is to build resistance. The more I see her as the new Jessa, the more I can move forward with my life.

Let her go once and for all.

"Text me all the details. I'll be there."

---

I'm toying with the idea of texting Jessa, though I'll have to get her number from my cousins. That itself isn't worth the drama. Both Millie and Ava will interrogate me, asking a million questions for which I have no time or patience.

All I want is to make sure she knows, not wanting to surprise her and have her act all awkward around me. If Benedict told her, she hadn't texted me either.

The butler opens the large door, welcoming me inside in a formal tone. I chose to wear a light blue buttoned shirt and black pants over jeans and a tee since Benedict didn't appear to be a casual type of guy.

The moment I step inside the grand foyer, Jessa walks down the stairs with Bentley in her arms, stopping halfway on the landing when her eyes fall upon mine. The knee-length navy dress she wears reminds me of a school uniform, pristine and nothing at all like the ripped jean shorts she would wear back home. Her hair is left out, the curls just how I remember, and the urge to tug on them is too much.

"A... Andy?" she stammers. "What are you doing here?"

"Your husband invited me for lunch."

Benedict walks in from another room as his gaze darts from Jessa to me. He extends his hand to shake mine, which I do so politely, considering I'm standing in his home. I'm thanking myself for taking a swig of the bourbon I had sitting inside a flask in the car, eager to take the edge off today.

"I invited him over. I thought it would be nice for you to spend time with family."

Jessa tries to hide her worry, forcing a smile. "Of course, what a wonderful thought."

"Shall we then?"

I follow Benedict as Jessa walks beside me, carrying Bentley in her arms. The little boy is happy to be in his mama's embrace, smiling back at me.

"Why did you say yes?" she barely whispers.

"Because it would look bad if I said no."

"What's that supposed to mean?"

We reach the formal dining room, and Benedict gestures for me to take a seat across from Jessa. The table is large enough for at least twelve guests, giving ample space for the servers to place trays of food in front of us. I notice the blood pudding, noting to stay away from it since its appeal is less than par.

Across the table, Jessa is trying to get Bentley to eat something, but he's more interested in banging his spoon on the plate. Benedict glances at his son, insisting he stop the incessant noise to which Jessa tries to retrieve the spoon from his chubby little hands.

"Tell me more about your work?" Benedict asks, focusing his attention back onto me.

I explain more about Lex and Noah's vision, not sure what else to talk about with him since this lunch is already peaking at an uncomfortable level. The more we converse, the more my mind questions precisely what made her fall in love with him. Sure, he's attractive and well-dressed, but his personality is stiff. He comes across as arrogant and entitled. Everything Jessa despised in men. At least, she used to.

The talk bores Jessa when Benedict segues to the stock market. In an effort to include Jessa, I nod my head but don't encourage the conversation to continue.

I place my fork down, fixating on Jessa as she finally gets a moment to take a bite of food. Bentley is distracted with fruit which he enjoys squashing in his hands.

"Have you managed to pursue your writing?" I ask, hoping the shift in topic will relieve her.

Her eyes fall toward the plate, and only now do I notice she's stirring her food around. "I... uh... I'm taking a break to spend time with Bentley."

"Banks women have very important roles in our family," Benedict states, placing his hand on Jessa's. My eyes instantly notice the gesture and how Jessa doesn't welcome it with a smile on her face. The muscles inside my chest begin to tighten, forcing me to turn away to ease the burning sensation while ignoring his sexist comment.

The butler enters the room, sliding a note to Benedict.

"Will you both excuse me? An investor from Hong Kong insists I jump on a video call right now. Normally, I would decline, but he's putting a lot of money into our next project and would only ask if it's important."

"It's fine," Jessa says while attempting to clean Bentley's face. "I'll show Andy the gardens so Bentley can get out before his afternoon nap."

Benedict shakes my hand, thanking me for joining them, then insists on dinner in London when he's back from a business trip. I nod, neither agreeing nor disagreeing with the suggestion for dinner.

As soon as he leaves, Jessa lifts Bentley from his highchair and suggests we take a walk outside.

The day isn't as overcast, with pockets of blue skies appearing here and there. The grounds of their property are large, manicured hedges and what seems to be a maze toward the left. Everything is so green, a vast difference from the desert environment we grew up in.

There's a small outdoor setting near a patch of grass. Jessa places Bentley on the ground so he can explore. He notices a plane in the sky, pointing to it while trying to mouth out the word. It gives me a moment to ask the burning question on the tip of my tongue.

"So, you just quit writing?"

Jessa folds her arms across her chest with a gaze that flicks upward. My honesty has struck a nerve, yet perhaps it needs to.

"I didn't just quit. As I said, I'm having a break."

I nod, then purse my lips.

"What?"

"Nothing," I say, shrugging my shoulders.

"Your nothing is always a something."

"You're taking a break, I heard you."

"No, you didn't. You think I quit because Benedict's family insisted I be a wife and mother."

"Well, did they?"

"You know what, Andy?" Her sudden change in mood is so typically Jessa. "Life isn't easy. Sometimes we have to make sacrifices."

"There's making sacrifices, but you should always come first."

Jessa shakes her head as her lips press into a white slash. Then a smile plays on her lips, oddly so. Finally, she lowers her gaze, but whatever I said appears to be amusing.

"What's so funny?"

"Nothing," she's quick to respond.

I cock my head, sighing heavily with exaggeration. "Go on. You know you want to say something."

"It's inappropriate."

"We crossed that line when you offered to give me a manscape of a lightning bolt," I remind her.

A sly grin graces her beautiful face, giving me a glimpse of the Jessa I remember.

"I was drunk on various liquor we poured into a bowl

because it was all we could find in your apartment. Thankfully, you rejected my offering."

"Best decision of my life," I mutter. "So, what was so funny about what I said? I mean it, you should always come first, Jessa."

She clears her throat, but with her lips pressed flat, suppressing her smile, I can see something is still amusing her.

"I guess coming first wouldn't be so selfish."

And then the penny drops. How stupid of me not to see that. Being around professional people who have no sense of humor has rubbed off on me.

*If Jessa were mine, she would be first every goddamn time.*

My pants leave nothing for the imagination, forcing me to look into the sky and think of anything to calm my dick down. Seriously, the last time I slept with a woman was Nina, and that didn't turn out great.

"Some things never change with you," Jessa muses. "Lucky, you're single."

"Why? Because you think I sleep around?"

"Well, you're a handsome man who has needs." She lowers her gaze, unable to look at me. "Part of the food chain."

"You're making me sound like a piece of meat."

She manages to chuckle softly. "I'm sure many women want the great Andrew Evans-Baker in their bed."

"Yeah, but when it's not the one you want, then it doesn't matter, right?"

Her smile wavers, and with a quick glance, she clears her throat. I've made her uncomfortable, but dammit, the truth needed to be said. All the women I've slept with have meant nothing. There were moments of lust, a quick fuck to clear my mind, which always did circles back to the original source of my problems. The woman sitting beside me.

I've spent hours imagining her naked, in my bed, picturing just how perfect she would feel. Each one of those times led me to jerking off, the only relief. But it's been a while since I'd done that, realizing the only one who suffered was me.

"So, Benedict understands we're family," I mention to shift the tension. "Therefore, he'll have no issues if I take you out for the day, maybe show you what I'm working on?"

"Uh, sure," she hesitates, fiddling with the skirt of her dress. "When are you thinking?"

"Tomorrow."

"Tomorrow? I'm not sure Eliza can watch Bentley."

"Bring him along. We can take him to the park and feed ducks."

She rolls her eyes, then furrows her brows. "You know how I feel about lakeside animals."

Some things never change.

But fuck, how I missed it all.

"Maybe it's time to face your fears," I muse at the same time Bentley crawls over to me and pulls himself up using my legs. "We'll have fun, won't we, little dude?"

Beside me, Jessa's lips curve upward, and her shoulders finally relax.

"I know just the place we can visit."

# TEN

## JESSA

The day is relatively warm with a slight breeze in the air.

I'm sitting on the grass with Bentley in his stroller at Greenwich Park. He keeps himself busy with a toy attached to the handle, a squishy caterpillar making a crunching sound he enjoys.

I welcome the momentary break, especially since last night he woke up three times crying. His appetite has resumed, so I didn't think it was his teeth again, but his tossing and turning ultimately led to him waking.

Eliza doesn't spend the nights at our house, despite Benedict insisting she occupy the room beside Bentley's. I'm not going to change my mind, even though I'm utterly exhausted and can use the help. It's times like these I wish Benedict would just offer instead of me nagging and a fight erupting between us.

This is what happened at precisely four o'clock in the morning before he left for a flight to Milan.

"A spot near the lake. Is this really, Jessa?"

Andy is standing beside me, carrying a tray of coffees like

he could read my mind. Wearing a black tee, jeans, and sneakers, this is the old Andy I remember. So casually sexy, and the guy doesn't even know it. His body has changed, much more muscular than I remember, but quickly, I glance elsewhere so not to be caught.

He rattles the toy in front of Bentley, making him giggle before Bentley finds the cracker he dropped earlier and places it in his mouth.

"There are no swans, I checked. Ducks, I can handle."

"You know ducks can attack," Andy chastises while sitting beside me on the grass.

I roll my eyes, then let out a yawn. "Don't mess with me. I'm tired. Someone decided to wake up three times last night."

"Who?" Andy asks, tickling his little chubby hands. "This innocent little boy?"

A huff escapes me. "Innocent until it's three in the morning, and he's crying for no reason."

"So, coffee then?"

"Yes, please."

Andy passes the hot beverage over, the smell lingering in the air so deliciously. As soon as the warm liquid hits my throat, I instantly let out a sigh.

"That good?"

"So good, heaven... almost."

"It's good." He nods, then wrinkles his forehead. "Different is perhaps the word more suited."

I laugh. "Let me guess. You're still used to our coffee back home?"

"Yeah, odd, I guess since everyone raves about European coffee."

"You get used to it." I raise my eyes, watching the clouds begin to hover. "Much like the weather."

Andy drinks his coffee with a sly grin on his face.

"C'mon, how can you pick this over the Californian sunshine?"

I place my cup down to remove Bentley from his stroller so he can sit between us and play with the leaves scattered on the grass. He loves to be outdoors, playing with nature and things he probably shouldn't be touching. Although he will be soon, he still isn't walking but can pull himself up if he wants something.

"Sometimes..." I add to the conversation, "... change is good."

It's a more straightforward answer than admitting the truth. Of course, I miss home and everything about it, but this place is my home now.

"So, how is the job with my dad coming along?"

Andy shrugs. "Some days easy, some days hard. When it's difficult to focus, it takes me a while to get the images right. The last few days have been hard..."

His words trail off at the same time he glances in the opposite direction. When it comes to his creativity, Andy needs to be focused. It's how he has always performed best.

"You're such a perfectionist. Much like Uncle Lex."

Andy chuckles softly. "That man is a next-level perfectionist."

"How is he?"

"Knee-deep in grandchildren."

"Seriously, Millie and Ava are crazy. Just one child is hard enough. I can't imagine two or even three in Millie's case."

"Hmm," he murmurs, passing a leaf to Bentley as he scrunches it up in his hand. "You know Will and Austin, they're like our dads. They make it look so easy."

I lower my head, knowing how much it hurts that Bentley doesn't have the same experience. Having children or how they would be raised was never a discussion Benedict and I had when we decided to get married, which is why the pregnancy took us both by surprise. In hindsight, I realize just how meaningful these conversations are, or you can end up in my shoes. Married to a man who thinks providing money is the same as being a dad.

"What's wrong? You've gone quiet for minutes."

"Nothing."

"Okay, say I pretend it's nothing and move on from the conversation. You and I both know it will come up randomly in the middle of another conversation, and I'm supposed to remember what we spoke about."

He knows me too well, of course.

I clear my throat. "It's nice Millie and Ava have help, that's all."

"It's not help, Jessa. It's a joint effort as it should be with parents."

"Right..."

Andy grabs my cup along with his own and tosses it in the trash can not too far away, choosing to keep his opinion to himself. I know he wants to say something, but I don't try to get it out of him, which ultimately will lead to us arguing over my husband.

"So, that woman at the ball, you never said her name?"

"Anastasia?"

"Nice."

"Nice?" he repeats. "And you asked because..."

"Because that's what friends do."

"I'm not dating her if that's where you're going with this."

I turn to face him. "I wasn't going there. Besides, why would I care? You're single as if I'd care who you date."

He nods. "Or fuck, right? Because you know I don't date but still need to get laid."

A painful tightness restricts my throat, causing a wave of nausea which I try to ignore. I'd be stupid to think he would stay celibate for the hell of it. I just don't understand why him being with other women still gets to me.

"Yep, just a typical guy," is all I say.

Bentley fusses, rubbing his eyes. Andy tries to distract him with a plane in the sky which works for a few minutes, but he has those hangry eyes—a combination of hunger that turns into anger.

"I need to feed Bentley, plus it's time for his nap." A small trickle of rain hits my forehead. Great, so London. I scoop Bentley in my arms as the rain begins to fall heavier, trying to protect him.

"My hotel is across the street. Take him back to my suite and out of this rain."

Andy reaches his arms out to take Bentley from me. I pass him over, making sure everything is inside the stroller as I follow Andy to the hotel.

I welcome the warm air inside the lobby, but as we make our way up, Bentley becomes more tired and cries while Andy manages to calm him down enough until we're inside the room.

"Can I change him on your bed?"

"Of course, inside there."

The room is a typical hotel suite, but five stars, of course, because no chance in hell Uncle Lex or Dad would let Andy stay anywhere else. I'd barely caught a glimpse of the lobby, worried about Bentley's tired tantrum.

Andy passes me the diaper bag, trying to distract Bentley on the bed while I quickly change him. When he's all clean, I grab his bottle and cradle him in my arms, knowing he'll be asleep in a few minutes.

I sit on the bed as Andy puts a pillow behind me, a simple gesture I welcome. Just as I predicted, Bentley closes his eyes halfway through his bottle.

"He must be so tired. He's going through this stage. Aunt

Charlie said it's normal but will test my patience," I say, unaware I'm just rambling. "I'm always so exhausted, but he's my son. He's not Eliza's son. At least that's what I keep trying to tell Benedict."

Andy is sitting in front of me, only an arm's length away, as he watches Bentley with a soft smile.

"It's not wrong to ask for help if you need it."

"My mom didn't have help, neither did Kate or Aunt Charlie," I remind him, the guilt weighing heavy on my shoulders. "Or your mom."

"True, but they had each other. What's the saying about it takes a village to raise a child?"

I smile. "Millie says that all the time."

"She does. Look, Millie and Ava have so much family around them to help. Don't compare yourself to them. It can't be easy here without our family around."

I bite my lip, holding back the stupid tears, but unfortunately, one falls down my cheek. Being alone is more complicated than I want to admit, but I hadn't breathed a word to Mom or Kate, scared they would tell Dad, and all hell would break loose. He'll say, 'I told you so,' and I'll get angry and stop talking to him for good.

"Hey," Andy whispers, then leans forward to wipe the tear from my face. His touch is soft, making me close my eyes momentarily. "What's wrong?"

"It's hard," I whisper. "Doing this all alone."

Andy lowers his eyes, careful with his words. "For now, you're not alone, okay? I'm here if you need me. You just call."

I smile at his offering. "Maybe I haven't completely changed. I'm still somewhat of a hot mess."

His eyes sparkle followed by his mouth twisting. "No comment from me."

Beside me, my phone rings, but I quickly hit reject not to

wake Bentley up. Benedict's name appears on the screen. I switch the phone to silent and send him a text.

ME

Bentley is asleep in my arms. I don't want to wake him.

BENEDICT

Where are you?

I hesitate, unsure what I should say. The truth, while honest, doesn't sound great. 'Oh, hey, I'm sitting in bed with Andy.'

"Is something wrong?"

"Benedict wants to know where I am."

"So, tell him you're with me? I'm family, remember?"

"Um, yeah, but it won't come out right if I say we're in your hotel room."

I send a quick text.

ME

About to head home.

"I should probably go," I tell Andy, not wanting to leave but knowing I can't stay here forever.

I place Bentley into his stroller with his blanket as he continues to sleep. I text the driver to meet me, and he responds, saying he'll be about ten minutes.

"My driver will be here in ten minutes." I slide the phone back into my purse. "Thank you for today. I'm sorry we didn't get a chance to see the hotel you're working on. Rain check?"

"Of course," he says and pauses before continuing. "And hey, no need to thank me. I didn't do anything."

My eyes drift until they lock onto Andy's. He may not even realize it, but everything he gave me today is what I need—the support, the courage, and the offering to help out of his own will.

"You did more than you know," I whisper.

As I begin to push the stroller, Andy grabs my arm gently, causing me to stop. My chest hitches, but I turn around anyway.

"Jessa, what I said before, I didn't mean it."

I tilt my head. "Which part?"

"About the other women."

I lower my gaze, biting my lip. "We both know it's true. You're not a priest."

"No, I'm not a priest."

"So, you do fuck other women?" I repeat, wondering why I can't let this go.

"It's not as brutal as you make it sound."

With a slow, disbelieving head shake, I ignore the tightness inside my throat. "You're not the one hearing it, Andy."

His gaze flickers, then he pinches his lips together.

"Well, you're not standing in front of a married woman."

As our eyes battle with words spoken and the words which remain unspoken, the deep stare coming from my former best friend evokes emotions I've long buried. Then, a wave of guilt consumes me.

"I need to go."

"Of course, to play happy families," he mutters under his breath.

"That's where you're wrong, Andy. You can believe everything you want to believe, but surely, you know me better than anyone else. I'm going home because I have no choice."

"You always have a choice, Jessa."

"It's not my life anymore," I whisper. "But you, you have everything."

He drops his head. At the same time, I notice his chest begin to rise and fall. Then, slowly, he lifts his eyes, and his penetrating stare touches every part of my body. I try to stand still, ignoring the voices urging him to touch me.

But all these feelings are wrong. I'm a married woman, and I'll never betray my husband.

"That's where you're wrong," he finally says, moving his fingers toward a loose curl where he tugs it softly, causing my breath to hitch. "I don't have everything. If I did, you wouldn't be going home to another man."

# ELEVEN

## JESSA

The phone rings while resting on the bathroom countertop.

Bentley is sitting inside the bathtub, splashing around and playing with his bath toys. I reach over to see *Benedict* on the screen. Then, with a deep breath, I answer the call.

"Jessa," he greets in a formal tone. "It's nice of you to finally answer."

"I'm bathing our son, hoping he'll relax and sleep through the night."

There's silence between us even though I can hear noise in the background. Benedict is in Milan for two days, nothing unusual. Rarely do I ask questions anymore, unable to keep up with what's going on because my focus is always on Bentley.

"Where were you today?"

I bite my lip, knowing the truth is better than being caught in a lie.

"I went to visit Andy in London. We took Bentley to the

park, drank coffee..." I pause, but quickly continue, "... then the weather turned, so I came home."

"You never mentioned you were going to meet him?"

"It slipped my mind. Bentley woke up several times, and you were leaving for Milan."

Someone calls his name, distracting him momentarily. Benedict's voice muffles, assuming he's talking to someone else while I wait in annoyance.

"Next time, I insist you tell me where you're going, especially since you are taking our son out."

My lips curl as the pound of my heart becomes louder. Heat flushes through my body, causing me to breathe heavily.

"Andy is family. I shouldn't have to justify my actions when it comes to family. So, I went out. God knows what you do, Benedict, on these work trips. Have you ever wondered why Bentley has never called you Daddy?" I ask hastily.

"Jessa," Benedict growls. "I don't need this now."

I release a sinister laugh. "Right, you never need your son."

My fingers move to the screen, slamming the red button to end the call as I tighten my grip on the phone—the nerve of him to question me and use our son as an excuse. The anger continues to fester inside of me while Bentley continues to play. I need to vent, and now, so I press dial on Ava's number.

"Hey!" she cheers over the phone. "Is this my long-lost English cousin?"

I smile, barely. "Yeah, hope it's okay to call you?"

"It's always okay to call me, except maybe when my husband is on night shift, and I'm mauling him like a feral animal during the day when he's supposed to be asleep."

"How is Austin?" I chuckle.

"Tired," she tells me, then lets out a sigh. "He just came home from night shift and is trying to get Emmy to eat, but, of course, she wants to run around. Poor guy, he looks beat."

I can imagine it now, Austin still giving his undivided attention to his daughter. When Austin and Ava got married, a particular moment stuck with me—their vows.

The exact words, while lost on me at this very moment, were powerful. They evoked so much emotion, remembering how both Millie and I were in tears. Austin promised to love and protect their family, their marriage, but more importantly, he promised to be the best man for their daughter and future children.

"You've got yourself a good man. Please tell him I said hello."

"I know. He's a keeper. And of course, I'll pass the message on." Ava pauses momentarily, then lowers her voice. "Is everything okay?"

My gaze shifts toward Bentley, wishing things were different. Just hearing Ava's voice on the phone makes me realize how much I miss her and everyone back home. Bentley would have so much fun with his cousins.

"I'm sorry I've been MIA," I say quietly.

"Oh, Jessa, we've all gone through this. Remember when Millie was sneaking around with Will? She barely spoke to us, and when she did, she always lied about her whereabouts."

"I remember."

"And what about me? I didn't speak to anyone when I was trying to hide my pregnancy. I kept telling you guys I was busy with work."

"We believed it." I sigh.

"So... it's fine, okay? Just life."

"I saw Andy," I blurt out, desperate to get this off my chest and to someone who'll understand. "Correction, I saw him, and we're talking again. In fact, we hung out for a bit today with Bentley."

There's an absence of sound on Ava's end, prompting me to check to see if the call is still connected.

"Ava, are you still there?"

"Yes, I'm trying to process," she informs me. "God, it explains why he never responds to me, like ever."

"This only happened a few nights ago."

I explained to her about the ball, and typical Ava wants every detail, not a single thing left out. She needs context, so she can understand exactly what happened, then give her brutal opinion.

"Okay, so this is a lot for me to take in."

"Really? I think Will and Millie screwing behind your dad's back was a lot to take in."

"Yes, that was a lot to take in. But, so, you and Andy…"

"There's nothing going on."

Ava falls quiet again.

"Ava!" I almost yell. "Don't go all quiet on me. Say what you need to say. I need a reality check here. Benedict is acting all weird, and his behavior doesn't make sense. One minute he's inviting Andy over for lunch, and the next he wants me to report my every move."

"Are you sure you want my honest opinion?"

"I wouldn't have called if I didn't. If I need someone rational, I'd have called Millie."

"Andy's still in love with you."

The moment the words drop, Bentley latches onto the edge of the tub and attempts to climb out. He's done, and despite me wanting to talk to Ava, he needs to get out and dried off.

"I'm not ignoring you, I promise. But Bentley needs to get out of the bath. I'll call you tomorrow, okay?"

"You better, and hey…" Ava trails off.

"Yes?"

"I miss you, girl."

"Me too, Ava," I say with a smile. "Me too."

After I dry and get Bentley dressed in his onesie, we head downstairs together to make his bottle. The staff always offers to help, but I assure them it's fine and to take a break. The one time Rosemarie heard me say that, she went straight to Benedict to complain we were underworking our staff.

Somewhere out there, a broomstick is calling her name.

We head back upstairs to Bentley's room. With his night light on and lullaby music playing, I place him in the crib with his bottle and kiss him goodnight. I linger for a while in his closet, sorting his clothes before finding him fast asleep with an empty bottle beside him.

Back downstairs, I wash his bottle, then decide to head to bed early.

I purposely take a long shower, relishing in the hot water to relax my tense muscles, then climb into the king-size bed, hoping to read before falling asleep.

But Ava's words are on repeat in my head.

*"Andy's still in love with you."*

I don't know what compels me, but I grab my phone to text Andy.

ME

Are you awake?

The bubble appears almost instantly.

ANDY

I'm always awake.

ME

I spoke to Ava tonight.

ANDY

Explains why she's blowing up my phone asking me what I've been up to.

ME

I had to go, I was bathing Bentley, but she mentioned something about you.

ANDY

Is it about the time you got drunk, and I drew that fake mustache on you but blamed Nash?

ME

I knew it was you! No way could he draw such a perfect curve.

ANDY

Like you said... I'm a perfectionist.

Without even thinking rationally, I dial his number needing to hear his voice.

"What's with you and calling mid text?" he asks, but I hear the smile in his voice. "You know it makes introverts uncomfortable?"

I take a deep breath, closing my eyes, but decide if I'm going to mention this, I'll change the wording slightly. Focus on the past, not the present.

"Ava said you were in love with me."

The expected silence is loud and unapologetic. I hear a rustle, then Andy releases a breath.

"Is that what she said?"

"Yes, is it true?"

"What does it matter now?"

"It matters, okay?" I persist. "Is it true, Andy?"

"Yes."

I try to think of something appropriate to say, but my mind wants answers more than anything. Between the small mention of him standing in front of me but unable to have me, to now this, it's a lot to take in. Life would've turned out very differently if this honesty had been conveyed two years ago.

"Why didn't you say anything two years ago?"

"Why?" His tone changes, laced with frustration. "I tried, Jessa. But you pushed me away. Then, you ran off to London and came back engaged."

My chest caves in, knowing I'm so much to blame for this. I did run away because I was scared. But now, I have this life and a son I can't imagine life without. The push-pull of regret is a constant battle, the eternal 'what-ifs' playing like a broken record.

"You still could've told me," I whisper.

"I kissed you, but you still walked away. I can't fight for someone who didn't feel the same in return."

I nod, even though he can't see, willing the pain inside my chest to disappear.

"I should go to sleep," is all I say.

Andy releases a heavy sigh. "Good night, Jessa."

The call ends, so I place my phone on the nightstand and turn the lamp off. As I lay in the dark, alone with my thoughts, the chain around my heart begins to loosen. For the longest time, I'd buried certain things, and my feelings toward Andy are beneath it all.

My hands reach out for my phone again, but this time I text.

ME

I ran to London because I was scared of how I felt about you. I was scared you wouldn't feel the same way, or if you did, we would ruin what we had.

ANDY

The timing wasn't on our side. A wise man told me timing is everything.

ME

Who's the wise man you speak of?

ANDY

Noah Mason.

ME

Of course, he would say that... good night,
Andy.

ANDY

Good night, Jessa.

With my phone still in my hand, I decide there's a call I need to make. So, I dial his number, hoping he'll pick up since it's midday in California.

"Jessa? Is everything okay?"

"Dad?" I call softly while toying with the edge of my bed sheet. "I'm sorry about everything that happened between us."

The weight of Dad's sigh is enough to tell me he's relieved to hear those words. I missed him so much, and nothing or no one can ever replace the void of which only your father can fill.

"Jessa, I only wanted the best for you."

"I know. I miss you, Dad."

"I miss you too, sweetheart. More than you know."

I briefly ask him how he is for him to tell me how Nash and Sienna are back at home and driving him crazy. Throughout the conversation, I find myself laughing, knowing I was always the mediator between them. Nash has middle child syndrome, and Sienna is spoiled for being the baby of the family.

"Maybe in a few months, I can organize a trip back home so Bentley can meet everyone."

"I'd love that, so would Kate," he says with ease. "I know your mother has a press tour coming up, so make sure you speak to her, coordinate with her when she's back."

"I will, Dad. Promise," I assure him. "Dad, I love you."

"I love you too, Jessa."

We hang up the phone as a smile graces my face. I'd never have reached out to my family if it wasn't for Andy.

It always comes back to *him*.

It's only just after nine now, and despite my restless night, my mind doesn't want to switch off.

Something compels me to hop out of bed and retrieve the brown leather-bound journal from my sock drawer. As I pull it out, the memories of how writing fueled my soul come fresh to my mind. Then, I hear Andy's voice from the past. He pushed me to finish my assignments, holding me accountable when I had deadlines. There was that one time I had an assessment to submit. He stayed up with me all night, so I wouldn't fall asleep.

There's a pen still inside it, buried in the internal spine. I walk back to bed to climb in, then open the first page. It's blank, but my thoughts are not.

The pen glides so effortlessly on the paper, writing words to a story that flows from page to page until I glance at the clock, and it's midnight.

Twenty pages are written, the most I have done in my entire time in London.

I shove the journal in my nightstand, turning off the lamp and resting my head on the pillow.

And for the first time, in the longest of times, I fall into a blissful uninterrupted sleep.

---

Benedict places his fork down, then wipes his mouth with his napkin. He arrived back home late this afternoon, and after the best sleep I've had in a long time, I somewhat have the patience for him to talk about work.

"Enough about work," he says, fixating his gaze on me. "I apologize for my behavior last night. I forgot Andy is your cousin, and spending time with him is important to you."

I place my fork down, too, wondering where this is leading.

"I should've told you."

"You were right. Bentley can be a distraction. He's getting older and more demanding." His expression hardens, but his stare remains controlled. "I can't even remember the last time we—"

Our butler, Fredrick, walks in carrying a glass jug of water. I thank him politely, despite Benedict's annoyed expression.

"As I was saying..."

"Look, we're both tired all the time. It's just a phase. It will pass."

I smile through the lie, knowing part of this is my doing. Yes, I'm half-dead when I hit the pillow with barely any energy and knowing Bentley will wake up again in a few hours. But also, I began to resent Benedict for his absence in our son's life. If he has the time to make love to me, he has the time for his son.

He tried, on occasion, but I played the same card, and he gave up trying to convince me. I can't even recall the last time we had sex, let alone had an orgasm. I'm certain that the changes in my body after having Bentley are another reason Benedict gives up trying. My breasts, along with the rest of my body—aren't the same as the woman he met on that rainy day in London.

Benedict doesn't entertain the conversation any further, calling Fredrick back to bring him some coffee.

"I was thinking, how about dinner in London? I have this Friday night free, and don't forget we have the polo match to attend on Saturday."

"If Eliza is free, that would be nice."

"And why don't you invite Andy? I'm sure he can bring a date. That woman he brought to the ball?"

"Oh," I stammer, blindsided to this now double date. "I can ask him."

"Ask him now," Benedict insists. "Call him."

I have no idea why Benedict is being persistent, but I pick up my phone and attempt to call Andy, somewhat praying he won't pick up.

"Hey," he answers in a rush.

"Oh hey, sorry, have I caught you at a bad time?"

"Can you hold on a sec?" Andy pulls the phone away, but I hear him tell someone to take five. "Okay, sorry. Angry women were judging me for answering the call?"

"Angry women?"

"Photoshoot."

"Photoshoot, of course." I glance at Benedict, who's watching me. "I don't want to take up too much of your time, but Benedict would like for you to join us for dinner in London this Friday if you're free."

Andy remains quiet, but I hear him breathing. "I see..."

"And for you to bring a date, the woman from the ball."

"Are you kidding me right now, Jessa?"

I'm trying to think of something to say without giving away that Benedict is watching me.

"Hold on, Andy, Benedict is beside me, so let me ask what time."

My palm covers the speaker, then I turn to him to wait for an answer. Benedict leans back in his chair, crossing his arms. "Seven."

I nod, removing my hand.

"How is seven? I know you're busy, but hopefully, you and Anastasia can make it."

"So, he's there beside you?"

"Great," I say with a smile. "I'll text you the details?"

"Jessa, you're pushing my limits."

I can hear him strain, knowing he wasn't exactly fond of Benedict, and I don't blame him either, especially if there's any merit to what Ava said.

"I'll let you get back to your photoshoot."

"Jessa..."

"Bye."

I end the call before he says something else to me, knowing my face can be reactive at times.

"All set," I say, taking a breath. "I'm looking forward to it."

Beside me, Benedict continues to watch me with a tenacious stare. It's making me uncomfortable like I've done something wrong, which I haven't.

Nothing is going on with Andy because, as far as Benedict is concerned, he's my family.

Not the man who admitted he was in love with me all those years ago, or the man Ava says is still in love with me.

Or the man I just can't get out of my head.

# TWELVE

## ANDY

"Oh, hello, stranger."

Millie's voice slightly echoes, sounding like she's answering from the bluetooth in the car. Since Jessa's unexpected call with an invitation to dinner with her and Benedict, my head has been a mess. When Jessa said Benedict was beside her—the odd behavior made sense. What didn't make sense was him wanting me to bring a date. I wasn't sure what difference it would make since the whole dinner idea is ludicrous. Declining the invite sounds like a much better plan, but I can tell by the sound in Jessa's voice, it isn't a good idea.

"Can you talk?"

"As long as you don't use the 'f' word."

"Kids?" I ask, scratching my jaw as I settle with my fifth coffee of the day.

"Yes, on the way home from swimming lessons."

"Maybe I should call you another time."

"Ashton has his headphones on. Archer is the sponge to worry about. So talk, looks like he's about to crash anyway."

I take a deep breath. "I don't have time to get into the

details, but Benedict has requested I join him and Jessa for dinner."

"Oh..."

"And to bring a date."

"Wait, I'm confused. You know what, I need more context. Why would he invite you? Are you guys talking again?"

"Yes, as I said, I don't have time to get into it."

"Okay, well, who does he think you are?" She questions, then quickly continues, "I mean, how were you introduced?"

"Cousin."

"Does he know you're not *actually* cousins?"

"Yes... it was said, though Jessa skirted around the introduction."

We were brought up as cousins our whole lives, so I didn't blame Jessa for introducing me that way. It was never a big deal, and no one ever questioned us.

"So, this invitation, it's a big deal because?"

My patience is wearing thin. It shouldn't be a big deal. It's the last thing I want to do and bring a *date*. What kind of fucking request was that? Something doesn't sit right with me, especially after our conversation last night when I was forced to admit my *past* feelings for her.

I close my eyes momentarily, remembering when Jessa asked, and I was done lying about it. There's nothing left to lose, not when she's married to another man.

"You know what, you're right. It shouldn't be a big deal," I agree reluctantly.

"Andy?" Millie says softly. "Can I say something?"

When it comes to my relationship with Millie, I consider her like an older wise sister. She knows me better than I know myself and never pushes me unless warranted. If this exact conversation happened with Ava, she wouldn't ask for

permission to say something. She would blurt it out unapolo-
getically.

"Go on..."

"It sounds to me like Benedict suspects something."

"There's nothing to suspect, Millie. She's married."

"Yeah, and I was engaged."

"But you didn't have a kid."

"No, I didn't," she concedes. "You know what? Maybe
I'm wrong."

My chest begins to move up and down at a fast pace,
knowing there's a possible truth to Millie's comment. "Or
maybe you're right."

"Andy, don't do it if it makes you uncomfortable."

"I hate seeing her like this."

"Like what?"

If anyone understands the complexity and emotional
well-being of being a mother, it's Millie. She adopted a son,
who was born from a woman Will had a one-night stand
with. Then, she gave birth to Archer and is now pregnant
with their third. She's voiced on several occasions the battles
she faces daily but, in the same breath, wouldn't have it any
other way.

"Like a mother who's overwhelmed but won't ask for
help."

"Do you want me to talk to her?"

"No, I just feel helpless." I sigh.

"As long as she knows you're there, she'll ask for help
when she's ready. Being a mother is hard work. I couldn't
have done it without Will or our families."

"Exactly... listen, I should go. Hug my nephews, okay?"

"Call me anytime. You know I'm here."

"I know."

I hang up the phone, thinking about what Millie said, but

time doesn't allow me to think longer since I'm needed for a meeting a few blocks over.

The meeting is held in Lex and Noah's office building with the entire team in attendance. Lex and Noah video conference from Manhattan where they're currently working. Most of the meeting is centered around the marketing campaign. It runs for three hours, and when it's finished, I'm told I need to travel to Spain next week.

When I finally get back to my hotel, I fall onto the bed and rub my face from the sheer exhaustion of it all. The sleepless nights are becoming too much. I'm lucky if I can get three hours, and even then, it's broken sleep. Between the change in time zone, long working hours, and everything happening with Jessa, the nightmares about my father are only getting worse.

Jessa hasn't texted after calling me about the dinner. Not even the location, so possibly, this isn't going to go ahead, which will suit me just fine.

I hop into the shower, willing the day to be scrubbed off me, then climb into bed and pop a sleeping tablet, hoping to get some rest. Then, my phone pings beside me.

JESSA

Dinner tomorrow is at the restaurant beside the hotel you're staying at. The Italian place Francisco's.

ME

I know of it...

JESSA

7 p.m. and your date?

ME

What about her?

JESSA

Anastasia agreed to come?

ME

Yes, I asked her while we went out for drinks last night.

JESSA

You went out for drinks, like a work thing?

ME

No, more like two grown adults keeping each other company thing.

There's no instant response, but there's no need to lie to her either. Contrary to what she may think, I somewhat enjoy Anastasia's company. When she's in work mode, she's in work mode, but after hours, she knows how to liven things up and knows of all the best places in London.

And the truth still remains—Jessa is a friend.

I'm still single.

My mind replays our conversation from the other night, where I was forced to admit my past feelings all because Ava opened her big mouth. But then, something unexpected occurred—Jessa admitted she ran because she was scared.

The truth cut deeper than I ever imagined. The what-ifs, the regret, but none of it mattered, and digging up the past is a waste of time while the gold band sits on her finger.

When it's obvious Jessa is done with our conversation, I turn my phone to silent and close my eyes.

But once again, his face is in front of me, smiling while touching my cheek. His hand is awfully cold like ice, causing me to flinch. I beg of him to stop. Then Lex appears in his scrubs again. This time, he's carrying a black body bag.

*"It's time,"* is all Lex says with a stern face.

I reach out for him, but he turns his back on me and climbs in the bag. Before Lex zips it up, he says, "Take one more look at him, Andy."

My eyes spring open as my breath is caught in my throat. I'm covered in sweat, forcing myself to lift my shirt over my head and toss it to the side of the bed. On the clock beside me, it's only just after midnight.

Great. Here we go again.

I can't get back to sleep, no matter how I try. By four, I hit the streets with my sweats on, running through the park to build up some energy for today. Then, I head to the gym for a two-hour workout. Since these sleepless nights started, I've frequented the gym more than usual, my body in the best shape it's ever been.

Back at the hotel, I jump in the shower but take my time to relax my muscles. When I close my eyes, I see her face and hazel orbs staring at me. The smell of her skin is engrained in my memory as is the taste of her lips.

Jessa has grown into a beautiful woman. Motherhood has changed her body, but the curves only make her sexier.

Fuck! Control yourself.

My dick instantly turns hard, but I shut my eyes tight, trying to ignore the pressure. It will be impossible to stop once I start this wicked fantasy again. I turn the cold water to full blast, needing to calm down.

By the time I get out, change, and grab my things, the sun is rising.

Another long day, but this isn't any ordinary day.

It's Friday, the day I'd been dreading all week.

———————

Anastasia is sitting beside me, across from Benedict. Directly in front of me, Jessa is drinking her wine. I purse my lips, watching as she tries to control her nerves by drinking, but also doesn't want it to look obvious, so she slows down.

When Jessa stepped inside the restaurant not long ago, I forced myself to keep my expression strictly platonic because

the low-cut black dress she wears leaves nothing to my imagination—an imagination I've been trying to tame.

Benedict's handshake was the ultimate distraction, and so
the introductions began. I informed Anastasia of Jessa's
connection to Noah and me. Of course, being a publicist
means Anastasia always knows the right thing to say. Plus, I
have to give it to her, she looks hot tonight. The slim white
dress is fitted nicely against her toned body.

When we drank the other night, she joked about her
sexual antics, teasing me about how sexy I am and how she
has a thing for American men. It would've been easy to take
her back to my suite and fuck her, but instead, I just pushed
more wine in front of her until she was too drunk to
remember anything.

The server appears at the table and takes our orders. The
conversation centers around work, of course. There isn't
much else to talk about, so I keep quiet and let Anastasia do
the talking, which Benedict seems to enjoy.

"And so we're nearly done here in London," Anastasia
mentions. "Then we're off to Spain."

"We're?" Jessa questions, her gaze flicking to me.

"Yes, me and Anastasia," I concede, keeping my expression flat. "Anastasia works for your father, so she'll be accompanying me across Europe."

Anastasia knocks into me playfully. "I'm becoming fond
of this old chap."

"Old?" I turn to her with a sly grin. "Cougar would be an
appropriate name for you."

She shrugs with a playful smile. "So, I like my men
younger."

Across the table, Benedict laughs while drinking his wine.
Jessa lowers her head, then takes her glass and downs it all in
one go while glancing sideways. A blush spreads across her

cheeks, and if I didn't know better, she appears to be consumed by jealousy.

When the waiter arrives with the food, we've already drunk two bottles of wine. Benedict orders another two, each of us drinking more than we should.

The conversation moves onto the history of England, with both Anastasia and Benedict being passionate about the topic. As I sit here, bored, I glance over to see Jessa release a huff.

"I remember when we were kids, Jessa put Stonehenge on her bucket list. Along with driving around the Big Ben, all of which she got from watching *European Vacation*."

The corner of Jessa's mouth quirks up at the same time Benedict places his arm around her. The gesture is enough for my stomach to harden, but I fight it off. If he wants to parade his affection, then I'm more than happy to bring up the past, all of which doesn't involve him.

"Are you sure that was me?" she questions jovially. "More you, I had Oktoberfest and drinking beer."

"From memory, you wanted me to dress up in Lederhosen."

"Oh yeah, maybe we did watch the Griswolds too many times."

Benedict drinks his wine, then pours himself another glass, bored by our trip down memory lane.

"Those movies are horrid," Benedict grumbles, rolling his eyes. "Entitled Americans traveling through Europe? I can't think of anything worse."

"They weren't entitled," Jessa argues back. "And as an American, I take offense to that."

"Oh, sweetheart, you're nothing like them." He brings her close to kiss her cheek. I purposely turn away, pretending to be distracted by someone at the next table over, this close to leaving this fucking dinner. "Please tell Andy and Anastasia about how we met."

"Yes," Anastasia responds cheerfully. "Please do."

I purposely place my arm around Anastasia, touching the tip of her exposed shoulders with my fingers. If they want me to sit through this, then time to play a game Jessa will absolutely hate. Jessa instantly notices the gesture, pursing her lips with wide eyes.

"Well," he begins with a smug expression. "It was two years ago in the middle of a torrential storm. I wasn't looking where I was going. Then, of course, I run into the most beautiful woman. We were both soaked, so I took her back to my flat to dry off and—"

"We got engaged, then had Bentley," Jessa finishes off.

Anastasia laughs. "Between us adults, I'm sure you taking her back to your flat wasn't just to dry up."

A slight growl escapes my throat. All my muscles begin to tighten as a burning sensation spreads all over me. I can't fucking sit here any longer, watching them across from me like I stopped loving her all those years ago.

Like she means absolutely nothing to me.

I was wrong to think I can move on.

Abruptly, my chair scrapes along the ground when I push it back. "Excuse me. I need to use the restroom."

The anger drives me to walk away without even turning around, escaping to the restroom to calm the fuck down. My hands rest on the basin, willing the rage consuming me to slow because the thought of going out there and facing them isn't worth it anymore.

I thought I could be the bigger person and remain friends, but the more this goes on, I realize I can't torture myself any longer. I'm the only one with everything to lose here. My fucking heart is on a tightrope, ready to fall without a goddamn safety net beneath it.

Just like it fell two years ago, smashing into pieces when I found out she was engaged.

Slowly, I inhale a deep breath to release, then open the door the same time Jessa pushes me back into the men's room.

"What the hell are you doing in here?"

"Why didn't you tell me you were going to Spain with Anastasia?"

I tilt my head, furrowing my brows. "Because I didn't think you would care."

Jessa crosses her arms beneath her chest, pushing her tits up, catching my attention.

*Now isn't the time to think about it.*

"I care, okay?"

A sinister laugh escapes me. "Why the fuck would you care, huh? You've got your husband. I mean, lust at first sight, right?"

"Andy, please don't—"

"Don't what? Ask you how it felt to fuck a stranger within five minutes of meeting him?"

Jessa bows her head. "It's not like that."

"Well, he painted an obvious picture of just how it happened," I grit.

"Just like Anastasia painted a very clear picture of all the fun you both have and how she can't wait to get her hands on you," Jessa throws back in haste. "And you didn't dispute it. I mean, for all I know, you're fucking her now."

"And so what if I am? What difference would it make to you?"

"I care!" Her eyes are wild, the hazel almost burning with fire. "God, Andy. You have no idea what it's like to be in my shoes. To battle with mistakes but count the blessings of my son at the same time. Then, you walk back into my life and..."

"And what?"

Jessa lowers her gaze to the floor, her chest rising as she releases a breath. "I won't cheat on my husband."

The words are like dynamite, but they also don't make sense.

"I've never asked you to—"

"No, Andy," she breathes, shaking her head while clutching her stomach. "I think about you all the time. I've imagined over and over again what it would've been like to have this life with you."

"Jessa..." I murmur, struggling to process this.

"But none of it matters. I'm married, and I won't cheat on Benedict despite how I feel about you."

Between the silence, I know we don't have long until Benedict questions where Jessa is and possibly punches me in the face. I'm prepared for it, confident I can hold my own against the bastard. Aside from my height, I'm much more built than him and have been practicing my swings against the punching bag at the gym.

Still, I don't want to put Jessa in that position. Not when Bentley is at stake.

"We need to get out of here," I warn her.

Jessa nods, but as she turns her back to exit the restroom, I grab her arm, turning her back around to face me.

"What Ava said wasn't true. I wasn't in love with you..."

"Oh," Jessa exhales, her lips pressing into a tight grimace. "But you said on the phone..."

I reach out and lift her chin with my finger. Our gaze locks, and I decide once and for all to seize the moment, admit the truth because I'm sick of running away and living in misery.

"I'm still in love with you," I begin, then stall as my breath hitches. "It's always been and will only ever be you, Jessa."

# THIRTEEN

## JESSA

After my admission to Andy in the men's restroom, dinner took an unexpected turn.

We returned to the table separately, and while we were gone, both Anastasia and Benedict had drunk the remaining bottles of wine.

Before I took a seat, I paused to observe their interaction. Anastasia was showing Benedict something on her phone, and whatever it was, it caught his attention. She placed her hand on his arm. Then his eyes fell to her chest. I saw the lick on his lips and the way she flicked her hair back to better expose her chest.

I waited for the jealousy to tear through me, but it never came.

The night ended with Anastasia lacing her arm into Andy's, begging him to join her at some club. Our goodbyes were amicable, yet the stolen glance before I stepped into the car with my drunk husband spoke a thousand words.

The cards have been laid out, and Andy made sure to tell me exactly how he felt about me.

Just as I made it clear of my intent to remain faithful to my husband.

Now, even after all those admissions, I'm going home to a place where I don't belong.

On the drive back home, Benedict continues to drink, purchasing a bottle of scotch from the bar but drinking it straight out of the bottle. I beg him to slow down, but he laughs like a delirious maniac, slurring his words which make no sense.

When we arrive home, he disappears to his study, which is for the best since I want to be alone. I remove my dress, take a quick shower, then climb into bed dressed in my paja-mas. With Benedict still gone, I quickly take out my journal, feverishly writing two pages to clear my mind.

Two becomes six, and for fear of being caught, I slide it back into my drawer before Benedict appears in the room. I'd done this the past few days, sneaking a few pages here and there whenever I got a moment. The words came fast, and it became an instant stress reliever to unload my thoughts from pen to paper.

I lay in bed, staring at the ceiling while my hands play with the wedding ring on my finger. Slowly, I remove it and spin it between my fingers.

My body aches for him, the touch of his hands against my heated skin. Of all the times we would lay beside each other, the opportunity was there, but both of us were torn, and only now do I realize just how much we were both fighting the same battle—protecting our friendship at all costs.

But then, I remember how Andy's eyes bore into me, how the one kiss we had sucked the breath out of me, sure I'd pass out from the overwhelming intensity.

Just for a moment, as I lay here in the dark, I wonder what it's like to have him touch me. Trace the curve of my breasts with gentle ease. Move his hands down the trail of my stomach until he reaches down, causing me to gasp. A pool of wetness forms between my legs, the urge to pleasure myself hard to ignore as my hands wander to my swollen clit. I gasp at the sensation, continuing to rub in a circular motion, followed by a hard swallow as my head pushes back into my pillow, and the overwhelming need to come is just moments away.

My fingers move inside, relishing in the warm pool of wet I'm expelling until the swell in my belly rises. My skin tingles all over, and the final moan escapes my lips as a warm sensation rushes to every part of my body.

My chest is rising and falling while I try to open my eyes, only to see bursts of light. It takes a few moments to calm my racing heart, and more than ever, I need to talk to him. Feel him in any way possible at this very moment.

Though given Benedict is lurking somewhere in this house, I opt to text, not wanting to be caught mid-conversation on a call.

I smile oddly, remembering all the times he would say that to me until the one day he admitted my texts always came at the wrong time when he was jerking off or watching porn.

ME

What kind of answer is that? Stuff? From
memory, stuff meant wrong time because
you were 'busy.'

ANDY

It's my answer to keep this message platonic.

ME

I wish I could say the things I want to say.

ANDY

Now you're just being a tease.

I hear a shuffle down the hallway and quickly text.

ME

Sorry, I have to go.

I turn my phone off, so no other messages come through. Pretending to be asleep, I close my eyes to hear Benedict moving around the closet. Moments later, the bed moves. I can smell the liquor between us. Its stench is so potent, I'm certain he drank the entire bottle.

Then, he moves closer to me and presses himself into my back, his cock rock hard. His lips move to my shoulder, spreading kisses against my skin.

"Stop, Benedict. You're drunk."

"And? I want to fuck my wife." He slides his hands between my legs, moaning in delight. "And you're so wet for me already."

His arm is forceful, but I try to remove his hands from between my legs.

"Benedict, stop," I say firmly. "I don't want to have sex."

Instead of pulling away, he yanks my panties down and presses his cock into my ass, causing my body to tremor with panic.

"If I want to fuck you, you'll fuck me."

My stomach flips with ill feelings, the fear crippling my

movement. But then, I knock his chest when he forces my legs apart, my blood pumping as adrenaline bursts throughout me.

"What the fuck did you do that for!"

"I said no!" I raise my voice, jumping out of bed, my heart racing like crazy. *"Why aren't you listening to me?"*

"What the fuck do you want from me? You've always loved being fucked spontaneously. At least you did before Bentley."

The way his tone changed at the mention of our son sends a wave of anger throughout me. He has no goddamn clue just how hard it's been to adjust since I gave birth, and here he is trying to take me so selfishly despite me saying no.

"I want to be respected for my decision, and I don't want to be raped in my marital bed."

"Oh, c'mon," he yells, almost spitting. "You're being dramatic. You're my wife, Jessa! Not anyone else's. And I demand you get back in this bed now."

My jaw sets as my hands clench into fists. With a tightness in my chest, my nostrils flare while I stand here in silence and listen to this monster I married.

If he dares to lay a finger on me, he'll have what's coming.

"I'm sleeping in the guest room," I tell him in an arctic tone. "Don't you dare come near me."

Grabbing my phone, I head to the guest room and lock the door behind me. Suddenly, this house feels like a complete stranger's home, and Benedict's actions begin to form a scar destined to stay with me forever.

The feeling of isolation is a cold reality in the dead of night, and slowly, the tears begin to fall against my cheek as I cry myself to sleep, alone in the bed I made for myself.

"Mama!" I hear Bentley's playful giggles in the morning while he calls out.

My arms reach out to grab my son, kissing his head as I change his diaper. Eliza walks in with a bottle, surprised to see me given I'm supposed to be attending the polo match with Benedict.

"What time are you leaving, Mrs. Banks?"

The exhaustion is weighing my thoughts down, unable even to think, let alone string a sentence together. My eyes are puffy, making me all the more aware of last night's events. Eliza doesn't comment on my appearance, ignoring any eye contact.

"I'm not sure," I say with a dry swallow. "I'm going to go downstairs and make myself a coffee. Will you be all right with him?"

"Of course, Mrs. Banks."

I can't be bothered changing, wearing my pajamas beneath my robe in a hunt for caffeine. Benedict is seated at the table in the dining room dressed in a white-collared dress shirt with a navy blazer on top. For someone who drank his weight in alcohol, he looks remarkably fresh.

Pulling the chair out beside him, I take a seat as Fredrick serves me coffee. I smile politely, then wait for him to leave the room.

"We need to discuss last night."

"There's nothing to discuss, Jessa."

I bite my tongue, but my patience is less than accommodating.

"I suggest you put your phone down and look at me, okay?"

He releases an exaggerated breath, placing his phone down to glance my way. His expression is unforgiving, not a hint of remorse for his uncalled-for actions last night.

"What would you like me to say, Jessa?"

"Let's begin with, what you attempted last night was fucked up."

His lips press into a grimace. Then he shakes his head with a sneer.

"You've never had a problem before," he says calmly. "I remember our honeymoon in Greece. You were fast asleep in our private cabana and woke up with me inside you. According to you, it was the best sex of your life."

"That was then..."

"So, what has changed for you to be disgusted by your own husband wanting you?"

"Don't over exaggerate, okay?" I argue, still waiting for a goddamn apology. "Things between us have been hard. You're always away for work, and you're barely here for our son."

"I'm sorry, so I'm being punished for providing for my family?"

I shake my head as a sharp pain hits my temple. The impending headache is worsening, and the last thing I want to do is fake my marriage in front of society.

"I won't be attending the polo match today."

"Excuse me?" He tilts his head, eyes widening as his jaw tightens. "You agreed to attend. How will it look if I arrive by myself?"

I push the chair out to then stand still as I look directly into his angry eyes. If Benedict can't see what he did wrong, then I can't be anywhere near him and sacrifice my mental health for *his* society's expectations of our marriage.

"Maybe ask your mother? I'm sure you'd much prefer her company."

"Can you please stop embarrassing me?" he grits, eyes blazing. "You're my wife, and you better not forget that, or you'll pay the consequences."

He leaves the room before I do, only for the front door to

slam and his car to screech against the gravel during my walk up the large staircase.

Back in Bentley's room, I sit on the floor and play with him while Eliza goes downstairs for breakfast. My racing heart still hasn't calmed down, tired of this life and the burdens I carry. The flashbacks of last night plague me, and all I want right now is to feel safe again.

When Eliza returns, I kiss Bentley on the forehead, then stand up.

"Eliza, I'm going to run some errands in town. Do you mind watching Bentley today?"

"Of course not, Mrs. Banks. That was the plan anyway." She smiles at Bentley. "We're going to feed the ducks today. Have you seen the beautiful black swan at the lake in town?"

I grin, knowing if Andy could hear this, he would be laughing right now.

"Yes, I have," I drag. "It's big and black."

"Beautiful creatures, aren't they?"

"Sure, from afar."

We talk more about her plans for the day before I say goodbye to Bentley and head to my shower. Once out, I opt to dress in my white buttoned blouse, olive skirt with knee-high boots. Again, the weather looks cold, so I grab my coat to wear over.

With my phone in hand, I quickly send Andy a text.

ME

Where are you?

Our driver pulls up while waiting for a response since I called him earlier. On the drive to London, Andy finally responds.

ANDY

Lobby of The Gilmore Hotel.

ME

I'll see you soon.

Andy is standing behind the tripod, his focus on the camera, pressing buttons, but his expression is serious. He runs his hands through his hair, a gesture he does when he's frustrated and can't focus.

As I take steps closer toward him, he catches my movement and tells the team he needs to have a break.

Reaching out, he touches my arm with concern. Then, I see him examine my face. Quickly, I drop my eyes, not wanting to break down here, of all places. If he knew what happened last night, he would hunt Benedict down and *kill* him. The whole ordeal has left me humiliated, but I bury it all to remain as calm as possible.

"You want to go somewhere?"

"But you're working?"

"How about you go to my suite, and I'll meet you there in an hour. I'll finish this up."

I nod without a word. Before Andy steps back to the crew waiting, he touches my cheek. "It's going to be okay, Jessa."

Andy doesn't push, knowing me too well and how my silence speaks words my head and heart can't seem to connect.

Inside Andy's suite, I take a seat on the lounge and pull my journal out. With my pen in hand, I begin to write but stop to glance at my surroundings. The hotel suite is luxurious, but the scent inside the room is all Andy. I close my eyes, breathing it in, then release my breath and place my pen again on the paper to write.

The emotions evoked from the words spilling out bring

on sudden tiredness. After last night's restless sleep, I slowly doze off until my eyes can't stay open any longer.

"Jessa," Andy murmurs when my eyes begin to flutter open.

"Andy?"

"I'm here."

I stretch my back to relieve the ache. "Did I fall asleep?"

He nods. "You looked tired."

When I move again, my journal falls to the ground. Andy reaches down to pick it up and hands it back to me.

"Is this the journal Noah gave you the Christmas before you left?"

A thickness forms in my throat, yet I fight back the tears willing to fall. Andy's recollection only makes me realize how much of myself I'd sacrificed to be here. My family, our friendship, but most importantly, all of me.

"It is," I say faintly. "I've started writing again."

A slow smile builds on Andy's face. "I knew you would."

All of a sudden, a familiar smell lingers in the air. The savory scent brings back fond memories. Then, beside Andy, I see a brown paper bag.

"What's inside the bag?"

"A surprise."

"It smells good." I grin, rubbing my hands.

"For you, I'm not surprised." Andy passes the bag over. I open it up and see the familiar purple bell logo. "Stomach ache waiting to happen."

"No way! Did you get me Taco Bell? I didn't even know they had it here."

"Oh, they do," Andy responds less than enthused. "I thought it might cheer you up."

I take the wrapped taco out of its packaging, desperate to taste it. As soon as I bite in, I moan in delight. It's just as good as I remember.

"Oh, God, I love you."

Andy lowers his gaze, a smirk playing on his lips, only for me to realize what I've said. My chewing slows down while I try to work out how to backtrack on my sentiment.

"Um, you know what I mean."

"You're in love with a taco. You always have been."

I welcome his humor, taking another bite until the taco juice squirts onto my shirt and skirt, causing me to gasp.

"My taco squirted!"

The taco sauce is stained across my clothes. Great, how on earth will this come out?

"You know, if Eric were here, that would've been interpreted differently."

My shoulders begin to rise and fall, unable to control my laughter. "I remember this one time. He told me there are actual squirting competitions. Ava and I were mortified. Luna was just like... yeah, I've heard about this."

"Please don't with my sister."

"I'm just saying. She appeared to be educated."

Andy purses his lips. "And we'll leave it at that. Now, if you were to mention anyone else who isn't related to me squirting, that's a conversation right there."

"You're such a guy," I tease.

"Why? Because I'm willing to have an open discussion about women who squirt."

I place my taco down. "Fine, have you ever seen a woman do it?"

"Maybe, kinda, I don't know."

"What kind of an answer is that?"

"The kind of answer you give to someone in a mood because she's possibly ruined a good shirt and skirt," he deadpans, gazing at my shirt.

"That's not an answer," I tell him. "Are you into it?"

Andy cringes. "Jessa. I'm a guy. I'm into everything."

"Hmm, I didn't think that was true, that all guys were into everything. At least, certain English men aren't. Quite possibly explains our marriage turning stale," I blurt out, only realizing just who I said those words to.

My eyes lift to meet Andy's as his prolonged stare causes the pound inside my chest to beat louder. The blue orbs are like staring into a calm ocean, the serenity washing over and filling me with a sense of calm. As the beat of my heart begins to slow down, Andy slowly inches forward.

"If you were mine, I wouldn't be able to keep my hands off you..." His fingers inch closer to my shirt as my stomach flutters with a warm rush. "I think we should take these off and have them cleaned immediately."

His fingers move of their own accord, unfastening each button at a slow and agonizing pace. Finally, when my chest is exposed, he removes my shirt and requests I stand up. I do so, watching him unzip my skirt for it to fall to the ground.

The desire to have him is too great, my body betraying me as I grow wet from just the sheer act of him stripping me down. With his expression still, he walks toward the bedroom then returns a moment later with his favorite oversized Dodgers t-shirt.

He spreads the shirt, placing it over my head as I put my arms in. The shirt falls mid-thigh, an interesting look with my boots.

"Um, so..." I try to catch my breath, willing to clear the dirty thoughts consuming me. "Thank you."

"You're welcome. I'll call housekeeping to come collect this to be washed and dry-cleaned straight away." He grabs my shirt and skirt, then leans over to whisper. "No rules were broken. Just so you know."

As he walks away, I let out the breath I'd been holding in.

No rules have been broken yet.

But the night is still young.

# FOURTEEN

## ANDY

Housekeeping came to the door and took the garments from my hands, promising to return them as soon as possible.

As the door closes, I intake a breath, squeezing my eyes shut for a moment.

Fuck, how am I supposed to walk back inside the room and pretend her body isn't the forbidden piece of fruit I desperately want to taste? When I removed her shirt, the swell of her tits teased me as did her nipples hidden behind the white lace bra.

My dick stirs again, making it difficult to walk back without seeming obvious. Thankfully, she's sitting on the lounge with her head bowed down while I walk over and sit beside her.

"You look good in my shirt," I say with a grin.

"I'm channeling some *Pretty Woman* vibes with the tee and boots."

"Hmm, you look hotter."

She throws a cushion at me. "When did you become such

a flirt? No wonder women are always throwing themselves at you."

"Throwing themselves? A bit of an exaggeration."

Jessa shakes her head with a simper. "Every time we used to go out, girls would always ask if you were my boyfriend. If I said no, they would try to get in your pants. So, I started to lie and tell them you were. I should apologize since I stopped you from getting laid several times."

My shoulders move up and down while I chuckle at her comment. "Don't feel bad. I used to do the same. I said you were only interested in girls. It was a mixed reaction at times."

This time, she slaps my arm, but I stop her and latch onto her wrist. "This explains why every time I was with my girlfriends, guys would walk past sticking their tongues out!"

I let go of her wrist and instead tug a lock of her hair with a pout. "Sorry."

"You're not sorry," she drags.

"You're cute when you're angry."

"Cute is what you call a fluffy teddy or puppy. Cute is not me. Look at me?" she complains. "I look like death. I didn't sleep last night, there are bags under my eyes, and if Eric saw me, he'd throw around the word Botox, then offer to book me in."

She crosses her arms beneath her chest, and when she does, the hem of the shirt rises, exposing all her thighs. Fuck, I need a distraction.

"Why didn't you sleep?"

Jessa shrugs, pressing her lips together. "Long story."

"The reason why you're here and not with your husband?"

She remains quiet, but I can read between the lines. I suspect they had a fight, not surprised at all since he was drunk last night. Toward the end of the night, he began mouthing off. The only one amused was Anastasia.

"If you want to talk about it, I'm not here to judge."

"I don't want to waste my breath."

I won't push her, distracted by her phone ringing. She lifts it up to see the screen, then lets out a huff before pressing reject. It's an easy assumption the person calling is her husband, and he has no idea she's here with me.

As I go to open my mouth, my phone rings this time, the name *Noah* appearing on the screen.

"It's Daddy," I tease her.

"What does he want?"

"Probably work," I answer, then hit accept on his call, placing him on speaker. "Noah."

Jessa waves, mouthing for me not to mention she's here. I poke her with my fingers, watching as she tries not to laugh, only for her to twist my arm like when we were kids.

"Andy, huge favor, and don't kill me because my wife is already giving me death stares, which will undoubtedly result in no sex for the rest of the year."

I hold in my laughter as Jessa's eyes widen. She grabs the cushion and covers her face, keeping it there as Noah continues speaking.

"There's been a last-minute change to one of the hotels. I need you to meet Anastasia in an hour, and we'll conference in. I'm sorry, one of my employees fucked up, and if this isn't fixed, we'll pay for it."

"Of course, I'll head over in an hour."

"Thank you, seriously. This has been the day from hell."

We hang up the call while Jessa continues to cover her face.

"It's over now. You can breathe."

"My dad and Kate are still having sex?"

I pull back, amused. "Why are you looking at me that

way? I don't ask the questions nor chat about these things. I believe it was said as a joke."

"Once, I came home early from soccer practice. It was senior year." She furrows her brows. "There was moaning. I thought we were being robbed. I grabbed the frying pan, and when I got to the butler's pantry, I heard..."

"What?"

"You know what, never mind. I don't need to relive the trauma."

My eyes glance at the time on the phone, knowing I need to shower and change before the meeting in the office. I lean forward, then tilt my head to face Jessa.

"I have to shower."

"Do you have to go?" She tugs on my shirt to annoy me. "What will I do by myself until my clothes come back?"

I drop my gaze with a smirk. "I could give you some ideas."

"There you go again. Acting all sexy with your casually messy hair and big muscles." She leans over and ruffles my hair. "I'm a good girl, remember?"

My head shakes smugly. "Of course, one who won't let me shower."

I stand up, but something compels me to pause for a moment. The last few hours with her have been amazing, but like everything, it has to come to an end. Just like now would be the perfect time to tell her I'm leaving for Spain in two days.

"Jessa, I need to tell you something."

"What is it?"

"I'm leaving for Spain in two days."

"Oh," she mouths. "With Anastasia?"

"Yes, but we've spoken about this. Nothing is going on."

"But she wants you, right?"

I stare into Jessa's pained eyes. "Maybe, but it doesn't matter if I don't want her."

"Yeah, um..." she mumbles, but I move in closer, caressing her cheek, for her to raise her eyes. "Andy?"

"Yes?"

"You need to shower."

"I do."

Jessa takes my hand without saying another word and leads me to the bathroom. Inside, she turns on the water, then slowly shifts her gaze to mine. Her hazel eyes are laced with desire, but her oath isn't to betray her husband. Perhaps, my imagination is wild with sexual thoughts, not thinking clearly.

"You better get inside. No one likes to waste water."

The bathroom fills with steam, causing the temperature in the room to increase. But her mixed messages leave me wondering what I'm supposed to do right now.

"I have to take off my clothes."

"It's a given."

I yank my shirt off, tossing it on the floor as her eyes wander down to my chest, then to my abs, stopping at my hips where my jeans sit. My dick stiffens beneath my jeans, and if they're to come off, it's going to be damn obvious.

"So, I kind of need to take my jeans off," I tell her, keeping my prolonged stare on her. "Are you staying or going?"

"*Stay*," she whispers opening her mouth with a slight pant. "I'm not breaking any rules by watching."

She broke the rules the moment she told me she couldn't stop thinking about me. But it wasn't my place to sway her opinion on the matter. If she wants to watch, I'm going to make sure it's a damn good show.

My hands move toward the top of my jeans as I unclasp the button. The zipper is next, my fingers pulling it down, so my jeans are loose.

Slowly, I take them off while kicking my sneakers off at the same time. Jessa keeps her gaze fixated on my every move, not a single flinch even when I remove my socks. As I stand here in my boxers, my dick stands hard, and I swear her neck moves with the large gulp she just took.

"This is your last chance," I warn her. "There's no turning back once these come off. And when I get in the shower, I'm free to do whatever I please."

She reaches out to graze my lips, exploring my mouth with her drawn gaze.

"Take them off," she commands.

I don't wait, not wanting her to change her mind. Pulling them down, she takes a deep breath, then lets her eyes fall toward my cock. Jessa's mouth forms an 'O' before she bites her lip and drops her head unbeknownst to her.

"*Fuck,*" she mumbles beneath her breath.

My hand moves to her chin, lifting her gaze to meet mine. "Just watch, okay?"

I pull away and step into the shower, splashing the water onto my face and hair. The water is warm, relaxing my muscles besides the one below. I'm unable to hold off any longer, bringing my hand to my shaft as I begin to stroke myself.

Fuck, it's incredibly sensitive, every tug bringing me closer to a finish. I focus on myself, knowing she's watching, imagining how wet she is right now and just how sweet her pussy will taste. The swell in my stomach builds, leading the charge to increase my speed until my entire body shakes, and I expel a grunt when I explode all over my hand.

I'm barely able to breathe, leaning forward with my eyes closed to even my ragged breathing. When I'm finally able to open my eyes, I turn to see her standing there, eyes full of lust like I've never seen before.

I turn the water off, leaning over to grab a towel. Quickly

drying myself off, I wrap the towel around my waist and step out. My feet move closer to her until we're standing only inches apart.

"That was..." she trails off.

"Perfect."

"Perfect in every way I've ever imagined," she barely manages, a slight croak evident in her voice. "You're..."

"Hmm." I move closer, our bodies almost touching. "What am I?"

"Hung."

"Hung?"

"Yes," she says faintly. "It's thick."

"I thought you just said hung?"

"Hung and thick," she reiterates, biting her lip. "Eric would be proud of you."

I shake my head as laughter escapes me. "I'm bothered and also afraid for my life."

"You should be," she muses, but then her expression fixates on me with a nervous smile. "Andy? Please be patient with me, with us. There's a lot I have to work through."

"I will be, and I know," I remind her softly.

"Just promise me something?"

"What's that?"

Her fingers reach out to touch my lips again, but I kiss the tip of her fingers this time.

"Please don't fall in love with someone else," she murmurs.

As I stare into her eyes, what she's asking isn't even possible. It's always been Jessa and always will be. But the roadblocks and hurdles will prove difficult to overcome. How much she's willing to fight to be with me remains unseen, especially since her son is at stake.

"I promise you, Jessa. It will only ever be you."

She releases a sigh, followed by her lips curving upward in a devious grin.

"Oh, and, Andy, one more thing?" She moves her hands beneath the shirt, then slides her white French panties down to step out of them. Bending down, she retrieves them from the ground and places them in my hand. "In case you're wondering how I felt about watching you in the shower."

In my hand, her panties are soaked.

Fuck, there goes my dick again, hardening beneath my towel.

I shake my head with a smirk. "You lied about being a good girl."

She shrugs, cocking her head to the side. "You only live once, right?"

With a sexy wink, she leaves the room to answer the door. I hear her thank the person, then the door closes.

Exiting the bathroom, she turns around to face me.

"I have to get changed," she reminds me with a simper.

"You'll need your panties back."

"I have spares."

"With you?"

Jessa shakes her head. "No, not with me. So, I need to get changed."

I lean against the wall, crossing my arms. "Don't let me stop you."

"Some things are better left a surprise," she adds, passing by and entering the bathroom. Moments later, she returns dressed, though still commando.

"There's something about you going commando in the same room as me."

Jessa moves toward me, pressing her hands on my chest.

"When are you back from Spain?"

"I don't know," I answer honestly.

"So, we don't know when we'll see each other again?"

"You need to do your thing, and I need to do mine," I remind her, then I lower my gaze to hide my jealousy. "You have a husband."

And as if she knew of my insecurities, how difficult it is to be in this situation when I'm forced to watch her live with another man, she caresses my cheek with her hand.

"I won't let him touch me. That's all you need to know, Andy."

The pain inside my chest eases from the words she spoke, which I trust, and the conviction in her eyes when she held my stare.

"Promise me that, Jessa."

"I promise."

# FIFTEEN

## JESSA

Everything changed between us the second I let my guard down.

From the moment I coerced Andy into the bathroom to take a shower, I knew resistance was futile. I was tired of lying to myself, beaten down to barely anything, and caught in a life I didn't want to live.

Though, the internal battle continues to be fought for the sake of my son. Bentley deserves a good life and loving parents, but even with my unconditional love for him, I'm not his father. The disappointment runs deep, not understanding how Benedict turned into a cold-hearted man, the complete opposite of the man I fell in love with.

Then, there's Andy.

*My safe place.*

The only place to ever make me feel alive and secure at the same time. When I'm with him, I can't explain it, as nothing else matters, and I'm free to be the person I want to be.

I think back to all my moments with Benedict. Our foundation was built on lust, a large fog that plays with your mind and leads to foolish decisions. I'd placed Benedict on this throne, wishing he would be everything I wanted, but in the end, I was distracted by all the changes in life to notice what was missing between us.

All-consuming love.

The kind of love you can't or will not breathe without.

From the moment we met, it was the thrill of new things —new places, new people. The proposal came as a surprise, and the wedding was so intricate to plan. The awaited honeymoon in Greece, then finding out we were pregnant. The preparations while pregnant again distracted me, and then the birth of Bentley.

Since the day my son was laid in my arms, his entire being has been my sole focus.

But now, I'm torn. My desire for Andy is greater than I ever imagined possible. Every time I'm around him, I struggle to ignore how devastatingly handsome he is. He always has been, but it's hard to resist him when you're finally looking at him while wearing clear glasses.

I did, though, sort of.

He gave me every chance to walk away and say no. But more than ever, I wanted something intimate from him without pushing myself to the extreme.

And that's what he gave me in the shower.

I watched every move, every stroke, mesmerized by how sculpted his body is to his perfect cock. I was fixated on how delicious it looked while hard inside his palm.

My hands moved on their accord into my panties, but I came while watching him explode all over his hand with only a few rubs. My moans filtered out inside the steaming hot bathroom, but my chest could barely catch.

When Andy stepped out, his devious smirk echoed my exact feeling. We both got what we wanted without *technically* crossing the boundaries.

He hadn't touched me.

Saying goodbye to him was hard, given his upcoming work trip to Spain. The thought of him traveling with Anastasia evoked jealousy, but I have to trust him, just like he needs to trust me.

Back at home, I quickly head to the room to shower and change into some sweats, planning to spend the late afternoon playing with Bentley. We settle for staying in the den, watching *Toy Story*, which he loves, and a plate of fruit we both snack from. Surprisingly, his attention is on the movie, his eyes perking up every time he hears the name, *Andy*.

Benedict opens the door during the pizza planet scene, still dressed in his clothes from today. Leaning against the wall with a stiff stance, his arms are crossed over his chest, and his expression remains hard.

"Where were you today?"

Bentley briefly looks up at him but doesn't falter, shifting his gaze back onto the screen. No surprises, he hasn't even said the word 'Dada' yet.

"Out."

"Out?"

"Yes, out."

"Would you like to explain where?"

"Not really," I answer back, uninterested in his interrogation. "Kind of like you not wanting to explain your behavior last night."

Benedict drops his arms straight for his hands to lock into fists. We've had arguments before, but nothing like this.

"I don't have time for this, Jessa. This sudden attitude like you're too good for this place."

"Maybe," I say, lifting my eyes to meet his. "This isn't a sudden attitude, but who I've always been."

With a pinched mouth, Benedict shakes his head in annoyance. "I'm going to my office to work."

He leaves the room as I breathe a sigh of relief. I have no idea how long I can do this for, trapped in a loveless marriage while absolutely miserable. The dreaded 'd' word plays on my mind, but I'm too tired to think about anything depressing. Instead, I grab my phone to send Andy a text.

ME

Are you still in your meeting?

ANDY

Yes… Noah is on the warpath, and his marketing director is in the firing line.

ME

That's my dad for you. He always gets what he wants in the end.

ANDY

Judging by his short temper, he's not getting what he wants in the bedroom.

ME

YOU'RE EVIL.

ANDY

I know, but you still love me, right?

I smile at his last text, wishing I could admit the honest truth, but in some ways, it feels too soon, and I don't want to rush things.

ME

The taco… I love the taco.

ANDY

I love tacos too… ones that squirt.

ME

Of course, you do, though I'm yet to understand its science. Perhaps I should research it, but I'm scared of what my search engine will come up with.

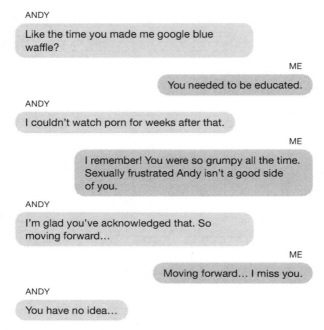

ANDY

Like the time you made me google blue waffle?

ME

You needed to be educated.

ANDY

I couldn't watch porn for weeks after that.

ME

I remember! You were so grumpy all the time. Sexually frustrated Andy isn't a good side of you.

ANDY

I'm glad you've acknowledged that. So moving forward...

ME

Moving forward... I miss you.

ANDY

You have no idea...

And just like that, I miss everything about home because that's exactly what I associate Andy with—home. My eyes wander around the den, looking at all the furnishings which were chosen and decorated by Rosemarie. This house belonged to their family and was given to us as a wedding gift. All you need to do is take one look around to see none of my own touches are here because it's not my home.

It was never supposed to be.

Bentley loses interest in the movie, setting his sights on a bookshelf instead. I feed him dinner, then take him upstairs for his nightly routine since he's tired from his day out at the lake with Eliza.

When I finally climb into bed, exhausted from today's events, Benedict joins me soon after. It's unusual for him to join me so early, making me slightly anxious he'll try something again like last night.

Suddenly, the guilts hit me. I feel guilty for watching Andy perform something so intimate, knowing that's not fair to Benedict. But also guilty for sleeping in the same bed as my husband and knowing the pain it must inflict on Andy.

No matter which way I look at the situation, everyone will get hurt.

"Jessa, perhaps we should talk," Benedict begins at the same time my phone rings.

I glance over to see Ava's name flashing on the screen.

"I need to pick this up. It's Ava," I tell him before answering, "Hey, Ava."

"Okay, so, you know how Bentley turns one in exactly twenty-nine days?" She doesn't catch a breath, waiting for my response.

"Um, yes, but also that quick?" I swallow the lump inside my throat. "This has gone too fast."

"Tell me about it," she mumbles, then releases a sigh. "So, your dad mentioned you may be visiting soon?"

"I mentioned it briefly, but nothing's planned."

Beside me, Benedict remains quiet.

"So, Millie and I were thinking about throwing a small birthday party here for Bentley. Just us family, and, of course, Eric because everyone knows he loves to gift Gucci loafers to one- year-olds which they hate to wear."

I laugh softly, remembering how Ashton kicked them off his feet and walked away when Millie tried to put them on.

"You would do that for Bentley?"

"Of course! He's our nephew, silly," she affirms. "So, will you get back to me with when?"

I clear my throat. "Of course, I'll speak to Benedict and get back to you."

We hang up the phone. Then I place it on the nightstand.

"Millie and Ava want to throw Bentley a birthday party back home. She said the family only," I inform him, knowing this won't go down well. Benedict has been very vocal about his distaste for California.

"You were already planning a trip?" he questions, his voice cold.

"No, I was talking to my dad and said I'd like to visit soon to see everyone. There was no planning, no dates."

"Bentley should be celebrating his birthday here. Mother has already found the perfect venue."

"Is there a bouncy castle?"

"Don't be ridiculous, Jessa. Mother's friends will be spoiling him with gifts."

"Money, you mean?"

"Yes, and what's wrong with that?"

I purse my lips, too tired to get into an argument. "Look, I want Bentley to spend time with his cousins. Plus, I want to see my family. Do you think you can get some time off work?"

Benedict refuses to travel with Bentley unless Eliza is with us. I wait for his answer, his expression deep in thought.

"Will Andy be there with you?"

It's so left field, or maybe not if you're suspicious something is going on. I think of something to say, to steer him off track for the sake of my sanity right now.

"Andy went to Spain with Anastasia. I believe they're an item."

"He told you that?"

I bite down, force a smile, ignoring the tightening inside my chest. "Yes, he did. They've been sleeping around. She's Andy's type, so I think it's a good thing."

Benedict remains still until he sighs dejectedly.

"I can't leave. I need to be in Venice for a meeting, then Milan again. Also, Mother has an appointment with the cardiologist. I'd like to accompany her to that. But you take Bentley, take Eliza with you."

Rosemarie and her so-called heart problems. They conveniently strike when she doesn't get her way.

"Eliza can stay here. I have my family to help if I need it."

"Are you sure?"

I nod with a smile. "They'll be fighting over him anyway."

---

Planning the trip back home is the only thing I can think about. Thankfully, Bentley has a passport which is usually half the battle when attempting to travel internationally.

When I mention it to Dad over the phone the next day, he insists on taking care of the tickets. In Noah Mason's language, it means first-class. Although Kate offered to fly over and fly back with me if I needed help, I kindly refused. If I time everything correctly, Bentley should sleep for most of the flight.

Upon confirmation of my itinerary, my cousins are relentless with their messages. The group chat blows up to the point even the husbands are involved.

MILLIE

How many bouncy castles can we fit in Uncle Noah's yard?

AVA

However many we want, money isn't an object.

ADDY

You really are Dad's clone, Ava.

MILLIE

LOL, Lex Junior.

AVA

Hey! That's Will. Everyone knows it.

WILL

I'm trying to work. Leave me alone.

MILLIE

Sorry, Addy, Ava has nothing on Will.

ADDY

Okay, Charlie Junior.

AVA

Why is there no Eric Junior?

MILLIE

THANK GOD. Can you imagine?

ME

Eric is going to give me the Botox lecture. I know it.

LUNA

Don't worry, Jessa. I'd already gotten it when I frowned in front of him. It was an hour of my life I'll never get back.

BTW excited to see you.

ME

Excited to see you!

AVA

We need a night out. We'll dress up and drink the night away.

AUSTIN

Did you forget something important?

AVA

What?

WILL

Uh… you're knocked up, as is my wife. So, no drinking??

AVA

Damn, I forgot.

MILLIE

How can you forget? I just left the toilet and need to pee again! Granted, two kids walked in on me because they had to show me something on their iPads. Oh, and the cat followed too.

WILL

I told you not to get that damn cat.

ADDY

It's so cute though!

AVA

Yeah, who doesn't want to have a pussy around?

WILL

Well said, Ava.

MILLIE

Don't you have work to do, Mr. Romano?

AVA

Can we get back to the bouncy castle talk?

The chat is still continuing, but I welcome the back-and-forth banter, feeling sorry for the men because Mille and Ava are nonstop. It's not just them, Kate is over the moon and continually messaging me about all the things she's buying for Bentley. Mom is excited, too, organizing a day out so we can take Bentley to the zoo.

In just under a week, I'll set foot back home. Being with family is just what I need. My son spending time with his cousins will be an experience I'll never forget.

The only thing missing is Andy.

I ache to hear his voice or even send him a text, but with my husband asleep beside me, I settle for my imagination instead—the only thing keeping me sane while the man I want is hundreds of miles away.

# SIXTEEN

## JESSA

"They're here!"

Kate claps her hands as Dad stands beside her with a relieved smile. We all embrace until Kate begs to take Bentley from my arms the moment we reach them. I welcome the help, my arms dead from carrying him through the passenger terminal.

Bentley fusses for a second, reaching out for Dad instead.

"I feel so rejected," Kate voices with a grin. "Let me take that bag off you. Surely, you must be exhausted."

The first part of the flight involved distracting Bentley in every way possible. His obsession with planes meant he called out *planes* every two seconds. Packed inside my bag was any small toy I could fit, a few books, plus his food. All of that lasted two hours until he started to get bored.

Given he hasn't begun to walk yet, I allowed him to crawl where there was some space but thoroughly cleaned his hands because all I could think about was the germs. Bentley pulled himself up to walk along where he could hold on for support. Most of the passengers enjoyed the smiling baby greeting them hello—all but one man dressed in a suit. The typical, arrogant jerk who gave me daggered stares suggesting I move my kid away from him as far as possible.

I could barely eat without Bentley wanting to touch everything when the food was served. I fed him first, to which he made a mess, but thankfully the hostess was more than gracious enough to help me before I managed to get him to sleep.

And what a relief that was.

I should've slept when he did, but instead, I took out my journal and just wrote. Page after page, again. The words have now become a story, one my imagination so desperately wants to tell.

"I'm exhausted. Why is London so far?"

"Let's get you home, showered, and fed," Kate insists, placing her arm around me. "Plus, we have a surprise for Bentley."

"Oh, what is it?"

Dad shakes his head with a knowing grin as Kate rolls her eyes at him. "Ignore your father, please. So, I went a little crazy shopping for him. How often do I get to spoil my only grandchild?"

"You did only a few months ago."

Kate purses her lips. "That doesn't count."

I brought only one large suitcase with me given the warm weather, so there isn't a need for thick sweaters or coats. After we pick up my suitcase, we make our way to Dad's car, which is securely fitted with a car seat.

"Gee, Dad, you've thought of everything."

"Smart man, right?" Kate turns to face him, his lips tightening at her judgmental stare. "Until he's buying diapers and comes home with swim diapers instead of regular diapers."

"In my defense, they all look the same."

My lips pout, but I'm unable to hide my smile. "They kinda don't, Dad."

"You're back for one minute, and the two of you are already ganging up on me," he muses.

On the drive home, the familiar sites are a welcome change, all of which have some memory attached from my childhood. It doesn't take too long for the house to appear before us, catching my breath as I release a long-winded sigh.

Finally, I've made it back home.

"Nash and Sienna will be back home tomorrow but only for the weekend," Dad mentions while taking Bentley out of his seat. "Why don't you go shower and have a rest. We'll have dinner tonight before the rest of the family wants your attention. I hope it's okay that your mother will be joining us?"

"That sounds perfect, Dad."

As soon as we step inside, the scent in the air consumes me, a smell reminding me only of this house. I can't even describe it. A mixture of many things and happiness is one of them.

Kate, of course, wants to show me the surprise, which happens to be the guest bedroom all decorated just for Bentley. The walls are painted a light blue with a white crib and changing table against one wall and a dresser and small bookshelf on the other. There are stuffed bears, cushions, books, and other toys positioned perfectly in the room.

"This room is adorable," I say in admiration, gazing at the light fixture, which happens to be a plane hanging from the roof.

"Mama," Bentley calls, "Ppp...pane."

"Yes, baby, it's a plane."

"Okay, listen. Please get some rest. I'm going to bathe and change Bentley, get him down for a quick nap, so he has some energy for dinner."

"I can't thank you enough."

"Your tired eyes are thanking me." Kate laughs.

I leave the two of them to catch Dad walking down the hall. Just like Kate, he insists I get some rest. When I open the door to my room, nothing has changed. Everything is the way I left it, from the king-size bed in the middle of the room with my favorite lavender sheets to the white bedside tables beside them.

Across the bed is a complete wall of bookshelves. Every single book I read and loved is sitting on those very shelves. My teal velour armchair is seated next to the window—my treasured reading spot.

After taking the longest shower known to mankind, desperate to wash all the plane smell off me, I'm barely able to climb into bed as my limbs are weighed down with exhaustion.

Jetlag—the bane of my existence.

Before I fall asleep, I want to hear Andy's voice since it's been days since I could last speak to him. Benedict was always in and out of the house or hovering near me. For fear of being caught, I thought it was best to wait until I arrived in LA.

I dial Andy's number, forgetting what time it is in Spain.

"Can it be that I'm speaking to a Californian?"

A laugh escapes me, followed by a yawn. "Yes, though I feel like I'm in some sort of twilight zone. I don't even know what time it is."

"Bedtime?"

"Yes," I yawn again, although it's only midday.

"How was the flight?"

"As expected with a child who wants to say hello to everyone and eat everything. Oh, and I think I counted he said the word plane like a thousand times."

"Aww, poor baby," Andy murmurs. "You, not him."

"I'm so tired that I'm too tired to sleep. Does that make sense?"

"Yes, but you should get some sleep."

"But I want to talk to you," I whine, followed by a string of yawns this time. "How has work been? Has Anastasia been behaving herself?"

This time, Andy chuckles. "Busy, never a moment to stop. As for Anastasia, well, she's just her."

I sit up against the pillow, suddenly wide awake. "What does that mean?"

"It means you have nothing to worry about because if I could be there with you, I would."

A sigh escapes me as my head falls back. "This is so hard, the distance thing. Amongst everything else."

Andy falls quiet for just a moment. "We both know this was never going to be easy. But Jessa, for now, we need to keep this between us. I don't want Bentley nor you to suffer because Benedict finds out."

"I made up a lie and said you're seeing Anastasia," I admit, then continue. "He asked if you would be here, and I said no, you and Anastasia are a thing, so you stayed in Spain for work."

"If he finds out..."

"How will he find out? I promise I'm careful."

"I know, but I don't want to put you in danger."

I bite my lip, trying to ignore the stir down below. To lighten the mood, I shift the conversation to something more thrilling other than my husband finding out.

"You're making us sound so forbidden."

"Well, we are. You're married," he reminds me.

"And you're supposedly my cousin."

"Thankfully, you're not actually my cousin," Andy muses, reiterating the facts since our whole life we were brought up as a family. "God, our parents are so twisted even calling us that."

"Taboo is the correct word to define us."

"I mean it, Jessa. Until you end things, we have to be careful." Andy is speaking only the truth, but this is the first conversation we're having about me leaving Benedict. Every time I think about it, the whole thing feels too overwhelming, and I start to feel sick to my stomach. "You're going to end things, right?"

"Andy, I need to get some sleep, but we can talk more about it when I get the chance. Right now, I just want to spend time with my family."

"Sleep well, Jessa."

"You too, Andy."

We hang up the phone, but I continue to hold onto it. There's so much to think about, and the more I think about it, the more the panic consumes me.

Right now, I need sleep, praying for some miracle when I wake up.

It's rare for me to be having dinner with all my parents, the last time being my wedding if I recall correctly.

Kate and Mom both cooked, and, of course, Dad and Jack talked about work because that's what they always did. On occasion, the conversation shifted to motorsports, but only after a few drinks.

"It's so good to have you back," Mom says, touching my hand. "And, of course, to have Bentley visit. What are your plans for the next week?"

"Tomorrow is catch up with Nash and Sienna, then Saturday is the party, which you both can come to, right?"

"We wouldn't miss it for the world," Mom assures me. "It's a shame Michael and his family are traveling in Asia. He would've loved to see you."

"I know, Mom. I miss him too."

"There'll be another time. So what day are you free so we can take Bentley to the zoo?"

"Um..." I try to do the math in my head of how long I have and who I planned what with. "I have some time next week. My flight back home is next Saturday."

I see Mom glance over to Dad, who drops his eyes like he's guilty of something. Upon seeing this, I look over at Kate, who's definitely forcing a smile. That, I'm sure of. Jack is in his own world, enjoying the chicken casserole.

"It's such a short trip," Mom continues. "And Benedict was unable to join you?"

"He has work. Besides, it's easier without him. He doesn't exactly have a lot of patience for Bentley."

The moment it escapes my lips, I regret painting him out to be the villain when I'm the one doing the wrong thing.

Bentley accidentally knocks his plate onto the floor, the loud bang causing him to cry.

"Oh, honey," Mom soothes. "Come here."

*This kid is so spoiled.*

Mom and Kate take Bentley upstairs to clean him up and change him into his pajamas. Jack turns on the football in desperate need to find out who won, leaving Dad and me to tidy up.

In the kitchen, we load the dishwasher until I still my movements, eager to talk to him.

"Dad, can I ask you a question?"

"Anything, of course."

I bow my head to get my thoughts right, so they don't come out in a jumbled mess.

"When you and Mom decided to separate, was it hard?"

Dad stops scraping the food off the plate into the trash, his expression stilling, but then continues his task before speaking.

"Yes, of course. When you marry someone, it's with the

intent it's forever. But life doesn't always work out that way, and marriage can have its ups and downs."

"After the conversation with Mom, did you know that straight away? That it was the right thing to do?" I shake my head to better communicate. "I mean to say, at the time, did you have regrets?"

"I think when you're making life-altering decisions, especially if it involves a child, there's initially regret. You only want to give your child everything they deserve, so regret comes from your own insecurities of failing as a parent because you couldn't keep fighting for your marriage anymore."

I nod with understanding, then release a breath. "You made the right decision."

Dad smiles with his eyes focusing on me. "Yes, we did. It doesn't mean it wasn't the hardest time of our lives."

"What did you do after? You know, to move on?"

A smirk plays on Dad's lips. "Well, your brother was obviously a result of me trying to forget your mother existed."

"Oh, I forgot the one-night stand," I say honestly. "It's easy to forget because Olivia feels like part of our family, you know?"

"Yes, she does," Dad agrees.

There was never a secret about how or where our parentage came about, including Nash. His mom, Olivia, is the nicest woman you'll ever meet. She's been joining us for Christmas for as long as I can remember and joined us on a few family trips. Kate once told me it took years for Olivia and Mom to get to know each other since things were tense between them. Though the affair happened while my parents were separated, Dad and Olivia's one-night stand was the final nail in the coffin known as my parents' marriage.

"Jessa, is there something you want to tell me?"

I shake my head, remembering what Andy said during our call earlier.

We need to remain a secret. Not a single person can know about us.

"No, Dad." I smile, then close the dishwasher. "Everything is just fine."

# SEVENTEEN

## JESSA

I'm barely able to breathe as my cousins pull me into a group hug, squeezing me tight while refusing to let go.

Millie and Ava examine me with glassy eyes. The pregnancy hormones have everything to do with their emotional greeting. Both look radiant with the glow everyone speaks of when observing someone pregnant.

"I've missed you so much," Ava says, pulling me into the backyard as Austin stops to hug me hello.

"It's been a while, stranger." Austin grins, carrying Emmy in his arms. I touch her cheek, mesmerized by how much she has grown and how she looks exactly like Austin, except for the emerald eyes, of course. I don't think it's possible for that gene not to be passed on. "How is motherhood treating you?"

"Tired," I cite, only for my eyes to gleam. "But worth every minute."

Will joins us, embracing me tightly, to pull away and say hello to Bentley. Sometimes, I have flashbacks to when Will was a teen and would annoy us with his attitude. Millie was the one he tormented the most, not that she ever backed down. Ava, Andy, and I would just watch on the sideline while they fought over the dumbest things.

"Let me take Bentley off you," Ava extends her arms. "Will he cry?"

I hand him over, but his lips begin to tremble upon seeing an unfamiliar face.

"Maybe try a man," I suggest, turning to Will since Austin is carrying Emmy. "He doesn't seem to be bothered by them."

Will reaches out for him as Bentley leans over, no tears following.

"He must be a daddy's boy," Millie mentions.

I almost snort at the comment but instead change the topic. "You guys, this is amazing. I mean, I went for a walk with Bentley and came back to all this. Cotton candy?"

"That's for me, darling."

I turn around to see Eric posing in a way only Eric poses. Throwing my arms around him, he's quick to warn me to watch his hair.

"Before you say anything, I'm not going to get Botox, but I'll entertain photoshopping or filters of your choice."

"Oh, honey, you don't need Botox." Eric laughs, patting his chest, and then his expression becomes flat. "I'm kidding. You really should see Gilda. She can make you look sixteen again."

"Why would I want to look sixteen again?"

"Don't listen to him." I hear a familiar voice behind me to see Aunt Charlie. "Let me look at you. Motherhood looks good on you."

I hug her tight, missing her so much. For some reason, emotions overwhelm me while we embrace, but I quickly play them off as I notice Uncle Lex next to her.

"Uncle Lex," I breathe, swallowing the lump in my

throat, wondering why the hell I'm choking up over seeing my uncle and aunt.

He pulls me into a tight embrace, just like he did on my wedding day before he stepped aside, and my father walked me down the aisle. I have only fond memories of him, always treating me like one of his daughters.

"It's good to have you home, Jessa."

"It's good to be home," I tell them both.

Will comes over as Uncle Lex asks to take Bentley. Bentley is drawn to him the moment he does but then points to the bouncy castle and demands to be taken over.

"The last time Lex got into a bouncy castle, it didn't end well." Aunt Charlie laughs, only for Will and Eric to join in.

"Oh, what happened?"

"Ashton's friend got sick and didn't tell anyone, so when Lex went in to get Emmy, he kind of sat in it." Will chuckles, bowing his head.

My chest rises and falls, the laughs escaping me. "How awful but also hilarious because Uncle Lex would've been disgusted."

Aunt Charlie nods. "Oh, he was, trust me."

Nash and Sienna walk into the yard carrying trays of food while arguing. I'm sure it has everything to do with Nash stealing food off the tray Sienna is carrying as she almost loses her balance and drops the whole platter.

Addy and Alexandra follow, stopping by for more hugs and comments about my hair being darker.

"We have so much to catch up on," Addy tells me, pulling me aside as Alexa walks over to Eric. "I hope you've got some free time while you're here?"

I smile, then hug her again. "For you, always."

Luna and Willow walk in next, with Julian and Adriana behind them. The second my eyes lay on Adriana, her gaze is longing, and I wonder if she knows what's been happening between her son and me. The chances are low, given what happened in Andy's bathroom has stayed between us and not exactly something he would discuss with his mom.

I exhale a breath, willing the speculation to disappear. Julian extends his arms, welcoming me back. Adriana stops just shy of where I stand, grabbing both my hands to examine me closer.

"You're a heartbreaker, always have been."

"You're just saying that because you want to steal my son, right?" I tease, tilting my head. "Aren't you notorious for your raspberry kisses?"

"Some memory on you." She grins, then winks. "And yes, I am."

She touches my cheek, then goes off to steal Bentley from Uncle Lex. Julian stands beside me, glancing at Adriana with a genuine smile.

"Are you still managing to write?" he asks, shoving his hands in his pockets. "I can imagine your hands must be full with Bentley."

I gaze over, watching Adriana blow raspberry kisses into Bentley's cheek as he giggles, only for Uncle Lex to scold her for overwhelming him. They get into an argument, typical sibling behavior.

"I started a few weeks ago. It's not much but something."

"That's where it all begins, with a few words."

"I'd love to chat with you someday when I'm ready to write professionally again."

"Anytime, you know where to contact me."

I clear my throat, shuffling my feet on the ground. "Andy, um, he's the one who pushed me to write again."

Julian's expression remains blank, but he's never one to give opinions unless asked for. Slowly, his lips curve upward into a proud smile.

"That sounds like my son."

With my shoulders relaxing, I find myself grinning. "Persistent, perhaps, is the best way to describe him."

"That too." Julian chuckles.

Rocky and Nikki arrive last, fresh off a plane from New York. Rocky smothers me in an overbearing man hug, then makes an inappropriate joke about age-gap couples. Eric's face says it all, disgusted but also intrigued as no doubt he has some story he wants to share.

The party is just as I imagined Bentley's first birthday. Tables full of food, bouncy castles, and those balloons you shape into animals or objects. Rocky is in charge of the balloons, and surprisingly, he's quite good until Millie's eyes widen.

"Is my son walking around with a giant dick?"

Ava snickers beside her. "I think it's a sword."

Eric crosses his arms with a satisfied nod. "That's a pee-pee, sweetheart."

"Why do I get the father-in-law who makes balloon penises!"

"It could be worse." Will sneers, shaking his head in disgust. "It could be your *actual* father making the balloons."

Both Ava and I whistle at the same time. "Thank God our dads are different."

"Yes, they are," Eric asserts, though I don't like where this is leading. "Arrogant, stubborn, and extremely needy in the bedroom."

I let out an involuntary groan as Ava growls. "Why would you even say that to us?"

"Because, sweetheart, the truth will set you free."

"Free from what? Eric?" Ava almost yells. "You're banned from birthday parties."

"Please, you said that last time when I said your mom enjoys her pearl necklaces."

This time, I laugh. "God, I miss this."

I'm trying to give everyone my attention as I walk around the yard. As people speak to me, my mind drifts off, wondering what it would be like to raise Bentley here, surrounded by family. My memories of California are fond, aside from my argument with Andy, when I returned from London engaged to Benedict.

The kids are all happily playing, running around as Bentley crawls after them. I ate American food, something I've missed so much. All of it is delicious until I grab a few pigs in a blanket, and Eric begins a story about a guy he once dated, Ariel, who had the most petite dick he's ever seen. The more he went into detail, the weaker my appetite became. When he brought out the words 'duck butter,' I put my plate down.

"What the hell is duck butter?"

"It's a combination of sweat from the ball sac and anus which creates a buttery—"

I raise my hand. "No more, I don't want to know anymore."

Rocky intervenes. "Oh yeah, a few buddies of mine in college had killer DB. You know, from playing gridiron and stuff."

*"Killer DB?"* I repeat, eyes wide.

"Yeah, that shit is nasty."

I have no more words left to say, walking away with a headshake, trying to erase the whole 'killer DB' conversation. My focus moves toward the table of gifts, all for my baby boy. Even though it's still two weeks until Bentley turns one, the emotions are overwhelming. My fingers trace the silver ribbon on top of one of the gifts, releasing a sigh of contentment.

"I hear California is a beautiful place to visit," I hear a

voice say behind me.

I turn around swiftly, to be met with blue eyes I've missed all day. Andy is standing in front of me, looking incredibly sexy in a white polo shirt and navy shorts. He wears his signature pristine white Nike sneakers because he loves his shoes more than anything.

"Andy, you're here? But how?"

"You know those things that fly in the sky? They're called planes."

A smirk spreads across my face. "Oh, I'm quite familiar with the word plane."

He nods, glancing over at Millie and Ava, who watch us. When I turn to see them, they quickly bow their heads, pretending they have nothing to do with this.

"No chance I was going to miss the little fella's birthday."

"I...I..." I stammer, speechless as to how thoughtful his intentions are. "I want to hug you, but people are looking."

"So? You're my bestie," he says, mimicking a woman's voice.

I break out into laughter, only to feel my shoulders relax. "Come here, then."

As he wraps his arms around me, everything feels just right. The smell of his aftershave causes my body to shiver in delight, despite the warm sun gracing my skin. I wonder if he feels the same, but judging by his tight grip, I'll say he does.

Together, everyone we love surrounds us, celebrating my baby turning one. The emotions, again, overwhelm me, forcing me to pull away, but Andy's expression softens.

"Argh, why is this hard? It's like him turning one means he's going off to college."

"Remember when I left for college? Mom bawled like a baby."

"I bawled like a baby. You and Millie gone at the same time was too much."

Andy gazes around the yard. "Full circle, it always comes back to this."

More than anything, I want to spend time with him but remember this day isn't about me. It doesn't take long before the family smothers Andy and for Eric to comment on Andy's muscular physique. Rocky throws in a joke about European women and full bushes, only for Will to warn his dad to shut the fuck up and not mention Nikki.

Ava pulls me toward the large table where Bentley's birthday cake sits. It's three layers, covered in sprinkles and chocolate with a big number one on the top. Beside it, there's a smaller cake known as the smash cake.

I take Bentley from Mom, who's carrying him, to stand where Ava lights up the candle. At the count of three, everyone sings Happy Birthday while Bentley watches with a confused look on his face. When it ends, I pretend to blow the candle to make him follow. He figures it out, and with my help, we blow it out together as everyone cheers.

Across the table, standing beside Uncle Lex. is Andy. My gaze fixates on him as I begin to tear up, his eyes soft and filled with an inner glow as he smiles in return.

None of this would've been possible if he didn't walk back into my life and remind me of everything I'd been missing.

My family.

The ones who raised me, the uncles and aunts who treated me like their own, the cousins who made memories with me, to the close friends we call family.

Every single person here has played a role in my life.

Unconditional love is the only thing I want for my son, and as I stare longingly at Andy again, I realize it's the only thing I want from him.

To be loved, and only loved, by the man I have *always* loved.

# EIGHTEEN

## ANDY

When Jessa texted me to mention Millie and Ava throwing a birthday party for Bentley, I didn't want to tell her they asked me days before if it was a good idea.

Frankly, Jessa needed to reconnect with everyone, so it made sense to celebrate Bentley turning one and a trip back home for her.

Noah had been in a great mood since his daughter called him, and they mended their broken relationship, insisting I fly back home for a week to join everyone.

Considering Noah is technically my boss, I wasn't in a position to say no but still played my cards, not wanting to allude to anything going on between his daughter and me.

The only person I'd confided in was Millie. I trust her with all my being, even though I insisted both Jessa and I keep things to ourselves. Millie is somewhat of my sounding board with the mess I've found myself in. While I never mentioned what happened in my hotel, Millie knows my feelings are strong, but the predicament isn't so easily resolved when Jessa is married to another man.

Yet seeing Jessa again, I just want to hold her and kiss those beautiful lips of hers which continue to tease me. But I held back when I surprised her, aside from the friendly hug, knowing my nosy cousins would be watching.

More importantly, I don't want my appearance to be the focal point—this day is all for Bentley.

It doesn't mean the smell of her perfume doesn't drive me wild. It's getting harder and harder to be in her presence without thinking about her completely naked and spread out for me to devour.

This is a kid's party, so now I have to control my rampant thoughts once again.

After saying hello to everyone, I find myself near the bouncy castle with Lex and Mom.

"It's good to see you, kid," Mom says, lacing her arm into mine. "Why do you look older?"

I chuckle softly. "Because you're watching a bunch of kids jump around in a bouncy castle, and I'm towering over you now?"

Lex and Mom laugh. "You towered over me at the age of ten. It doesn't help that I'm the shortest in the family."

"So, whose genes did I get then?"

"Definitely Elijah's," Mom informs me, but then she slows her movements as if something is bothering her. "I've been thinking a lot about him lately."

My throat thickens, wondering why his presence is being felt everywhere. I still haven't told Mom about my recurring dreams, not wanting to upset her. She's always been an open book about him, but truthfully, I've never really felt the need to ask questions.

Lex puts his arm around Mom for her to rest her head against him.

"I... uh... me too," I manage to stumble out.

"You have?"

"Yeah." I rub my face, then let out a sigh. "I told Dad about it the last time I was here. It's the same recurring dream. I see his face smiling at me, then Lex comes and takes him away."

I leave out the parts of the body bag and other gruesome things, not wanting to stress Mom since she has her own memories of him.

"I believe he must be trying to tell us something," she almost whispers. "My dreams are... somewhat similar."

"But what, Mom? I can't go on with these sleepless nights," I admit out of desperation. "Nothing is working, not even the sleeping pills I'm taking."

"Is there anything that helps?" Lex asks, his expression one of concern. "Anything which stops this from happening?"

I glance over at Jessa, watching her try to feed Bentley, who's far more interested in the balloon Rocky hands him. Oddly so, the balloon looks like a giant dick.

"A long time ago, there was," I murmur with my stare fixated on her.

"You know, sometimes it just all works out," is all Lex says. "But maybe, for now, Elijah is trying to tell you both something."

Mom's lips curve upward into a smile. "I think he is. As for life, when you least expect it, it works out."

Lex's words continue to play in my thoughts. I wish I knew the reason why these dreams are so vivid, thinking just like him, something is trying to be said.

The birthday party goes on for hours with the kids starting to wear themselves out and Bentley's overtired tears coming hard and fast. He crawls over to me, pulling himself up to my legs and begging for me to pick him up, calling, "Andy."

"What's wrong, buddy? Too much excitement?" I ask

while carrying him, only for him to rest his head on my shoulder.

"He needs a nap," Jessa says, reaching out for him, to which he shakes his head. "No, Mama. A... Andy."

"You know he only remembers your name because of *Toy Story*?"

"Great movie." I grin, then remember something Mom once told me. "Mom said I used to always write my name on my shoes, just like the movie."

Jessa laughs. "Why am I not surprised?"

"I'll help take him for his nap," I insist, wondering if he'll fall asleep on the walk upstairs.

I follow Jessa through the house, welcoming the silence. My ears are still ringing from the noise outside, only realizing now how loud kids can be. It doesn't help that Rocky insists on riling them up, chasing them around the yard pretending to be a dinosaur on the hunt for kids to eat.

It's been years since I walked down these halls, the nostalgia coming back until we're inside what appears to be a room for Bentley.

"Noah and Kate went all out," I mention, scanning the room.

"First grandchild, you know how it is."

"Imagine what my mom will be like."

"The closet will be bigger than the nursery," Jessa muses.

Jessa motions for me to place Bentley down so she can change his clothes as I keep him occupied so he doesn't fuss. When he's freshly changed, she places him on the ground for him to crawl to a toy beside the rocking chair.

Then, I remember his gift, buried in my back pocket. I pull out the little blue box and hand it to Jessa.

"For the birthday boy."

"You didn't have to get him anything, just being here is enough."

"I wanted to," I murmur, then draw in a breath. "Open it."

Jessa pulls the little ribbon off, her eyes sparkling with anticipation. When she lifts the lid, she gasps in complete shock.

*"Andy..."* She barely breathes. "You remembered?"

"A wise girl once told me the importance of first birthday gifts."

She removes the gold chain from the box to rest the pendant of a plane in her palm. Unable to speak, Jessa stares at it with admiration.

"Bentley is obsessed with planes."

"I know."

"You don't know how much..." her words trail off at the same time her chest rises and falls. "How did you even find this?"

"With much-needed patience to scour every jewelry store in Madrid."

I'm about to mention my dealings with one of the sales assistants when Jessa lunges forward, grabbing my face with both her hands to smash her lips against my mouth.

The jolt electrifies every inch of my body, the cravings for her only intensifying with every taste of her beautiful mouth. A soft moan escapes her, but then she pulls away, eyes wide with heavy pants following.

"I... uh... wanted to thank you."

I try to catch my breath, my gaze falling upon her pink lips with a primal need to taste more of her. It was her rule, the no-touching thing, so I wasn't going to force myself on her.

"That was quite a thank you." I reach out to touch her face, seeing her expression torn for her sudden move. "Don't feel guilty."

Her eyes fall to the ground. "This is harder than I thought."

My hand reaches out to her arm, eager to hold her. With her face against my chest, I kiss the top of her hair, trying to ease her guilty thoughts.

"We'll get through this."

Jessa moves out of my arms, creating a small distance. "How? You know what, I don't want to think about it."

"We'll get through this because I need you all to myself."

Jessa's mouth twitches for a grin to appear slowly. She places her hands on my chest, expelling a long-winded sigh.

"You know, the sexual tension is killing me."

A smirk falls upon my lips. "Oh really? You. I thought you were all vanilla."

"More like Neapolitan, a mixed assortment of flavors depending on my mood."

"What's your mood now?"

"All flavors," she teases. "But I'm going to behave."

We both still our movements to turn around at the same time, only to see Bentley fast asleep on the floor hugging a stuffed bear.

"He's knocked out," I whisper.

I move toward him, bending down to scoop him in my arms. Slowly, I carry Bentley to his crib, where I place him down, then cover him with his blanket.

"You're so good with him," Jessa says, watching me move a strand of hair away from his eyes. "He adores you, you know."

"He's a good kid, and you're doing a great job. I hope you know that."

Jessa smiles, her face lighting up so beautifully. "We should head back downstairs."

Before we go, I stop her at the door.

"This isn't going to be easy. He'll fight you for Bentley," I remind her because the weight of the cold hard truth is too heavy to ignore. "But I need you to know I'm here for you every step of the way."

"I don't want to think about it right now," she barely whispers. "We should go."

When we walk back downstairs, we go our separate ways, not to seem obvious.

The parents move inside the house with the younger kids, who grow tired and rest in the den with a movie. My younger cousins join them, and Nash, of course, because he likes to talk throughout the movie to annoy the kids when they annoy him by asking so many questions.

Outside, Will turns on the fire pit when the air starts to cool slightly. Will sits beside Millie, who looks incredibly tired, rubbing her stomach. Ava sits on Austin's lap, but unlike Millie, she's not as far along in her pregnancy and has more energy. I take a seat across from Jessa, keeping my distance.

"I don't know how to thank you guys for today," Jessa mentions, nursing a wine in her hand, which Will passed to her.

"You move back home?" Ava jokes.

Jessa smiles. "I wish I could."

"Anything is possible," Millie says wistfully.

"It doesn't feel that way at times."

Ava glances over to me, our eyes trying to speak which, of course, hers never listen to me.

"Is everything okay?" Ava asks softly.

Jessa drinks her wine all in one go, forcing me to bow my head because she's known to blurt out her true feelings when intoxicated. Will extends the bottle out again, in which Jessa willingly accepts his offer to pour more into her glass.

"No, it isn't."

Millie leans over and places her hand on Jessa's leg. "It's just us, okay?"

Jessa nods then takes a deep breath. "Benedict isn't the man I thought he would be."

My lips remain flat, not wanting to give my opinion on this subject. The very fact I told her to keep this between us is lost on her the more she speaks of her imperfect husband. A husband she chose over me.

"I mean, people change, but also, they can change back," Ava says, trying to remain impartial and hold back her opinions. "Maybe, he's going through things?"

"I think I chose not to see it," Jessa admits in a low voice. "Rose-colored glasses, right?"

"So, does this mean you want to leave him?" Ava asks.

I beg Jessa not to look my way, but she steals a stolen glance in which both Will and Austin notice. Neither of them has questioned me on my rekindled friendship with Jessa, but I suspect the next time we're alone, it will come up.

"It means I have no idea how."

Will clears his throat. "Benedict is a man who's used to getting his way. The chances are, Jessa, he won't accept your decision without a fight."

"That's such an awful thing to say, Will," Ava argues, crossing her arms much to Austin's amusement. "Why do men think it's okay to make women into objects like their feelings mean nothing?"

Austin tries to calm her down. "It's a pride thing, more than anything."

"Screw pride, Jessa isn't happy. He needs to let her go. End of story."

"It's not that simple, Ava. Not when a child is involved," Millie informs her.

"You're right," Ava agrees, calming her tone. "I'm sorry, Jessa, whatever you need, we're here."

"Whatever you need, Mom and I can help you, legally," Millie adds.

"Thanks," Jessa mumbles. "For now, I need to enjoy the rest of the week."

Jessa's back-and-forth, let's talk about, let's not talk about, escalates my frustration. Here I am, always offering to help her get through this so we can be together, yet all she does is cut our conversations off, making me feel like it will never happen. The truth is, next week, she'll be back on the plane and sleeping in the same bed with her husband.

The jealousy floods my veins, running wild like a current building from an impending storm. My insecurities fight for attention, telling me I'm not good enough again because this is just a 'fling,' and soon she'll be back to playing the role of Benedict Banks's wife.

I stand up, unable to look at anyone, allowing the anger to consume me. "I need to go. I have somewhere to be tonight."

Without a goodbye, I turn around and walk off, knowing I'll pay the price later when everyone contacts me to make sure I'm okay.

Well, I'm not okay.

Far from it.

But I'm my own worst enemy, fighting for a girl again who places someone else above me.

Déjà-fucking-vu.

# NINETEEN

## JESSA

Andy storming out isn't how I imagined the night would end.

We all sat in silence upon his departure. My cousins aren't oblivious to what's happening, despite Andy wanting to keep things between us. Just because I said my marriage isn't working out doesn't mean something is going on between Andy and me.

I don't want to be known as that woman.

The one who cheated on her husband and destroyed her marriage.

Yet as I sit here, lost in my thoughts, the truth is I'd crossed all the boundaries, even when I said I'd never cheat on Benedict.

The lie I continue to feed myself has run its course.

*The damage is done.*

The guilt eats away at me as I sit here across the other side of the world. The poisonous seed is implanting itself into me, and no matter what I do or say, it's there for good.

It only dawns on me now, Benedict hasn't even checked in to see how Bentley or I are doing. The last communication between us was when I landed. I texted him a quick we made it, to get a thumbs-up response. Not even an 'How was Bentley on the flight?'.

I excuse myself to a quieter part of the yard and dial Benedict's number. It rings out as I tap my foot impatiently until it goes to voicemail. I redial the number, my frustration growing while the seconds pass.

"Jessa," he answers coldly. "I'm in the middle of something."

"Can you please talk to me, just for a few minutes?"

"I'm with people." I hear the grit in his voice. "Can this wait?"

"No," I choke, clutching my stomach, willing the guilt consuming me to admit the truth finally. "I need to talk now."

"Listen to me. I can't talk. You chose to go with your family. Now I'm with mine. Whatever you need to discuss with me, can wait for a more appropriate time."

And just like that, the call ends.

I shake my head in anger, then storm toward the kitchen where Mom and Kate are cleaning up.

"I need to go do something," I tell them with my hands clenched into fists and arms straight. "Bentley is—"

"Honey, go do whatever you need to do. Kate and I are here to take care of him, okay?"

With a sharp intake of breath, I nod, though unable to string a sentence together, let alone say thank you. My head is rampant with thoughts and emotions, all screaming for attention and causing my heart to race abnormally.

"Jessa," Kate calls softly. "Take all night if you need, no judgment from us."

As I look into their eyes, I only see the unconditional love from two women who raised me as their daughter. I want to thank them for everything they've ever given me and tell them the truth, but they aren't the ones desperate to hear me speak—it's Andy.

---

As I ring the doorbell, I note Andy's black Wrangler is sitting in the driveway.

Julian, Adriana, Luna, and Willow were still at my parents' house. The adults began drinking when I left, and if Rocky has anything to do with it, they'll be there well into the early hours of the morning.

When there's no answer, I contemplate ringing again but instead text Adriana for the code. She quickly responds with no judgment or questions asked. I've always had a great relationship with her, and I'm glad she hasn't pushed to why I'm asking.

Inside, the lights are off, and the house is covered in darkness. Like a road I've driven on several times before, I walk down the long dark hall to the other end of the house where Andy's room is located. The door is closed, and behind it, I have no idea if Andy is in fact in here, but it doesn't slow my erratic heartbeat. The voices telling me it's now or possibly never.

The suspense cripples me, so I turn the doorknob and open the door quietly.

The lights are off in here too, yet the sun has just set, and the moon is illuminating the sky, emitting a beautiful light in the room. Andy is sitting on his bed, still wearing the clothes he wore earlier, staring out the large window which overlooks the city. In the distance, the buildings begin to light up, the entire panoramic view so mesmerizing.

Every step closer to Andy, he doesn't flinch nor move, not one time. I sit on the edge of his bed, keeping my distance.

The nerves overcome me as sweat builds in my palms, but I can't run away anymore from him.

The force between us is too magnetic, and my shield against it crumbled the moment I allowed my heart to beat for him.

"I'm terrified, Andy," I whisper, swallowing the lump in my throat. "I'm terrified he'll take Bentley away from me."

Andy lowers his gaze, remaining silent.

I want Andy to know the truth, just how I feel about him and the demons I carry, which weigh me down each time I breathe.

"The night of our dinner, Benedict..." I choke on my own words, trying not to break down. "He tried to force himself on me."

The moment it leaves my mouth, Andy's head snaps in my direction.

"He tried to force himself on you?" he repeats with malice.

I nod, followed by a downward gaze, the humiliation too much to bear. Thankfully, I managed to stop him, but my initial reaction of fear is something that will never leave me.

"I didn't want to tell you or anyone. I pushed him away and slept in another room. When I tried to talk about it the next day, he pretended it was nothing." I pause, then continue, "Sorry, he pretended it wasn't a big deal because I'm his wife."

Even in the pale moonlight, I can see Andy's muscles tighten and his jaw clench tight. I've witnessed Andy's temper before, usually involving me on some date which ended badly.

"Why are you telling me only now, then?" he almost barks.

"Because I'm sick of lying about everything. Of how miserable I've been these last two years married to a man who

I wish would be a father to Bentley. The older Bentley gets, the more I resent Benedict for treating him like a stranger." I draw in a breath, willing it all to come out. "God, Andy, I see you with Bentley, and I wish you were his father. I pray for a miracle to change everything that's happened between us, so he's your son."

"That's not how life works," Andy merely mumbles.

"I know that. God, I know that," I repeat in frustration. "I love you, Andy. I've been in love with you for a very long time. So many moments in the last two years, I thought about you. And each time I did, the guilt ate away at me."

"Jessa, I—"

I don't give him a chance to finish, speaking over him. "No, please don't say anything in return because you feel you have to."

The absence of our voices forces me to focus on my heavy breathing, confident Andy can hear the loud thumping of my heart. This surreal feeling of knowing I openly said the words I've so desperately wanted to say for years leaves me speechless.

Across the bed, Andy reaches his arm out for me. "Come here."

I place my hand in his, relishing in his warm touch as he pulls me toward him. He guides me to straddle him while he leans against the tall fabric headboard, our faces at the same level.

Andy caresses my cheek with the back of his hand, making me feel so safe, like the world doesn't exist outside this room. My eyes close momentarily, expelling a small breath as I focus on his touch.

"Look at me, please," he begs.

I open my eyes to stare longingly into his. Of all the times in my life where I stared into these very eyes, this feels entirely different.

"I've always been in love with you," he whispers. "It's why I took the job in London. It wasn't my intent to break up your marriage, but I needed to see you. My life, since you left, hasn't been the same."

My finger moves toward his lips, trailing the bottom with a gentle touch.

"I'm here," I barely whisper.

"Yes, you are."

"I know what I said in the restaurant that night..." I stammer, but this fight is only against everything I want at this moment.

"You don't need to say anything," he murmurs, trailing my cheekbone with the tips of his finger. "It's just you and me."

Andy tilts his head, placing his mouth to mine as we slowly kiss in the darkness. My hands run through his hair, our tongues battling feverishly until a soft moan escapes me. The taste of him is so pure, igniting every inch of my body and heightening all my senses.

"I need you, Andy," I beg faintly. "I don't want to wait anymore."

He places his hands on my thighs, lifting the hem of my dress until it goes past my shoulders and over my head. In only my black bra and panties, I wrap my hands around his head to bring his lips back to mine.

His hands wander all over my body, then back around to the hook of my bra, unclasping it to slide it off, so my breasts are exposed.

We break away, out of breath, for his gaze to fall to my chest, exploring every inch with lust in his eyes. He brings my neck to his lips, trailing my skin with kisses down my chest, causing me to arch my back as he circles his tongue around my nipples. My skin grows hot and feverish, the need to lose myself in him the only thing consuming me.

With ease, his lips wrap around my nipple with gentle sucks, teasing me so effortlessly as I moan at his touch. When he pulls away, he grazes my lips with his thumb, biting down on his own while trying to restrain himself.

"You sure you're ready?"

I nod, then shuffle off him, removing my panties while he unbuckles his jeans and boxers, tossing them to the floor. Unsure of how to bring up the whole protection thing, I take a deep breath.

"Do you have... you know?"

"I do if you want."

"I think we should," I suggest with a faint voice.

He leans over to his nightstand to pull one out, then rips the packet and slides it on.

As I climb back on top of him, I rub myself against his hard cock, watching him groan in delight.

"I've been waiting a long time for this." He breathes the words out, followed but a deep kiss, then pulling away to leave me out of breath.

"You don't need to wait any longer," I tell him.

Slowly, I angle myself by hovering near the tip of his cock. To savor the moment, I slide him in so softly, watching his face tighten until he's all in. I give us a moment to catch our breaths, especially me, before I start rocking gently.

Andy's muscles stiffen, and I know he's trying not to come at this very moment. I slow my movements, taking his mouth, devouring his tongue, and tasting him.

"I need to own every part of you," he demands, pushing my hips down so he goes deeper. It causes my skin to tingle, and I know I'm incredibly close, struggling to hold off.

"I'm yours," I whisper, "But... but... I can't hold back any longer."

He brings his palm around my head, then clutches my hair tight to grab a handful.

THE TROUBLE WITH HER

"Come for me," he commands. "You've seen me. Now I want to see you."

I rock my hips, building up the pace as he tugs on my hair, exposing my neck for the euphoric waves to crash against every part of me, exploding into a beautiful finish consuming every inch of my body.

Moans escape me, my breathing ragged and uneven. I slow down, only for Andy to trace his lips on my ear lobe. "I'm not done with you yet."

The exhaustion weighs in as he moves me, so I'm lying on my back. He thrusts harder with his body on top of me, the familiar build inside my stomach threatening to burst again. I warn him eagerly that I'm about to come again, but then he whispers, "I'm going to come now, and when I do, I'm going to fuck you nice and hard."

An involuntary groan leaves my mouth while Andy pushes deeper and drives me into another blissful orgasm. I bring his mouth to mine, moaning in his kiss while he thrusts one last time until his body stiffens on top of me.

Our heavy breathing echoes in the room, and he collapses on top of me as I stroke his hair, unable to speak.

We silently lay here until he pulls himself from me, yanking off the condom. Tossing it in the trash can beside his bed, he pulls the sheets over us.

"I don't want to leave this bed," I tell him honestly as he wraps his arms around my body from behind me. "But I should probably go soon."

"Stay a little while longer."

I playfully knock into him. "You're still hard."

"I am." He slides his fingers down between my thighs and enters me, causing me to gasp. "You're still wet."

As he continues to finger me, my body takes over once again. With every touch, his need to have me again turns me on. I love how insatiable he is, worshiping my body like it belongs to only him. Despite the exhaustion, I still crave more. I want him all over me.

"You gonna come for me again, baby?" he asks, withdrawing his fingers to place them in his mouth so he can taste me.

Fuck, how is this man so sexy?

I nod, unable to comprehend anything else.

"Good girl," he purrs, inserting his fingers in harder this time, causing me to moan in delight. "Because I'm hungry, and there's only one thing I want to taste right now..."

# TWENTY

## ANDY

For the first time in the longest time, I slept through the night.

Not a single dream or nightmare.

Jessa snuck out of my room somewhere after midnight. My parents weren't even home yet, probably still drinking away at Noah and Kate's. As much as I wanted to ask Jessa to stay, I knew she needed to be with Bentley, not wanting to put her in a position where she felt like she needed to choose between us.

So, I took what I could in the time I had her.

It didn't stop after I went down and tasted just how sweet her arousal was. I wanted more, so I entered her again, demanding she go on all fours because I needed her in every possible way. I altered from fucking her nice and slow to hard and fast until I came again, just as intense as the first time.

Every single inch of her body is just as perfect as I imagined—the right curves, the swell of her beautiful tits, her ass which I desperately wanted to smack but worried my parents would come home and hear us. Fucking hell, I'm hard thinking about it again.

I roll over, turning to face the window. The sunshine is out in full glory, with only a slight layer of haze in the sky. My hands reach out for my phone, noting it's just after eight. I want to text her but assume she's busy with Bentley. They have plans to go out today with her mom, so as much as I want her attention, I know I'm not the only one either.

My stomach growls, needing food so desperately. All my stamina was exerted last night, so I'm hungry as hell, no surprises.

I drag my bare feet to the kitchen, wearing my sweats and a ragged white tee I found in my drawer. Dad is cooking breakfast in the kitchen while Mom appears to be nursing a hangover. Her head is buried in her hands, and occasionally, she lets out a groan.

The stool beside her is empty, so I take a seat as Dad slides a coffee over to me.

"That smells amazing. I'm starving," I tell him, eyeing the bacon and eggs on the plate near the stove.

"It smells like vomit," Mom complains beside me with a scrunched face. "Oh wait, that's probably me."

"Your mother got herself drunk last night."

"I didn't get myself drunk. Rocky got us all drunk," she corrects him. "Did you see Lex? He was so far gone..."

"Lex, drunk? C'mon, as if, Mom."

Dad nods, pursing his lips to hide his smile. "It was quite some show last night."

"I'm sorry I missed it," I apologize but shift my gaze onto my coffee, taking a long-winded sip.

Across the countertop, Dad slides a full plate of food in front of me. I thank him, then scarf it down as Mom watches me with disgust.

"How can you eat all that?"

"Frankly, I'm still hungry."

"But look at you? Where does it even go?"

"I burn it off, Mother, like most boys."

The moment it leaves my mouth, Dad glances over with an amused expression. He doesn't say anything, but I assume he knows about last night. Quite possibly, it's why they didn't come home until the early hours of the morning.

"So, about last night..." Mom begins. "Are you okay?"

"I'm fine."

My phone vibrates in front of me, and when I see Jessa's name, a smile spreads across my face.

JESSA

I just walked over Rocky's half-naked body on the living room floor. When I say half-naked, he's only wearing boxers, and they have pictures of Nikki's face all over them.

I hold back my laughter, typing a response and hitting send.

ANDY

Take a photo. It might come in handy one day.

JESSA

Already did. I'm no amateur here.

ANDY

Mom is completely hungover. Apparently, Lex was just as bad.

JESSA

Oh yes, they were. I'll tell you about it later. So, are you free for dinner tonight? I'm spending the day with Mom. Then she's offered to take Bentley so I can go do adult things.

ANDY

What kind of adult things?

JESSA

Eat tacos...

Before I type a response, I glance up, then sideways, to see Mom watching me.

"You're awfully chirpy for someone who appeared agitated last night when you left the party."

"I just needed sleep."

"Sleep?" She questions with her brow raised. "Did you manage to get some? Sleep, I mean."

My gaze falls back onto the screen as I start to type a message back.

"Yes, Mom, I got some sleep. The best I've had in a while."

Across the counter, a smirk spreads across Dad's face as he talks to me with his eyes. Mom looks at him, then to me, letting out a huff.

"Okay, fine. Secret men's business, I get it. So, basically, you're getting laid, which explains why you ate three plates of food. Also, why you're smiling like a lovesick fool."

"Lovesick fool?"

"Adriana, leave Andy alone, and let him enjoy his breakfast." Dad then walks around the countertop, kisses Mom on the head, and grabs her hand. "You need to go back to bed. You don't handle hangovers well."

"Like you do?"

"Yes, I do. We had to get Luna to drive us home because I couldn't even count to five. I've showered, cooked breakfast, and am about to log into a zoom meeting."

"You're a showoff," she complains, smacking his chest with a sly grin.

"Okay, would the two of you lovesick fools leave me alone?"

Mom says something back, but I ignore her to text Jessa back.

ME

Sorry, Mom was questioning me about last night. The woman is relentless when she's hungover and grumpy.

JESSA

What did you say?"

ME

Nothing, I went to sleep, and that's it. What do you expect me to say? Oh, hey Mom, so I fucked Jessa three times and four blissful orgasms later, she went home.

JESSA

I think you should've said that just to goad a reaction from her.

ME

Such a daredevil... so tonight?

JESSA

Pick me up at seven from Mom's.

ME

Have fun today, and hey... I love you.

JESSA

Back at you, baby.

---

So I can say hello to Bentley before we leave, I park my Wrangler out the front of Jessa's mom's house and knock on the door.

Jessa answers the door, dressed in a very short skirt which catches my attention, a far cry from her usual attire worn in England. It's denim, matched with a camel-colored tank and wedges to give her height. At least, that's what I used to tease her about.

"My eyes are up here, just so you know," she muses.

"Yes, but I'm interested in what's down there, just so *you* know."

Jessa grins, pulling me in as Bentley crawls toward me. I bend down, picking him up.

"A... An... dee," he finally gets out.

"It's Andy." Jessa smiles, moving his hair away from his face.

"A man bun would look good on this kid."

"You know me too well." She laughs.

Morgan walks down the hall, saying hello before offering to take Bentley for his bath and then get him ready for bed. We say goodbye and head out to my car.

"God, this car brings back so many memories."

"She's a keeper."

Jessa furrows her brows. "She had a name... Greta?"

"Gerta," I correct her.

As soon as we're in the car, I glance over to make sure the front door is closed, then place my hand on Jessa's thigh to bury my head into the crook of her neck.

"We can't here," Jessa says in a high pitch as my hand runs up her thigh and beneath her skirt. "What if someone sees us?"

"Fine," I drag, pulling back. "So, am I supposed to behave throughout dinner?"

"Hmm, we'll see, but I don't see you getting through the main course, which is why we should probably go for something more chilled like—"

"Don't say it. I already spoiled you with it in London."

"In-N-Out," she finally says.

"Deal."

It's not like I don't enjoy fast food, but Taco Bell never agreed with me, so I welcomed In-N-Out over it in a heartbeat. Jessa went on and on about how much she missed this place and all the bland dinners she's had to sit through with

Benedict's family. To add to the whine she complained about all the questionable food she was forced to eat.

As much as I love conversing with her, it's still hard to hear about her life with him. I smiled but kept quiet, letting her talk.

"I'm sorry," she frowns, "I've been talking nonstop."

"It's fine."

"Okay, so tell me more about Spain. There's this restaurant I absolutely love that Ben..." she trails off, not finishing her sentence upon realizing she's mentioning him again.

I lower my gaze, picking at my fries. Across the table, she reaches out her hand and places it on mine. "I'm sorry I keep bringing him up."

"He's your husband," I remind her hastily.

Jessa retracts her hand with a distant stare only for me to notice the wedding band and engagement ring. She's worn it every time I've seen her, but only now does it catch my attention, throwing fuel to a very burning flame.

"Let's go," she pleads, standing up from the booth. "There's somewhere I want to visit."

---

I park the car at the edge of the cliff as we both unbuckle our seat belts and then exit the car.

Just like old times, we climb onto the roof, my hand extending to Jessa to help her up. I sit behind her, wrapping my arms around her body as she leans back against my chest.

We gaze at the horizon and ocean from this secluded clifftop, admiring it quietly. I've lost count of how many times we've come here, always to escape life and just sit or talk.

"I love this place," Jessa murmurs while taking it all in. "I never realized how much I miss everything about California until now."

"It's our home, where we grew up," I remind her. "It's not Manhattan, that's for sure."

"Manhattan is chaotic, although I do love it there. Just not as much as here."

"A completely different lifestyle."

"Yeah," she mumbles. "It's great for single people."

"Sure."

"Sure?" she questions, her tone pitched, which happens when she's jealous. "You know what, don't answer that."

"Answer what? You haven't asked me a question."

I sense her biting her tongue, which never lasts long.

"Your answer of 'sure' sounds like you enjoy Manhattan because of all the single ladies."

"Are you jealous? Is that it?"

Jessa tenses in my embrace, but I squeeze tighter until she finally relaxes.

"It's just... you're crazy handsome, and women look at you everywhere we go."

"Men, look at you," I inform her.

"Yeah, but you're single, and women are relentless. I mean, seriously, how often did you sleep around before London?"

I always wonder why women need to discuss every detail of the past. What did it matter anymore? I only want the woman in my arms who appears to be fixated on things she can't control.

"I'd prefer not to answer this. I was lonely, okay? And the one woman I wanted was across the other side of the world married to someone else."

"I don't know how to do this," she admits. "Be in love with someone I can't see all the time."

"You don't trust me?"

Jessa grabs my hand, kissing it gently. "When will we see

each other? How long are you in Spain? Then after, aren't you working in Italy?"

Drawing in a deep breath, I lace my hand into hers. "We just have to take it one day at a time. Right now, we're here, and we're alone."

Jessa shuffles, turning around, so she's facing me.

"We're alone."

"Yes," I murmur, running my hand up her thigh, then around to cup her ass. "We're alone, and you've been teasing me all night in this skirt which, by the way, is this old?"

She nods. "Found it at Mom's."

"The Jessa I met in England would never wear such a thing."

"Yeah, well, things change."

I bring my hand around the back of her neck, drawing her in for a heated kiss. Her lips taste just as soft as last night, and the moans she expels as we kiss drive me fucking crazy.

"I have a confession," Jessa whispers, wrapping her arms around my neck.

My hands wander back beneath her skirt, spreading her ass cheek as I grind against her. "You want me to fuck you up the ass, right now?"

"When did you become so dirty?"

"The moment I saw you naked beneath me and imagined all the things I need to do to your body." I place my lips on her neck, trailing kisses to her chest. "So, your confession..."

"Remember that black-tie event Eric made us go to?"

"There's been so many."

"The one where Eric's fly was down, and no one told him, but it appeared on some website?"

"Oh, yeah. That was hilarious."

"Do you remember how we came here afterward?"

I nod, vaguely remembering.

"I remember watching you, dressed in your suit, and I wanted to kiss you."

"You were drunk."

"And horny... but yes... anyway..."

My fingers caress her chin. "You're cute."

She lets out a huff, though keeping her smile fixed. "What did I tell you? Cute is puppies, stuffed teddies. I'm far from cute."

"Oh yeah? Prove it."

With a devious smirk on her face, she moves her hands to the top of my jeans, unbuttoning the top button. Slowly, she unzips the front, then yanks my boxers down, freeing my cock.

She holds my gaze, sliding down toward where I stand hard to wrap her hand around my shaft.

"How bad do you want me to be?"

I bite my bottom lip, watching her mouth open wide near the tip. My muscles begin to clench, fogging my thoughts with the only focus on her taking me all in.

My hands move to the back of her head, clutching her hair in my grip. I pull her head back slightly as she watches me with lust burning in her eyes.

"I'm yours, baby. Show me what you got."

Not wasting any more time, she glides her mouth over me, taking my cock as deep as she can. I watch her suck gently, teasing me as my body tenses, the fight not to explode quickly becoming harder and harder to battle against.

I can easily blow in her mouth, but I need to feel her all over me.

"Come here," I command, helping her slide up until she's back on top of me, and I ease myself in.

The sensation consumes me, no rubber to desensitize my cock inside her. I wait for her to stop me, which means I'll have to pull out and grab one from my wallet, sitting in the car. But instead, her gaze doesn't waver, and she slowly grinds against me as we fuck slowly on top of my car.

There's nothing more arousing than being outdoors, the fear of being caught only adding to the thrill. I watch her move so effortlessly, then observe the way her body grinds faster as she warns me she's just about to come.

I make sure she finishes first, riding out the wave of pleasure before I take myself out and demand she sucks me off until I come.

Like her, I see fucking stars, everything blurring when I blow inside her mouth into a blissful finish.

We both catch our breaths until she leans in and kisses me deeply.

"Am I still a good girl?" she teases.

I grab a lock of her hair, tugging it gently. "I'm not sure I was paying attention. Maybe you need to show me again?"

With a steady gait and gleam in her eye, the playful grin warns me we're not going home just yet.

"Round two," she whispers. "Reverse cowgirl seems the perfect way to admire the view and come at the same time."

# TWENTY-ONE

## ANDY

"Did you know Disneyland is the perfect place to pick up chicks?"

Nash is behind me, scanning his ticket while eyeing the two girls beside us. I pegged them for being college-age in their short shorts—right up Nash's alley.

"You're on uncle duties," Jessa reminds him.

"Although everyone knows kids are chick magnets," I tell them both.

Nash nods with a grin, trying to grab the handles of the stroller and move Jessa out of the way. "Give me Bentley."

With a heavy eye roll, Jessa gazes at me with annoyance. "This is your fault."

"How so?"

"You're giving him ideas and supporting his manwhore behavior."

Luna is standing next to Addy, who decided to join us last minute. Even though this was Ava's idea, she had to bail last minute because Emmy came down with a stomach bug. Millie chose to pass only because she's well into her third trimester and struggles to stand for long periods of time.

"Andy is an enabler," Addy voices with her head high. "That's the correct term to use."

"Okay, psych student, we get it," I drag, only for her to punch my arm.

We enter the park, and just like every time I've visited, you never know where to start with so much to do. All of us are standing on Main Street, collectively agreeing to head to Fantasyland. Just as we begin to walk, Mickey Mouse is hovering, waving to all the kids.

Bentley catches a glimpse of what's going on, his brows furrowing at this character he's never seen before in real life, only on television, according to Jessa.

Nash moves the stroller closer, only for Bentley to hide his face with a shake of his head and repeat the word no. He doesn't appear to be the only one resisting, a few other kids are doing the same thing in their strollers.

We try to stick together, but everyone wants to do something different. The usual wait times for rides make the day drag. Nash managed to grab a few fast passes, which meant we were forced to split up at times. I don't mind as it gives me time alone with Jessa.

There's a small grass patch near Main Street where we sit to take Bentley out of his stroller so he can eat lunch.

"Going to Disneyland with a child is a completely different experience," Jessa says while attempting to feed Bentley a small sandwich. He opens his mouth unknowingly, too busy watching his surroundings.

"I'll say, though I remember when Dad and Mom took Willow here for the first time. I begged them to let me walk around by myself, to which they said no. From memory, I sulked the entire time wishing she was never born."

Jessa's lips curve upward into a smile, followed by a laugh. I want so much to bring her lips to mine but being in public means we have to behave. We thought it wouldn't be hard when we spoke about it last night. Sitting next to her, it's a different story altogether.

"Can you not do that thing with your mouth?" I tease, watching her bite into an apple to lick her lips afterward.

"You're not allowed to talk smut in Disneyland." She grins, doing it again to annoy me. "I'm sure it's in the rule book."

"There's no rule book..." I chide, "... and do you still read your billionaire romance books, hence the word smut?"

"I don't, unfortunately. When Bentley sleeps, I sleep," she informs me. "And, of course, there's a rule book. No sex in the park would be on top of the list."

Her longing stare doesn't waver, even when she takes a deep breath, and I see her chest rise and fall.

A smirk plays on my lips. "Why did you look at me that way when you said that?"

"I have no idea what you're talking about."

"Sure," I jest, only to be distracted when Bentley lets go of the stroller handle he was holding onto and takes a few steps, stumbling into my arms. "Good job, buddy!"

"Oh my God, did he just walk?" Jessa rushes to get her phone out of her purse. "Bentley, do it again?"

Bentley watches her with a sly smile, burying his face into my chest.

"Sorry, Mama, game over," I answer playfully.

Jessa watches me with a slack expression, her lips parting with an appreciative sigh. She reaches out her hand to touch my cheek but quickly yanks it back when we hear Nash's obnoxious laugh.

"That ride was epic," Nash blurts out. "Especially when the chick's tits bounced for the entire ride."

I purse my lips to control my smile. Addy laughs, but Luna looks annoyed.

"It's Disneyland, can you not use the word tits? Kids might hear you."

"Speaking of kids, guess who just took his first steps?" Jessa mentions excitedly.

"No way? This little dude!" Nash sticks out his hand to high-five him. Bentley raises his palm with a giggle. "Did you walk to Andy?"

I nod, rubbing the top of his head. "He sure did."

Luna raises her eyes to meet mine, her expression pinched, and one I've seen many times before. She doesn't speak a word, remaining quiet while Nash and Addy jokingly argue over who is Bentley's favorite.

"He must spend a lot of time with you, Andy. To always want to go to you," Luna insinuates, forcing a smile on her usually jovial face.

"I'm charming. What else can I say."

Jessa fidgets with the grass in front of her, avoiding both of us. Thankfully, Nash wants to grab some lunch, so we move along, only stopping for some food.

As the day wears on, Luna distances herself from me. Considering my sister is known to be moody, I ignore her for the most part while Nash insists we try to do It's a Small World with Bentley.

The beginning of the ride went well. By the end, he cried, extremely overtired from what's been a long day. After we exit, he willingly sits in his stroller and falls asleep as we walk along the paths exploring the park.

"How about you and Jessa go ride something?" Addy suggests, taking the stroller from Jessa. "Bentley's sleeping anyway."

Luna shakes her head. "I don't think it's a good idea. What if he wakes up?"

I tilt my head to observe my sister better. What the fuck is her problem today?

"I think it's a good idea." I grab Jessa's hand. "Let's go. We'll be back in twenty minutes."

Jessa follows along beside me as we walk to Space Mountain.

"Why is Luna in a mood?" Jessa questions as we wait in line. "She's been avoiding me. When I try to talk to her, her answers are all abrupt."

"Who knows with her. Probably because she's got no boyfriend and is living at home again. You know her, she's always got some problem."

The line moves relatively fast, and before we know it, we take our seats in the neon-lit area. I scan around me as everyone is busy getting settled, placing my hand on Jessa's thigh to squeeze it tight.

A grin spreads across her beautiful face, only to widen when I move closer to her panties.

"You wouldn't dare," she challenges me.

"Watch me, sweetheart."

The ride begins to move at the same time I slide my fingers inside of her, causing her to gasp in her seat. Thank fuck she chose to wear a skirt. The carriage jerks with every corner and dip, which forced my hand to move on its own accord, in and out of her. I'm oblivious to the thrill of the ride and my head slamming against the headrests, focused on how wet she is while waiting for her to explode all over my fingers.

I speed up my movements as the ride begins to slow, allowing me to catch her eyes close until they spring open moments later while she gasps repeatedly. Slowly, I remove my fingers just before the ride ends.

"Satisfied?"

"Very much." She winks, only to laugh softly.

Upon exiting the ride, I think of anything to control my dick so people don't notice I'm hard as fuck. A child dry heaving with the impending vomit is enough to do the trick.

Back outside, the sunshine is blinding when we find everyone waiting near the exit.

"How was it?" Addy asks.

"Thrilling," Jessa responds with a knowing smile. "Great ride."

I nod, keeping my smile fixed only to see Luna's judgmental stare again. Seriously, this is getting old.

Bentley stirs to wake up. We continue to walk around the different lands, stopping to take turns on rides, then settle for the parade. It's been a long day, so everyone goes their separate ways when it's finally over. I say goodbye to Jessa with a quick hug, knowing I can't say anything else with everyone around us. Yet my eyes tell her I'll call her later to try to organize something tomorrow morning before she leaves in the afternoon.

My flight is a few hours after hers, a goodbye I've been dreading since the moment I arrived here.

Luna places her AirPods in on the car ride home to ignore me. I don't push a conversation, eager to get home and shower, exhausted from a long day.

We finally arrive home as I park the car in the driveway. Once again, Luna exits without even a thank you, heading straight for the kitchen where I join her because I'm thirsty too.

Luna slams the refrigerator door, releasing an obvious huff while trying to open the bottle of water in her hands.

My patience with her hits an all-time low. After a long day, I have zero time for her, ready to head to bed and crash for the night.

Turning my back, I mumble a good night until she calls, "Andy."

Closing my eyes momentarily, I clench my jaw then turn around, willing to listen to her sad and pathetic apology.

"What the hell are you doing?"

"I'm going to bed," I drag. "I'm beat."

"I mean..." she clears her throat though her eyes remain tight, "... with Jessa."

"Luna, now isn't the time to—"

"To ask you why you're having an affair with a married woman?"

The manic pacing of my heartbeat causes me to clench my fists into balls. "Jessa and I are none of your business."

"None of my business?" Luna questions with a sinister laugh, the same time Mom and Dad walk into the kitchen. "You're ruining a marriage! And the only person who'll truly get hurt in the end is you."

My blood pumps furiously as I gaze at my sister with contempt. She has no idea what it has been like for us, nor what Jessa has been through. Typical, she has formed an opinion based on her limited experience with relationships.

"You have no goddamn idea what you're talking about, Luna."

"I know when you marry someone, you vow to be faithful. What the two of you are doing is wrong," she responds hastily.

"Don't you dare tell me what's wrong!" I point my finger at her, my lips pulled back, baring my teeth. "What gives you the right to judge what we do, huh?"

Dad moves closer to me, trying to calm me down.

"Because you're breaking up a family!"

"I'm not breaking up a goddamn family. It was fucking broken before I even got there."

"So that makes the sneaking around okay? Don't you think her husband will find out? How fair is this to him?"

The pounding in my ears is enough for me to walk away from this conversation.

"I don't need this..." I mumble.

"Of course not. You don't need a reality check, right? I

bet you're going to sneak to Jessa's place now and fuck her pretty little brains out like she's not married to someone else. Jessa won't leave Benedict, and in the end, you'll be the one hurting the most."

"Luna," Dad warns. "Enough."

"No, Dad. What Andy is doing is wrong! What kind of person has an affair with a married woman? As for Jessa, what kind of woman cheats on her husband? Talk about being a selfish bit—"

A guttural roar escapes my throat. *"Don't you dare even think of calling her that."*

"Well, neither of you care. And you know what? You'll both get caught, and the one to suffer the most will be Bentley. What kind of a mother would do that to her child?"

The adrenaline rushes through my body, ready to lash out at my sister for being such a fucking bitch.

"Luna!" Mom snaps with furious eyes. "Apologize to your brother for this uncalled-for behavior. I didn't raise you to be so judgmental and trash another woman for her private decisions. Especially when that woman is your close friend."

"Was, Mom," Luna resigns. "Not anymore."

Luna walks out of the room without another word, leaving the three of us behind. With my head bowed, the anger refuses to subside, leaving me with a dry throat from my rushed breathing.

"Andy," Mom calls softly, placing her hand on my arm. "If there's truth to what Luna said about you and Jessa, you need to be careful. A lot is at stake."

"You don't think I know that, Mom?"

"I know you know, honey. But affairs can get messy. Far be it for me to raise this since the past is the past, but your father can tell you just how hard it is to be on the receiving end of this."

My glance shifts toward Dad, his expression tight as if this brings back memories he prefers not to relive.

"Adriana, I don't think bringing up my own experiences will help Andy."

"Why? I'm sure if Charlie ended things with you before jumping into bed with Lex, you would've preferred that over suffering the way you did."

"Yeah, maybe. But what's done is done."

"Exactly, so my point is, Andy and Jessa should come clean now before this goes further. You hold onto things because it's s safety net. Benedict shouldn't be her safety net because Andy won't let her fall."

"Right," Dad says, but his face begins to fill with anger. "Nothing worse than being second best, the so-called safety net."

Mom crosses her arms, then tilts her head. "What the hell is your problem? Everything worked out in the end."

"Exactly," Dad raises his voice. "It did work out in the end. It doesn't mean you forget the aftermath of a woman's poor decision. Yes, I had moved on from Charlie a very long time ago. It doesn't mean I've forgotten about becoming an addict and how I lost everything and almost my own life."

"Julian, I..."

"Adriana, people make mistakes. We weren't exactly innocent while hiding our relationship from your family. Andy and Jessa are adults. They have their own experience to live and their own emotions to work through. Not you, or Luna, or anyone else for that matter, should be voicing opinions of their relationship. End of fucking story."

Dad walks out of the room, leaving just the two of us. I've never seen Mom and Dad argue to this extent. They have fights, but they're petty over dumb stuff like how the bed should be made or which way the toilet roll should be facing.

The guilt weighs on my shoulders since this is my life and

shouldn't cause problems between my parents. As for my sister, I don't give a goddamn fuck about her right now, still livid over our heated argument.

"I'm sorry, Mom."

"Oh, Andy." She sighs, placing her arm around me. "Love can really test us. When Elijah passed away, I never imagined loving someone else, especially my best friend's ex-fiancé. I knew we were against all odds, but I didn't care. Love is a powerful feeling. When you feel it, you feel it. Sometimes the circumstances aren't perfect, but nothing in life ever is."

"No, it isn't," I say in a low voice. "I need to be alone."

"Whatever you need," Mom assures me, then she releases a breath. "Andy, just be careful. Leaving a marriage is one of the hardest things to do. I don't want to see you get hurt."

"I can take care of myself," I remind her, then close the door behind me.

I find myself driving in circles, my mind unclear and able to settle. Finally, I pull up in front of Noah and Kate's house. With my phone in my hand, I decide to text Jessa rather than knock on the door.

A few minutes later, I see her exit the front door until she's sitting in the passenger seat.

"Hey," she greets out of breath. "What's wrong?"

My focus is on the windscreen in front of me.

"Are you going to leave Benedict?"

"Andy? Why are you asking this, and now?"

"Answer me," I respond in an arctic tone.

"I'm tired, okay? It's been a long day and—"

"I'm not going to sit here and wait forever, only to get hurt at the end because you don't leave him."

Jessa angles her body to face me. "Are you giving me an ultimatum? As in a time limit?"

"I'm asking you a question in which you're not giving a straight answer!"

"Maybe I'm not giving you a straight answer because I don't know how to answer it," she argues back. "You show up, without warning, and expect me to say what?"

I swallow the lump inside my throat, wishing the sharp pain tearing through me to disappear for fear of it controlling my anger once again. It refuses to leave, and it pains me even to sit here any longer. I need to go before I say something I'll regret.

"I should go," I mutter.

Jessa places her hand on my arm, the touch so warm and inviting, which I try to resist for my sanity right now. I don't move, not even a single flinch.

"Andy, please look at me," she begs.

With a heavy sigh, I turn to face her, only to see the sadness in her eyes.

"I can't imagine my life without you, but I also don't know how to walk away without hurting my son. This won't happen overnight but promise me, please, you'll be patient with me. Once I'm back in England, I'm on my own. Trying to leave my husband and take care of my son will take its toll on me, so please, just understand you're the only one I want to be with."

I stare into Jessa's eyes as she pleads for me to trust her.

We have no plan or commitment besides the words spoken between us.

It all boils down to trust and the strength I'm forced to endure living in another country while she's in bed with her husband every night.

There's only one answer—I have to trust her no matter what because without the trust, there'll be no happy ending.

And without her, I don't know how to breathe or even exist.

# TWENTY-TWO

## JESSA

Saying goodbye to my family was always going to be difficult.

But saying goodbye to Andy—much harder.

Last night, our fight became more than a lovers' quarrel. The moment I entered the car, his posture was stiff, and he couldn't even look at me. I didn't understand what had changed since we said goodbye at Disneyland. We'd had so much fun along with Bentley taking his first steps. The act alone nearly had me in tears, my baby growing up way too fast.

There was our naughty moment on Space Mountain, Andy daring me because that's what he's always done—pushed me to live as if tomorrow doesn't exist.

Then, he threw the question hovering over our relationship. I wanted to be honest with him, but his anger only started a chain reaction from me. He isn't the one who has to face her husband after breaking the sanctity of marriage.

Nor is he the one to tell her husband she's unhappy and wants to leave him.

There are so many complications, and even though I

chose to keep my marriage troubles private from Dad and Kate, I knew they suspected something was wrong.

Kate organized a last-minute breakfast at a restaurant in Calabasas. Everyone came to say farewell, and it gave me a proper chance to thank Millie and Ava for planning a memorable first birthday for Bentley.

Andy sits at the other end of the table, keeping his distance. Luna doesn't show up, not even a text to say goodbye. Julian and Adriana are here, sitting beside my parents.

I try to talk to Andy a few times, but someone else always has his attention. Nash is relentless with his pursuit to hook up with women, voicing his excitement over a trip to Spain he's planning. I can see Dad is less than impressed, but he doesn't say a word when it comes to Nash.

Kate is beside me as Aunt Charlie takes Bentley for a walk.

"Are you okay?" she asks.

I nod. "Yeah, just sad."

"I know, honey. It's never easy saying goodbye."

"No, especially with a family as large as ours," I tell her honestly.

Kate rubs my back, then places her arm around me. "In the end, Jessa, this will all work out. Distance makes the heart grow fonder."

"We're not talking about you guys now, are we?"

"No," she whispers. "Time, my girl. Give it time to fall into place."

When breakfast is finished, the goodbyes begin but not without a few tears shed. I hugged everyone tightly, but when it's time to say goodbye to Andy, I notice many people turn away. It doesn't mean I can freely kiss him by any means.

I place my arms around him, but even in his embrace, he purposely holds back.

"Wait for me," I whisper. "Please?"

Pulling away, he simply nods with his eyes a darker shade, then turns his attention to Bentley. He picks him up, kissing his forehead with a dull stare.

"I'm gonna miss you, buddy."

"An-dee," Bentley stammers with a smile.

Andy touches the chain around his neck, placing the plane pendant on his finger.

"What's this, Bentley?"

"Plane, And-ee, plane," he says, then claps his hands.

"Good boy!"

With a small kiss on his forehead, Andy places him back down to look at me one more time. I know this hurts him just as much as it pains me. To not even be able to kiss him is extremely difficult.

And the truth is, we have no idea when we'll be able to see each other next because right now, all the cards are being held by the one man I'm dreading the most.

---

Before I leave for England, there's one important stop I need to make.

I sit inside the kitchen of Uncle Lex and Aunt Charlie's house, not long after our breakfast. My bags were already packed, and Dad offered to pick me up in an hour. Both he and Kate are back at the house, spending time with Bentley.

The Edwards' house feels very much like home because so much of my childhood was spent running around inside this very house along with my cousins. There were sleep-overs, parties—so many memories at this property.

Aunt Charlie slides a cup of coffee over to me while she takes a seat with her cup in hand.

"I'll leave you two ladies to chat."

"No," I call out. "Stay, Uncle Lex. Please."

He takes a seat beside Aunt Charlie, his posture straight and presence always felt inside the room.

As the steam of my cup rises, I run my finger along the rim and draw in a deep breath.

"I need some advice," I stall, then begin again. "About my rights should I leave Benedict."

Aunt Charlie doesn't appear shocked. Her expression is more concerned than anything. Her brows draw together. Then she looks inward. "For starters, are we talking custody rights?"

"Yes."

"Initially, you're both entitled to joint custody unless the courts see a parent as unfit."

"Court?" I ask, panicked.

"Yes, most of the time. There are, at times, couples who remain amicable and come to an agreement without having to settle in court."

I highly doubt Benedict can be amicable about anything, not if Rosemarie has anything to do with it. The coffee demands my attention, so I take a long-winded sip before asking more questions.

"But what if I want to move back here with Bentley?"

Aunt Charlie draws a breath. "It's a lot more complicated. Benedict would have to agree."

As much as I knew that would be the answer, hearing it from a family lawyer hits ten times harder. Benedict loathes California. If we live here, he'll never see his son unless I fly back and forth. That doesn't sound fair to Bentley.

"Divorcing a partner can be messy. There are assets to think about as well."

"I don't have anything," I tell them both as Uncle Lex just watches though remains quiet. "I have my apartment here, which is being rented out. I don't want anything from Benedict or his family."

Aunt Charlie briefly glances at Uncle Lex to then focus her attention back onto me.

"I'll help you, Jessa, with any legal representation. I have friends who work in London. They can assist with differences in our legal systems as I don't know all the ins and outs."

My shoulders curl, the heavy feeling in the pit of my stomach only growing.

"Benedict will fight me for everything," I stammer, suddenly feeling helpless. "I can't imagine your fees would be cheap."

Aunt Charlie places her hand on mine. "Sweetheart, you're family. Don't you dare think for a second you're paying for anything? This is what family does."

I nod, pressing my lips together, but a tear escapes me. "I'm scared of him, what he'll do."

Uncle Lex leans forward this time to place his hand on top of my other hand.

"You have us to help fight. I don't want you to worry about money. I'll take care of this."

I shake my head. "I can't ask you to do that."

With a small smile, he lets out a sigh. "Well, you're lucky I never take no for an answer. Just like Charlotte said, you're part of our family, and we do everything to protect each other."

My eyes fall to the table, choking on my thoughts. "I know Dad will be disappointed."

"Noah will love you no matter what," Aunt Charlie reiterates. "Life doesn't always go according to plan. There's not one of us who hasn't made a mistake, or in some cases, two or three, maybe even more. It's how we move forward, Jessa, which counts for everything."

"I don't want Bentley to suffer because I—"

I purposely cut myself off, about to mention Andy until I

remember just who I'm sitting in front of. Uncle Lex and Andy have an extremely tight bond, and I don't think he'll be pleased to know we're sleeping with each other while I'm married. Affairs are always frowned upon, especially when other people are involved.

"Jessa, please tell me to stop talking if this isn't open for discussion." Aunt Charlie glances at Uncle Lex again briefly. "Is there another reason you think Benedict will fight you for Bentley? Perhaps, a certain person he may be jealous of."

My hands wrap around the warm mug, but I find myself staring at the coffee inside blankly. We promised not to say anything, but this lie is becoming harder and harder to carry around. The weight on my shoulders begins to indent on the verge of permanently scarring.

"Yes," is all I say.

Aunt Charlie sighs. "I've only met Benedict the one time, so far from me to judge his character without knowing him better. However, this won't be an easy battle if he's like many of the husbands I deal with in court."

"I know. I just don't know where to begin."

"I can't tell you where to begin because only you know your marriage better than anyone else. We're here for you every step of the way, and if you need us in person, we are only a plane ride away."

"Thank you," I tell them both. Then I gaze up at Uncle Lex. "Please just be there for Andy. Things are complicated, and I know he's frustrated with me."

Uncle Lex nods. "You leave him to me, okay?"

And perhaps the small amount of relief came from the two people who would never judge me. After all, they had their own love story play out similarly.

But now, it's time I face the inevitable.

Bentley stumbles to Benedict with a grin on his chubby little face. The move catches me by surprise, given his crankiness in the car on the way home from being overtired to the fact he has never really demanded Benedict's attention.

His hand wraps around Benedict's legs until he picks him up in his arms to carry him. Of course, Bentley is quick to repeat the word 'plane' over and over again.

"He's walking?" Benedict asks.

I nod. "Yes, he took a few steps at Disneyland but has been wobbly since. I think he's getting the hang of it."

As I watch them bond as father and son, something I haven't seen in a long while, I begin to swallow repeatedly with a tightness in my chest. The guilt from my actions with Andy consumes me, knowing I allowed myself to get carried away back home when I have family here all along.

For the rest of the night, I busy myself by getting Bentley bathed and fed, hoping he'll settle for the night, and the time zone change doesn't keep him up. I welcome the distraction, trying my best not to check my phone for messages. Resisting is futile. When I finally cave and check, there are only texts from my cousins and parents.

Nothing from Andy.

I want nothing more than to call him just to hear his voice. But the way we left things wasn't exactly how I envisioned. With so much at stake here, my head is full of thoughts, and no answer is easy, no matter which way I look at the situation.

My eyes glance at the clock to see it's late and bedtime. After unpacking my things and safely storing my journal, I shower and head to bed even though I'd been dreading this moment.

When I exit the bathroom, Benedict is nowhere to be found. Placing my robe on, I wander the house, assuming he's in his office. Upon knocking, there's no answer. I search the common areas, then the den, until I see his shadow outside on the patio.

Opening the door, the stench of cigar lingers around me as does the cold.

My arms wrap around my body. "It's cold out. What are you doing here?"

Benedict is staring into the darkness with the cigar perched in his hand and a bourbon in a glass beside him.

"Were you going to tell me Andy was in LA?"

It was bound to be found out, especially since my family took so many photos which were posted online. I'm the fool in thinking this could've been kept a secret.

I take a deep breath, then release a sigh. "My father flew him in."

"Your father flew him in," is all he says with a nod.

It wasn't a question, more like an odd repeat of my answer. His tone is unusually controlled, confusing me as to how he feels about this or if his suspicions will be vocalized, making this the moment, the possible showdown between us.

"He flew him in because he knew it was important for family to be present."

"Except, your husband?"

My arms tighten against my chest. "That was your choice, Benedict. I asked you to come. You said work and your mother were more important. Don't make this out like it was my fault this all happened."

"My son, out of all people, was the one to tell me. He kept pulling the chain on his neck, a gift. I assume, repeating the name Andy," he explains with malice. "Were you alone with him?"

I keep my stare fixated on Benedict without a single blink. "What does it matter?"

He blows a puff of smoke away from his face, then stands up quietly. I'm waiting for his angered gaze to fall upon me or his callous words insisting I'm his wife. The possessiveness he only portrays when he feels threatened.

But none of it comes.

"I'm going to sleep in the guest bedroom."

I go to open my mouth but quickly close it, too tired to continue this conversation.

As he begins to walk away, he stops just shy of the door. "Mother is hosting Bentley's birthday next week. It will be held here. She has planned it all, so you don't need to do anything besides make sure Bentley is best behaved."

The information doesn't surprise me, nor do I argue or battle. Let Rosemarie do whatever she wants, for Bentley has celebrated in the perfect way already. I highly doubt there'll be anything for children to play with or explore—this party is more for herself than Bentley.

Inside our room, I sit on my side of the bed, staring at the empty spot beside me. Despite the jetlag and exhaustion, my mind refuses to settle to sleep, so I take my journal out and write.

The thoughts, emotions, everything I'm unable to say to myself appear freely on the page. When my eyes begin to grow tired, I place my journal away and decide to send Andy a text.

**Me:** *I'm back home.*

I wait for a response and the familiar bubble to appear. The longer I stare at the blank screen, the more I grow anxious. Andy is supposed to have arrived in Spain a few hours ago. I close my eyes for a brief moment, but the temptation is a devil's curse.

My fingers move to the Instagram app, opening the icon to type his name in the search engine.

He rarely posts anything personal, mainly shots he's

taken of buildings or for work. Then, I click on his story. There's only one, and it's a picture of a raised shot glass with liquor in it, maybe tequila, taken beside another shot glass held by a female. I recognize the nails belonging to Anastasia.

My stomach begins to churn as I stalk the app for her profile. I can't find it anywhere until I accidentally stumble on it through the hotels' website, which has her listed as the public relations manager. With a deep breath, I check her profile, but there's nothing. Then, I hover over her profile photo to view her stories. It's a video of her and Andy. They're taking shots and laughing.

The anger tears through me like a destructive storm ready to destroy everything in its sight. My body trembles, wanting so much to call him and ask him what the fuck is he doing. How is it possible for him to land in Spain, and the first thing on his agenda is to go drinking with *her*?

It's almost as if the exchange of 'I love you' or the sex between us meant nothing.

As the hurt creates a ripple, tearing me to pieces at the unknown, the familiar feeling of being alone is just as bad.

But this time, I'm isolated once again and trying to control my jealousy over a man I can't have right now.

At least, not in this very bed.

And perhaps that's what cripples me the most—the basic freedom to live my life and love who I want.

Easy for some, impossible for me.

# TWENTY-THREE

## JESSA

Misery indeed does love company.

For days after I stalked Anastasia, I did nothing but mope around the house. Andy never responded to my text, and I wasn't going to beg him to talk to me.

I spent nights in bed, crying myself to sleep, even when Benedict slept beside me last night for the first time. My appetite dwindled to nothing, my stomach barely able to hold anything from this constant ill-feeling consuming me. To add to that, I struggled to find the energy to do anything or talk to anyone unless absolutely necessary.

It became difficult to complete the simplest of tasks, my head foggy with this constant ache which refused to leave.

I wrote more in my journal, the pain a muse I didn't expect after my trip back home. Everything is darker, the clouds supremely gray, the air unbreathable. I'm drowning in my sorrows, and the only one keeping me afloat is my son.

Today is another milestone—Bentley officially turned one.

He woke up in a good mood, and for the sake of my son, I

make an effort to brighten my spirits since it's his special day. All my family FaceTime in, only confusing Bentley as he tried to grab my phone, then put it in his mouth.

The house is buzzing with workers setting up for the grand affair. Outside is a marquee with blue balloons scattered across the pitched ceiling. Tables are set up with pristine white tablecloths and exquisite china, the kind of expensive stuff you don't want around a now toddler.

I was privy to the guest list last night, noting only three young children were in attendance, and Bentley is one of them. The rest are all of Rosemarie and Benedict's acquaintances. Rosemarie asked if I wanted to invite my parents, even though it was out of courtesy, to which I said they were unable to attend.

"My dear, why aren't you dressed?"

The condescending voice is behind me, forcing me to turn around despite my reluctance.

"I was just about to get changed, Rosemarie."

She's dressed in a white Chanel suit, of course, with her gray hair tied back into its usual bun. Rosemarie raises her hand toward my loose curl, almost with a look of disgust.

"Please dress appropriately for the event. Unruly hair like this must always be placed in an elegant bun."

I force a smile, willing my patience to be granted. Rosemarie knows just how to push my buttons, and no doubt today will be a very long day.

Upon leaving the outdoor area to change, Rosemarie is barking orders at the staff for placing the tables too close to one another.

My dress is simple, navy with a tunic-styled skirt which reaches my knees. I chose to keep my heels not too high, especially if I needed to chase Bentley around. As for my hair, Rosemarie can bite me. I leave it out, knowing I'll pay for my disobedience later.

Guests arrive, carrying nothing more than envelopes that are no doubt filled with cash. I perform my duties, smiling and greeting all the guests, trying to remember everyone's names.

Benedict keeps his distance, his behavior odd, but I don't think twice about it. Since our conversation regarding Andy last week, we've barely spoken two words to each other, even when he slept in our bed last night.

The lunch continues just like all of Rosemarie's functions. People converse, mingle, and eat the meals served. There's wine, plus champagne, and nothing at all fun or edible for Bentley to eat.

After lunch, Rosemarie corners me to inform it's time to cut the cake and find Benedict since she's having no luck. I leave Bentley with Eliza, searching the marquee, then outside. Back inside the house, I check his office but still no Benedict.

Upon my walk to our room, my phone vibrates in my hand.

ANDY

Please give Bentley the biggest of hugs and wish him a happy birthday from me.

I miss the little guy.

My fingers type profusely, without a care in the world as to what's right or wrong anymore.

ME

We both miss you.

I take a deep breath, knowing we have to get this cake over and done with because Bentley needs a nap. As I enter the room, my eyes gravitate toward Benedict, sitting in the armchair beside the window with my journal in his hand.

"Wha... what are you doing?"

"What do you think I'm doing?" he questions in an arctic tone, deliberately raising his eyebrows with tension in his jaw. "You want to explain this?"

I'm overwhelmed by panic but at the same time anger. This journal is private, and my thoughts are yet to be edited to form a piece I want to share with the world.

"I've been writing again."

"You've been writing again," he repeats, raising his voice. "And this story of yours?"

"Is just a fictional story," I answer calmly.

Benedict opens the page, his eyes falling to the words. His sudden sinister laugh is disturbing until he opens his mouth. *"And no man has ever made me feel this way, a complete woman, in just a simple touch."*

"Benedict, how dare—"

*"But our bond was founded well before this intimate moment. It started when we were kids, raised in a world of the unknown, yet to experience the true love of another human being besides our family."*

I lower my head, clutching onto my stomach. "What do you want me to say?"

"Admit the goddamn truth!" he roars, running his hands through his hair like a crazed maniac. "You think I'm some idiot? Like I don't know my wife is being fucked by another man who's supposedly her family."

"It's not like that," I breathe, willing my chest to calm down. "You don't understand."

It's the moment of truth, the weight of this secret too hard to live anymore. It's come down to this, and because I couldn't find the courage to bring this up earlier, I've hurt Benedict even more.

"I understand we need to be downstairs." He throws the journal on the bed to storm out of the room, but I call his name for him to still his movements with his back facing me.

"Our marriage was over before Andy walked back into my life," I whisper.

Benedict slowly turns around with a corded neck and his pupils flared. It comes as no surprise he is angry, but I know him well enough to assume it's his pride hurt more than losing his wife.

"Don't for one second think you're going to walk away from our marriage," he snarls.

The battle to end our marriage is just beginning. Benedict would easily continue our loveless marriage and fuck me whenever convenient for him.

But I can no longer live like this.

"You can't force me to stay," I argue back.

*"You have no idea what my family is capable of."*

He exits the room without another word, leaving me here alone.

My heart is beating incredibly fast as my chest rises and falls, making it difficult to breathe. The ill-feeling in my stomach rises, forcing me to run to the bathroom, where I vomit profusely into the toilet. I hold back my tears, not wanting anyone to notice since everyone is downstairs.

In the marquee, we're forced to stand side by side to sing Happy Birthday to Bentley. Our façade masks the pain of the truth unveiled moments earlier, to which no one notices any different. If there's one thing this family does well, it's put on a show like nothing in the world is wrong.

When all is said and done, Eliza places Bentley in his chair as cake is served to all the guests. Rosemarie pulls me aside, away from Bentley, as Benedict stands beside her with cold eyes.

"My son has just informed me of the wondrous news."

I tilt my head in confusion, thinking this can't be true. Has Benedict mentioned our marriage is over?

"What news is that, Rosemarie?"

"Of your acceptance for Bentley to attend boarding school when he turns five. Now, the headmaster is a very good acquaintance of mine, so securing a place will be of no concern. I've already placed his name down."

My mouth slackens as my muscles begin to quiver. With wide eyes, my gaze darts to Benedict to see a satisfied smile on his face. Lightheadedness causes me to sway for just a moment, but then I finally find the strength to open my mouth.

"*Excuse me?*" I question with a strained voice. "Did you say boarding school?"

"Yes, my dear. All the Banks men have attended boarding school. It's only right to do so," Rosemarie insists with her head held high. "Bentley is English. It's expected he's raised in a proper manner."

My fists clench into a ball, the rage consuming me. The only shade I see is red, and even then, it's dark, almost like blood. If this woman thinks she can have any say in how my son will live his life or be raised, she's in for the shock of her life.

"Bentley is my son!" I yell as people turn around, stunned by my outburst. "I don't care what your stupid tradition is. I did not, nor will I ever agree to this."

"Young lady," Rosemarie scolds, gritting her teeth. "We do not raise our voices in public."

"We don't do it in private either," I argue back.

The second the words register, Rosemarie's face stiffens. The stare is cold, and I'm half expecting her to slap my face like some dramatic movie, but as she raises her hand, she moves it toward her chest, clutching her heart.

"Mother?" Benedict calls, his brows furrowing. "Mother?"

Rosemarie winces over until she collapses on the ground as everyone gasps.

"Someone, call an ambulance!" Benedict yells.

A fluster of panic circles around me, yet I stand here frozen, watching the woman I despise with all my being, the woman trying to take my son away from me, lie on the floor with a broken heart.

Benedict tries to talk to Rosemarie as a guest who happens to be a doctor rushes to her aide. I quickly instruct Eliza to take Bentley upstairs, not wanting him to see any of this, then ask the guests to stand back so the doctor can attend to Rosemarie without everyone watching on.

I don't know how long we stand here until the ambulance arrives. Rosemarie is conscious but barely able to speak, and her skin has turned pale. Upon placing her on the stretcher, she reaches out for Benedict and his brothers, who stand around her. I choose to stand back, allowing them to wheel her out to take her straight to the hospital.

---

The corridors inside the hospital are stark white with a sterile stench in the air. I'm sitting on the hard plastic chair, waiting for any news. It's been over an hour, and not one single person has come out.

I pull my phone out of my purse, quickly calling Eliza to make sure Bentley is okay, wishing I was with him, especially on his birthday. Eliza FaceTimes me so I can at least say good night to him, my heart extremely heavy from today's events.

As much as I want to hear Andy's voice, calling or texting him seems inappropriate while my husband is worried sick about his mother. Instead, I decide to call Kate to inform her of the news and exactly what happened.

"Oh gosh, Jessa," she calls softly. "This isn't your fault, okay?"

I nod, even though she can't see me. Despite her saying it

isn't my fault, why do I feel like it is? If I hadn't raised my voice and yelled at Rosemarie, perhaps the heart attack could've been avoided.

"I humiliated her..." I choke, barely managing to say the words, "... in front of her family and friends. That's all I seem to be doing lately, destroying everyone around me."

"Listen here, you're not responsible for this woman's health issues, especially since she had a heart condition to begin with. As for destroying people, you couldn't be further from the truth. If anyone had tried to take any of my kids away from me, I'd have done the same."

"Bentley can't go to boarding school," I sob. "I won't let it happen."

Kate sighs over the phone. "Jessa, no one will take Bentley away from you. Now, I'm calling Dad and telling him to go be with you."

"Dad's here?"

"He's in Madrid..." Kate trails off. "With, um... Andy."

"Oh."

"Just making sure he's okay. You know..."

"I'm glad Dad is making sure he's okay." I draw in a breath, wishing to God Andy will somehow persevere with me during this time. "I can't stand the thought of him hurting too."

The double doors open as Benedict appears.

"Kate, I'll speak to you later. Benedict is here."

"Of course, I love you, Jessa."

"Love you more," I respond before hanging up the call.

I stand up, but Benedict motions for me to take a seat. He sits down beside me, looking worn out as the shirt he wears looks crumpled with his sleeves rolled up. With a pained expression, he stares at the wall in silence.

"What did the doctors say?"

Benedict releases a breath. "She'll need surgery. Her

heart is a lot worse than we thought. Apparently, she's had a heart condition since she was a child but thought she was invincible."

"I don't understand. I thought you went to her cardiologist appointment with her?"

He shakes his head. "She lied, said the appointment was canceled. And well, here we are."

"Here we are," I repeat in a low voice. "I'm sorry."

"What's there to be sorry about? This is typical Rosemarie Banks. She controls everything and everyone around her," he states, staring wide-eyed at the wall still. "She's my mother, for all intents and purpose, but I don't know the woman inside that room begging me to be by her side."

"Sometimes, we don't know what we have until it's too late."

"For the longest of times, I just wanted a mother to show unconditional love. The kind of love you show to Bentley..." he trails off, his voice quivering.

I'm stunned by his admissions, given this man always chose her over me. My opinion meant nothing. Then I remember the boarding school.

"I don't want Bentley going to boarding school," I tell him firmly.

With his shoulders slumped, he buries his face into his hands. Moments later, he lifts his head to speak. "I only agreed because I was angry at you. I knew it would hurt you."

A tear falls down my cheek. "I might deserve your anger but not Bentley. Please don't make him suffer because our marriage didn't work out."

Benedict falls into a digestive silence, toying with the ring on his finger.

"Divorce is not an option in my family."

"And staying in an unhappy marriage is not an option in mine."

"I don't want to discuss this right now," he says with finality.

Staring down at his hands, then mine, my voice begins to break each time I open my mouth to speak.

"For now, I'm here for our family. No matter what happens, Benedict, we're family. You'll always be Bentley's father no matter where our personal lives take us."

*"Andy,"* he mumbles.

It isn't the moment to discuss my relationship with Andy nor admit the whole truth. I respect my husband is in pain, dealing with his life changing in so many ways. I know it wasn't easy for him to admit his struggles, and there'll be an appropriate time to discuss our future in more detail. Not here in a hospital corridor.

"You go home, put Bentley to bed. I'll stay here for a bit longer."

"Are you sure?" I ask, worried about leaving him. "Eliza is with him."

"I'm sure he needs his mother at home."

As I stand up, I grab my purse and sling it over my shoulder. I touch his shoulder gently, letting him know it will be okay. My feet begin to move to the exit when he calls my name.

I turn around to meet his sorrowful gaze.

"I'm sorry about what happened that night in our bed. I should've respected your wishes, along with apologizing the next day. It was wrong of me to do what I did."

My lips curl as I bite down with a nod. "We all make mistakes, Benedict. It's what we do moving forward that counts."

# TWENTY-FOUR

## ANDY

"Three, two, one..."

The shot glass tips back into my mouth for the tequila to slide down my throat without the usual burn it's known for. Perhaps, this is because it's our fifth round, and the supposedly potent liquor is beginning to taste flavorless.

"I'm done," Anastasia admits with a head shake, squinting her eyes to open them again.

She'd captured photos of us drinking, posting it to her stories, and yanking my phone off me to share on mine.

"You're not done." I push her, calling the bartender back, who warns me this is the last round. That's what the fucker said two rounds ago. "C'mon, who'll drink with me?"

"I will."

The bartender places the shot glasses on the table as Lex takes the one that's supposed to be for Anastasia. Until now, he'd been nursing a scotch. We clink the glasses, then drink them in one go.

"I feel sick just watching this," Anastasia complains,

covering her mouth. "I'm going to the bathroom. Please send a search party if I'm not back in thirty minutes."

I watch as Anastasia stumbles to the bathroom in her tight white dress, almost entering the men's instead, until she realizes when a man exits with an annoyed look on his face. She laughs, not at all embarrassed because she's beyond drunk right now.

"You remind me of my younger years," Lex mentions with a fond smile. "I could drink the night away. These days, I'm done after two."

"That's not true. You just choose not to drink your troubles away because you have no troubles." I point my finger at him. "You have a beautiful wife, four smart daughters of which two of them are happily married. Nothing at all is wrong in your life."

Lex gazes at me with an unrelenting stare. "I'm blessed. I'll admit that. It doesn't mean I haven't had my share of pain. Some things will never leave you."

When I waited for my plane last night, I was surprised to see Lex boarding the same flight at the airport. Firstly, he has a private jet so traveling on a commercial plane isn't something he does much anymore. Then, it clicked. The more he tried to explain the so-called business meeting he needed to attend in Madrid, the more I realized he was instructed to babysit me.

Everyone is worried about me. Poor Andy is going off the rails because Jessa is back with her husband. When I left home, Dad had a few words with me, but he's wise, and I listened with an open mind. Luna didn't even say goodbye, ignoring me to stay at a friend's house so she could avoid me. On the other hand, Mom worries about me like I'm some goddamn broken baby bird.

I'm fucking fine.

And the tequila is making life good again.

The bar we found ourselves in is quaint with a chilled vibe. There's soft music that plays, nothing overbearing or loud. The space is dimly lit with a few sconces on the wall and candles sitting on each table. The crowd is slightly older, missing the usual obnoxious singles group, who create all the trouble when out drinking.

"So, I'm guessing Mom sent you here to watch me, huh? Make sure I don't do anything stupid like fuck Anastasia into oblivion."

Lex glances to the table beside us, then back onto me. "Well, the night is young, and the two of you seem to have lost control of your ability to make good decisions."

"I'm not tied to anyone," I remind him, my vision blurring for a sudden moment before I can focus again. "No wedding ring on my fucking finger."

"You're right, there isn't. But we both know you're hurting, and trust me, I know it's not easy to sit back and expect miracles when the woman you love is sleeping in bed with someone else."

My eyes fall upon the table. "You have no idea how much it hurts."

I expect Lex to tell me he understands just how much, for I know he went through his fair share of turmoil to win Charlie back. But instead, he motions for the bartender to return and orders the last round of drinks.

When the shots arrive, Lex slides one over. "Last one for the night, then we head back to the hotel."

I stare at the glass, wishing it could numb the pain, erase her from my memory so I can breathe like a normal human being again. Her hold over me is far greater than I ever imagined possible. I see her everywhere in women who walk past with curly bronze hair, to my imagination which continues to torment me at every waking moment. I've tasted her and felt her body melt into mine.

And these memories refuse to disappear even after all the tequila shots.

The last glass sits in front of me, and with Lex, I drink it in one go.

"I'm glad you're here," I finally admit. "I could've done something stupid because... because I can't even fucking breathe right now."

Lex nods. "I've made mistakes, done things I'm not proud of. But you, my son, won't make the same ones."

"How do you know?"

"Because you have family who loves you and won't let you suffer in silence."

I release a breath, suddenly desperate to get out of here. No good can come of this anymore, and all I want to do is sleep and get through another day alive.

"It's been thirty minutes," I say to Lex. "Should we rescue her?"

Lex laughs. "We probably should. Just don't be surprised if we find her head over the toilet bowl."

"This isn't my first rodeo with her." I chuckle.

The only good thing about Lex being in Madrid is he insisted I attend meetings with him which distracted me from reality. The hotel's interior has been completed, with decorators finishing their touches by the end of the day. All in all, he's pleased with how it's turned out and expects the hotel to be up and running before spring.

I chose to purposely not respond to Jessa's text, wanting to give her space. It seemed like the right thing to do, not that it was easy. As hours passed, I battled with my morals and conscience, holding myself back from jumping on a plane to see her. I even go as far as to search for plane tickets, but just before I take the final step, only one thing comes to mind.

*Bentley.*

He doesn't deserve his family to fall apart because I can't control my jealousy or temper. So, this is the sick and twisted game I play with myself, fighting against good and bad.

But today is his birthday, so I sent a quick text to wish him a happy birthday, wanting so much to see him since I miss his chubby little face. I contemplate calling but don't want to make Jessa uncomfortable if she can't answer. My mind starts to conjure up scenarios, them playing happy family. I begin to feel sick, knowing I can't continue to do this to myself, so I switch my phone to silent so I can continue working.

Lex left only this morning, giving me some breathing space.

Then, Noah shows up.

The shiny leather shoes appeared beside me as I tried to focus on the lens and capture the hotel's pool area we were working on.

"If it isn't Mr. Mason here to play babysitter," I say with an annoyed huff.

Noah clears his throat. "I have no idea what you're talking about."

"Sure. First Lex, now you. Let me guess, is Dad next?"

"I'm here for work. I just thought I'd check in to see how things are going."

"Or make sure I'm not drunk in someone else's bed?"

One of the workers beside me watches on with curiosity until I glance at her to give us a moment.

Pulling away from the lens, I move toward the table and chair sitting by the pool and take a seat. Noah follows, then requests for drinks to be served.

"I'm fine, okay? See, sober and alive."

Noah stares at me furtively, and I hate how similar he looks to Jessa making his presence another reminder. Same eyes, same smile—all the things I want to avoid.

"Let me tell you a story..." he begins with, then continues, "... about when my marriage fell apart."

"Okay," I mumble.

"I was so angry, you know. At myself for failing as a husband, for failing my daughter, but most importantly, for never listening to my own voice." The young woman places two drinks in front of us, which appear to be sangria. Small pieces of diced fruit float on top of the beverage, mixed with ice cubes. Noah takes a sip, thanking the woman, then continues, "I never once stopped thinking about Kate. We had this connection that never left me. When things started again between us, I knew it would be difficult. On one side, I had a woman I wanted to be with for the rest of my life, and on the other, I had an ex-wife who, at the time, used our daughter as a pawn in her fight against me."

"I'm sorry," is all I say but listen on.

"I don't blame Morgan. We were both angry at the time and struggled with the idea of co-parenting, let alone bringing another person into our daughter's life. I wasn't a saint either. I mean, Nash was a result of me trying to bury my problems in another woman."

To hear Noah admit the truth isn't easy. He treated me just like Lex for pretty much all my life. I've always felt comfortable around him because he's an uncle figure to me. He's always trusted me, but years ago, when things began to shift between Jessa and me, I often worried about what he would say. He was always protective over his daughter, which I could never blame him.

"What I'm trying to say is no matter what happened, Kate always stood by me. At times, she knew she had to take a step back and let me and Morgan work through things for the sake of Jessa."

I lower my head, tapping my fingers against the glass tabletop. "You don't think that's what I'm doing now? I don't want to make it more stressful for Jessa, which is why I'm giving her space to think about what she really wants."

"She wants you," he tells me adamantly. "My daughter is stubborn, much like her dear old father. I respect your decision to allow her to work through things, but she needs you."

"I'm not the one married, Noah. Nor am I the one with a child," I remind him, my tone turning frustrated. "You don't think this has been hard? Every day I'm fighting the same goddamn battle. Imagine having to lie at night, and the woman you love is lying in bed with her husband."

The resentment grows deeper as I sit here, forced to admit my struggles, showing my weakness to another man. When I told Jessa in LA to keep things between us, it didn't take long for everyone to figure it out for themselves. But it's only now I'm admitting the truth.

Just as Noah begins to open his mouth, his phone rings.

"Hello?"

He turns silent, but his eyes fall to the ground as he nods quietly while listening to the other person.

"I'll leave straight away."

His finger taps on the screen to end the call for a sigh to escape him. The usually straight shoulders with perfect posture slumps as something is bothering him.

"Is everything okay?"

Noah takes a deep breath, then glances directly at me. "Benedict's mother had a heart attack. They're at the hospital now."

"Is Jessa okay?"

Across the table, Noah purses his lips. "She, uh, is upset. She thinks it's her fault."

"I don't understand?"

"Jessa had a fight with Rosemarie, and she collapsed."

My hands move to my face as I rub it vigorously. I can only assume the fight would've been over Bentley without all the details, given it's his birthday.

"I'm going to fly over." Noah stands up, the same time I do. "Stay here, okay? I'll check on her to make sure she's okay."

"I feel fucking helpless," I tell him.

"I'll make sure our girl knows she's loved by her entire family, including you."

As Noah walks away, I pull my phone out and see a text message from Jessa sent three hours ago.

JESSA

We miss you too.

I pace the area around the pool, willing the tightness inside my chest to dissipate. When I can't take it anymore, I pull out my phone and dial her number. It rings on loop, but no answer. I desperately want to try again but decide against it.

The sangria is too tempting, so I drink it all, willing my nerves to calm down. Nothing seems to work, so I tell everyone I'm heading back to the hotel where I'm staying.

Inside the lobby, I run into Anastasia at the counter. I quickly head over to tell her I'm calling it quits for the day, but she's trying to talk on one phone with her other phone on the counter when I get there. Why this woman carries both phones is beyond me.

When she sees me, she motions for me to wait one minute while she walks toward the exit for better reception, leaving her purse and phone behind. I can't leave now, so I wait impatiently until her screen lights up, catching my attention.

BENEDICT

I can't fly out. My mother had a heart attack.

Curiosity consumes me. How many Benedicts does Anastasia know? Quickly glancing to where Anastasia stands with her back toward me, I touch her screen, which has no password stupidly enough, then slide the message up to read the trail.

ANASTASIA

How dirty do you want me tomorrow night? I can be a good girl like your precious wife or bad just the way you liked it last week.

BENEDICT

I'll fly out after Bentley's party and tell her it's for work. Not that she'll care.

I turn away, not wanting to read more. It's enough evidence to prove her husband isn't a complete victim in this mess we've found ourselves in.

Anastasia rushes back. "Sorry, I had to take that call. Is everything okay?"

With a hard smile, my eyes fall upon hers with contempt. Did she know how much I'd suffered being apart from Jessa so she could do the right thing when all along, Anastasia was also a part of this tangled web?

"I'm heading up to my suite," I tell her, gritting my teeth, then shift my eyes toward her phone. "I'm sure somebody needs your attention."

She tilts her head in confusion, then glances at the screen. Her eyes widen as she shakes her head. "It's not what you think."

"I don't think anything. I'm leaving now."

Inside my suite, I sink into the lounge and close my eyes. The exhaustion begins to weigh heavily on my shoulders caused by the sleepless nights and the worry over Jessa's safety. After her admission about him almost forcing himself on her, I can't help stressing if he would try again.

*I would kill him.*

With my fucking bare hands.

The phone rings, only to startle me as I see her name appear.

"Jessa?" I'm barely able to breathe. "Are you okay?"

She falls into a digestive silence, but then she breathes heavily.

"Yes, no. I don't know."

"This isn't your fault," I remind her firmly. "You had no idea this would happen."

"I know, but I yelled at her in front of everyone. She wanted to take my son away," Jessa's voice begins to crack. "I was so angry."

My eyes close for a brief moment, trying to understand how it all came to this, but no answer comes to mind. My head is clouded and full of irrational thoughts.

"You had every right to be angry. Do not apologize for protecting your son."

"Andy?" Jessa calls softly. "He knows about us."

The bombshell comes as a surprise, and so many questions come to mind. But I can hear the tremble in her voice, knowing she's overwhelmed and the last thing she needs from me is an interrogation.

"I guess it was eventually going to come out. You knew we couldn't hide forever."

"I know. Look, it's late, and today has left me drained," she resigns, to then take a deep breath even I can hear over the speaker. "Andy, I need you to be patient with us. Right now, I need to be here with Benedict. Not as his wife, but as his son's mother."

Once again, my patience is tested. I know it's right for her to do this. It doesn't mean it hurts any less.

"Okay," I mumble.

"Andy, I love you. Please don't ever forget that."

I swallow the lump inside my throat, willing my emotions to calm the fuck down because nothing will change our circumstances right now. It was never going to be easy between us, despite our history. We were family first, then became best friends. I owe her the best of me, the man who stood by her side when things got tough.

It's too late to walk away and to lose patience is to lose the battle.

Just like Dad once told me, letting go for now doesn't mean it's forever. Sometimes you need to save yourself first because love can test us in unimaginable ways. It can bring out the worst in us, but it can also bring out the best in us.

All I know is that I love her, and if forever is it for us, I need to learn to step back when the time calls for it.

And that time is right now.

# TWENTY-FIVE

## JESSA

Two weeks after Rosemarie's heart attack, she passed away in the hospital.

It didn't come as a surprise since she refused all treatment, wishing to be left alone to die in peace. Even in her hospital bed, she brought in lawyers to make sure her will was just the way she wanted it, not a single cent spared for anyone she didn't care for in the slightest.

She planned her own funeral, down to the music and clothes she was to be buried in. Everything was organized, including her final resting place, next to Benedict's father, who passed away when Benedict was only ten years old from a stroke.

Dad, Kate, Mom, and Jack virtually attended the funeral since Rosemarie only wanted her family and acquaintances inside the small chapel.

Benedict and his brothers took it as well as you would expect. They rose to the occasion, spoke at the chapel with the appropriate words though without the usual sentiment from a child. Then, when she was laid to rest, they paid their respects and said goodbye.

Not once did I see Benedict shed a tear, even though I stood by him the entire day as support.

Rosemarie consumed our thoughts, which left us no time to discuss our marriage moving forward. There was never a right time to raise the topic, but as we sit inside the bedroom after attending the funeral, I need to say something for my own sanity.

Benedict removes his black suit jacket, hanging it up in the closet. We'd slept in separate beds since Bentley's birthday party, and kindly, Benedict allowed me to sleep in our bed while he took the guest room.

"There's no right time to bring this up," I begin with, toying with the black dress's cuffs. "I was thinking of staying at Dad and Kate's flat in London."

I wait for his response, but with his head bowed, I'm unable to see his facial expression.

"For how long?"

"Indefinitely," I respond with a croak in my voice. "Benedict, I know you just lost your mother, but we can't continue to pretend everything is fine between us."

"I know," he resigns, stilling his movements, but then he begins to unlace his shoes. When he's removed them, he takes them to his side of the wardrobe, then returns to the room. "I want to see my son."

"Of course, I'd never take him away. I think London is the perfect compromise. I also thought it might help for me to stay there so I can look for work."

"You don't need to look for work," he informs me with a stern voice. "You're Bentley's mother. I'll take care of you."

I bite my tongue, wanting to educate him on my capabilities of taking care of myself and where he can shove his goddamn money, but instead, I take a deep breath to calm my elevated pulse.

"I need to work, for me," is all I tell him.

"If you insist. What about Bentley when you need to work?"

"I was thinking of looking for freelance work so I can work around Bentley, plus maybe enroll him in daycare once or twice a week so he can make friends and learn to play with other kids."

"Daycare? We have a wonderful nanny."

"We do, but Bentley needs to be with other children. One or two days will be good for his development."

Benedict rubs his face, and I know I shouldn't push him further, but I continue the conversation since we're already on the topic.

"Maybe, when things settle, we can work out a custody arrangement." I choose my words carefully, aware this is like walking into a minefield. "I don't want a fight, Benedict. Not when it comes to our son. You can be angry at me, but Bentley deserves to have us both in his life. He shouldn't have to miss out on anything because we're no longer married."

"I don't want a fight either, Jessa. I'm tired, but how do you expect me to react when you've been having an affair behind my back?" He raises his voice, prompting another argument between us. "This is humiliating."

Averting my eyes to the bed, I dip my chin while trying to process his question. This is so much more than just Andy. Our marriage wasn't built with equality from the beginning. The expectations placed upon me didn't align with my own beliefs. Rosemarie allowed me to marry into this family, thinking I'd follow my husband's lead with no questions asked.

But in the end, it didn't work, my resentment grew, and once the seed was planted, there was no stopping the spread of its roots.

"It was never supposed to happen that way."

"But let me guess?" he questions, pinning his gaze on me. "You're in love with him?"

"Benedict," I mumble. "It's been a long day. Let's both get some rest, and we can talk tomorrow."

After Benedict leaves the room, I climb into bed and turn the light off. Twisting onto my side, I stare out the window to a full moon. Funerals are exhausting, from the planning to the unfamiliar emotions which come out when you least expect it. I should be tired, but my eyes refuse to close, needing so much to connect with Andy. It's been close to a month since I saw him last, and each day is becoming harder.

I grab my phone off the nightstand to send him a text.

ME

Are you awake?

The screen remains blank until finally, I see the bubble appear.

ANDY

Always.

ME

The funeral was held today. It was weird. I'm sad, but I despised her.

ANDY

I guess it's still the loss of someone. I'm sure there is some good in her.

I quickly dial his number, not even stopping to breathe.

"Are we doing this again? You calling me mid-text?"

"There was no good in her," I tell him, eager to get it off my chest. "On my wedding day, I heard her say, she'll have to do for now."

"Mothers can be overprotective of their sons."

"When Bentley was born, she asked the doctor if it was

possible to take some sort of medication or treatment to get rid of his small curls."

Andy clears his throat. "I'm not sure what to say to that."

"Exactly."

"Jessa, what's really bothering you about this?"

"I just miss you, that's all," I whisper.

"Look, I need to get some sleep. Try to get some sleep."

Andy hangs up the phone, without an 'I miss you too' or an 'I love you.' The missing sentiment begins to play on my mind. What if he's fallen out of love with me because I asked him for space. Worst yet, what if he's found someone else?

The vicious thoughts swirl around like a hurricane threatening landfall.

But then, I remember he's my best friend.

If I asked for space, and he respected my request, I need to trust him and not get caught up in my own insecurities.

But for now, sleep is imminent, and tomorrow is a new day.

---

A week later, I officially moved my things out of the house. Benedict is away for work, but I make sure to inform him rather than him come home to my wardrobe being empty. He doesn't say much because there's nothing left to say. After the funeral, he buried himself into work, never spending time at home or with Bentley.

He's constantly on his phone, taking calls or messages in private. But it's no longer my place to question him, though I suspected he'd gone back to his bachelor ways since he wore only his best suits.

My suspicions were confirmed when he left his phone in the closet while showering, and I happened to walk past when a message went off.

It was a normal instinct to glance at the screen until the name *Anastasia* caught my attention. I didn't know the pin number to unlock his phone so could only read what was on the screen.

ANASTASIA

> You know I'm a bad girl. Just like our first night when you fucked me while your wife was away.

I was shocked, speechless, but not in the way of a wife hurting because her husband was cheating. The night they first met was at our dinner. I didn't even know they'd exchanged numbers. This must have happened when I was in LA. Yet it didn't make sense. What excuse did Andy give to Anastasia of his absence? Surely, if she knew he was in LA, she would have said something to Benedict. Unless, Andy lied which is not out of the question.

But even with this revelation, there was no point questioning Benedict. He's not so innocent, and the truth is, he probably strayed before. The constant business trips and late nights added up. Our sex life dwindled, which I thought was because of my post-partum body.

Our marriage was a convenience for him. After all, according to Rosemarie, Benedict being single at thirty was a big disappointment to their family. It only really sinks in now just how arranged our marriage was for him.

I only wish Benedict stopped thinking about his dick and his newly found freedom to fuck around, to spend more time with Bentley, especially after voicing his desire to be more of a father. When I spoke to Mom, she suggested he may be grieving, and men do stupid things when they're not thinking straight.

Nevertheless, Dad and Kate were more than happy for me to stay at the flat. Dad is worried it's not big enough for

Bentley, offering to buy a bigger place. I tell him to calm the hell down. This is temporary until we figure out how it will all work out.

My boxes are strewn all over the living room, and I'll need to unpack at some point. They keep Bentley entertained as he plays around them with his toy truck, enough, so I can check my email.

A few days ago, I decided to email my resume to some of London's smaller newspapers and presses. I didn't expect a response so quickly, but I received an email from a company that promotes lifestyle products for women. They're pretty well-known with a vast following. If I got the job, I'd be writing articles for the working mom's sectors. Ironic since I haven't started working yet, so it feels out of my element.

The interview will be held via video stream because the CEO is currently in Singapore. I made sure to organize the time for when Bentley takes his afternoon nap, not wanting to call Eliza into the city to take care of him for only one hour.

Everything is going according to plan, despite my nerves. But I try to calm myself down when the video connects, and Brooke introduces herself. She's nice enough and down to earth, considering the position she holds.

She asks routine questions about my previous work, my studies back home, all of which I answer professionally. We converse well and have similar interests, laughing at the same things we both find humorous. By the end of the interview, she offers me the job.

I'm gobsmacked, not sure how to react since interviews rarely result in being offered a job on the spot. Brooke goes over the details, then advises me she'll get contracts sent over. By the end of the call, I've thanked her repeatedly.

Bentley continues to sleep, so I use the opportunity to call my dad. Within the first few rings, he answers the call.

"Hey, Dad!"

"And a hello to you too. Why so chirpy?"

"I have some good news. I got a job!"

"Jessa," Dad says with a smile in his voice. "I'm so proud of you, sweetheart. Tell me exactly what you'll be doing?"

I begin to tell him the ins and outs, plus how I'll manage with Bentley on my own. Of course, Dad worries, offering to fly over if needed to help, but I know he has his own work to do.

"I promise, if I need help, I'll ask. Okay?"

"I know, I know. I was thinking, though, why don't I fly over with Kate when you start. So that you can concentrate and not worry about Bentley. It's only a week, Jessa. Plus, your dear old father misses you."

"Old?" I snort, then laugh. "Ava sent me a link to some video online in which you and Uncle Lex feature as, let's just say, eye candy."

Dad laughs. "Oh, that video."

"You know there's a video?"

"Apparently, it went viral. Some BookToker created it."

"Okay, stop," I tell him. "How do you know what a Book-Toker is?"

"Eric." He sighs.

"Of course," I mumble, only to hear Bentley's babble coming from the room. "I need to go, Dad. Bentley just woke up."

"So, it's fine for me and Kate to come? No extra visitors I should consider possibly staying with you?"

My lips curve upward into a smile. "No, Dad. I've got to fix my mistakes, one at a time."

---

Quickly, I push Bentley's stroller through the revolving door until we're in the hotel lobby. The warm air is comforting, a far cry from the wintery cold outside. They predict snow in the next few days, something I actually enjoy since we don't have any in LA.

A lady stares at me rudely, looking down her nose at me like I'm not good enough to be here. She walks my way, advising me the hotel is closed and only staff are allowed on site. Considering my dad and Lex own the hotel, I wonder at what point I can tell her to go fuck herself.

"I'm here to see, Andy. Can you please tell me where he is?"

Dad informed me last night Andy had returned to London to finish some work. Conveniently, he slipped it out at the very end of our conversation before claiming he needed to answer another call.

"I'm sorry, staff only, and no children allowed."

"Oh," I mouth, then pull out my phone, pretending to play dumb. "Would you wait just one moment, please?"

I hit redial on Dad's number until he picks up.

"Is everything okay, Jessa?"

"Hey, Dad. So, I'm just standing inside your gorgeous hotel with your grandson, but one of your staff won't let me stay because I'm not staff. Oh, and children aren't allowed."

My mouth turns up into a fake smile, watching the woman's face turn bright red.

"Jessa, please put that person on the phone now."

I cover the speaker to whisper, "My father would like to speak to you. I'm sure you know who Noah Mason is?"

She closes her eyes to take a deep breath, but then I uncover the speaker to talk again.

"You know what, Dad? I think this was all a mistake. I'll call you later. Love you."

"Love you too, sweetheart."

The call ends as I glance at her once again. "So, let's start again. Where can I find Andy?"

She points to the room on the left, which appears to be some sort of function room. Without even saying thank you, I push Bentley over until I see all the white lights and cameras set up. The room has been transformed into a wedding reception.

My neck tips back as I glance in awe at the beautiful tables all decorated in white with a small amount of gold as a feature to the fairy lights strewn across the ceiling. There's organza hanging from the large arched windows, but the showstopper is the six-tiered wedding cake placed on a table in the middle of the wooden dance floor.

I take in all the beauty, the romantic scene of it all, but then, my gaze falls upon the man behind the camera.

Just the sight of him causes my lips to part. My chest tightens, heart pumping at a quick and erratic pace, knowing when he turns around, I won't be able to piece together the words I so desperately need to say.

"An-dee." Bentley points, then tries to wiggle out of the stroller.

I see Andy's posture stiffen. Then he turns around at a slow and agonizing pace, dressed in his jeans and a dark green hoody. I remember the hoody from years ago, often stealing it without his permission to only find out he'd sneaked it out of my wardrobe and back into his.

"An-dee!"

Andy's eyes fall upon me, the ocean blue orbs spreading warmth all over me as I'm finally home, where I belong. The deep breath I take is expelled slowly, relishing in this moment and never wanting his loving gaze ever to go away.

Bentley reaches out for me, demanding I take him out. I lean down, unbuckle his strap as he wiggles out, and runs straight into Andy's arms.

I watch the two of them hug, admiring how Andy's face lights up in Bentley's presence. Unable to hide my smile,

Andy tickles Bentley, who begins to giggle, showing his four teeth.

"What are you doing here?" Andy asks, standing up but taking Bentley in his arms.

"I came to give you something." I move closer to him while reaching into my bag to remove my journal.

Upon pulling it out, Andy's eyes wander to my bare hand. The ring that sat on my finger, symbolizing my commitment to another man is no longer there.

I extend my journal out to him, though staring at it with thought.

"This is your journal," Andy murmurs, his eyes still fixated on me.

With a nod, I move it closer to him. "I want you to read it, please."

"You want me to read your journal?"

"It's not so much a journal, but a story I needed to tell."

Andy cautiously takes it from me, almost as if I handed him a fragile vase he's scared to break.

"Jessa, you don't have to give this to me."

I shake my head. "I need to, Andy. I'm doing this for me, not just you."

And with those words said, I try to pry Bentley out of Andy's arms. It's harder than I thought, but I tell him we're going to look at the planes.

"You're going?"

"Yes." I smile, kissing Bentley's cheek to smell Andy all over him. The scent is intoxicating, but I need the strength to walk away right now. Not forever, but for as long as Andy needs. "I'm staying at Dad's flat here in the city."

"For the night?" he asks.

"No, indefinitely. Until I sort out what I can afford and where."

Andy touches the base of his neck to cross his arms while trying to process what I just said.

"I... I don't understand?"

"You're smart. I'm sure you can figure it out." I place Bentley in his stroller, handing him a cookie to keep him quiet. "Oh, and I got a job. It's not much, just some freelance work. But, still, it's something."

Andy continues to gaze at me, his head flinching back slightly.

"You did all this? Moved out and got a job?"

I nod, then I move close to him and place my lips on his cheek for a quick kiss.

"You know where to find me," I whisper in his ear, inhaling the smell of his skin as if my life depends on it. "Whenever you're ready, I'll be waiting."

Gently pulling away, he raises his hand to caress my cheek, releasing a sigh.

No more words are said, but they didn't need to be.

I trust my heart just as much as I trust his, and second chances count for everything.

Sometimes, we need them because, in the end, our love will come out stronger and forever will mean just that...

*Forever.*

# TWENTY-SIX

## ANDY

The journal sits on the coffee table in front of me inside my hotel suite.

I stare at it for minutes on end, jumping back and forth as to whether or not I open it to begin reading.

They are Jessa's thoughts.

Thoughts I may *not* want to hear.

The last few weeks tested me in ways I never imagined possible. The mental and physical endurance came with challenges, and, of course, my weaknesses were brought to the surface. To sit back to give the woman I love and want to spend the rest of my life with, time so she can help her husband grieve over the loss of his mother almost drove me to the brink of insanity.

There were times when the days became dark, and all I saw was pitch black. My mind conjured up thoughts in which she's fallen back in love with her husband, wanting to give it a second chance.

And in the pits of those dark moments, his hands wandered all over her naked body. Touching her in ways no one else can but me.

To add fuel to the burning fire, my nightmares persisted.

My father is back again, dying in front of my very eyes. My mother's screams are heard in the background, and my father's dead body is being placed in a corpse bag. It was one sleepless night after another, combined with sleeping pills that did nothing. The only thing able to keep my mind focused and clear was the gym.

The workouts began at three in the morning, sometimes lasting until seven. I ran the streets of Madrid before the city even woke up. I did everything I could to numb the constant pain.

Then, Noah insisted I head to London for another photo-shoot, making temptation harder to resist until she showed up to hand me this journal.

With a bare hand, she was missing her wedding ring.

My hands reach out to run my fingers along the leather-grained cover. The texture is soft, and unknowingly, my lips press together thoughtfully as I imagine Jessa's delicate finger tracing the very same spot.

Slowly, I turn the page with a deep breath to begin reading the words...

*There's always one summer that defines who you are. For some, it's a childhood moment, and for others, the teenage years.*
*For me, it was my first solo trip to Manhattan to see my best friend.*

The memory plays like an old-time movie—Jessa standing at my door wearing the Rolling Stones t-shirt she stole off me with ripped jeans exposing all her legs. I recall the joke I made, asking her what happened to them since it looked like someone was scissor happy, only for her to push me out of the way and head straight to my kitchen for alcohol.

My eyes move back toward the page, continuing to read her words as I find myself getting comfortable on the lounge, like catching up with an old friend as no time has passed.

The hour passed, my emotions taken on a wild ride with twists and turns I never expected. There were times when I laughed at the memories and others where my stomach was ill at the thoughts of her husband.

Night falls across the room, forcing me to turn on the lamp to read the final pages.

*And even though your heart can beat a billion times during the course of your life, if the man you're irrevocably in love with doesn't beat to the same melody, the pain will only lead to one thing.*
*A broken heart.*

The next page is blank, and the story she tells is far from finished. I hold onto the journal, then quickly check the time. It's after eleven, almost midnight.

But I know sleep is impossible.

Not when I need to know how this ends.

---

My knuckles tap on the door as my chest beats like a drum being played in the jungle. The echo is loud, demanding attention in all its glory. All my senses are heightened, desperate to see her on the other side.

The door slowly opens. She tilts her head to the side, then opens the door wide. Even though it's cold outside, Jessa's wearing a tank and shorts with bed socks. The robe sitting on top is completely open, with her hair falling past her shoulders.

Our gaze meets like a magnetic force, futile to resist any longer.

I step forward, cupping her face in my hands to bring her lips onto mine. Her mouth is soft, the taste of her lips sending a frenzy within me. Our tongues battle feverishly as if this is our first kiss but not our last.

"Andy." Jessa pulls away, out of breath, but our lips are still grazing against each other. "Are you sure?"

"Never been so sure of anything in my life."

My hands lift her thighs as she wraps her legs around my waist. We kiss all the way to the bedroom, which she directs me to since I've never been here.

With ease, I lay her on the bed, climbing on top of her like an animal who has just cornered its prey. Thirsty, eager, and desperate to taste every last inch like it's my last meal on earth.

We lose ourselves in heated kisses before I slide her tank over her head, exposing her tits.

"Do you know how beautiful you are?" I whisper, running my tongue around her nipple as she arches back. The tip of my tongue teases her relentlessly while she begs me to enter her.

"Please," she pleads while panting. "I need you now."

I want to savor this moment, a moment that's no longer forbidden. There isn't a wedding ring on her finger judging us for our wrongful actions anymore. Nothing to remind me she's legally bound to another man.

In my eyes, Jessa is completely mine.

So, I'm going to take her nice and fucking slow.

"Patience," I murmur, gliding my hand between her thighs, bathing in the pool of wet smothering her tight pussy. "Be a good girl, and you'll get what you want."

My fingers enter her slowly, a teasing finger-fuck that has

her on edge. I'm struggling not to blow either, watching her crumble at my touch to only pull out my fingers just in time.

I bring my fingers to her lips, insisting she taste herself, which turns me on like fucking crazy.

"Good girl," I tell her. "Now you can get your wish."

Carefully, I angle myself to taunt her entrance with the tip of my cock, but she moves on purpose, forcing me in.

"Someone is a little impatient," I whisper in her ear. "I think you're ready."

Jessa nods, then smashes her lips onto mine as we move together, our bodies in complete sync. Beneath me, her body tenses until she arches her back again, exposing her chest to finish while I come simultaneously.

The dimly lit room suddenly bursts bright. The euphoria consumes my entire body as we try to calm ourselves down, slowly working on our heavy pants.

I fall onto my back, swallowing with a dry throat. Jessa rests her head against my chest, running her fingers down my torso and trailing my abs.

"You don't know how much I've waited for this moment," she says faintly. "It's been hard without you."

"I'm here."

"To stay?"

"For as long as you'll have me," I answer with a grin.

"Forever?"

I turn to my side, then climb back on top of her. Without even asking, I enter her again, still hard. As our eyes meet, and the woman I love is finally mine, I kiss her lips gently.

"Forever."

———

"I can get used to this," Jessa moans as I spread kisses all over her beautiful tits.

I enter her slowly, knowing Bentley can wake up at any time since it's morning. We fell asleep only a few hours ago because of my greed to have her in every possible way.

We move together, out of breath, until she warns me she can't hold off any longer, and I feel her contract all over me. I'm fast behind the moment she comes, blowing inside her and expelling a grunt.

The morning is upon us, but it didn't stop me from waking her up so selfishly. I kiss the top of her shoulder as she pushes back into my embrace.

"Bentley will wake up soon, and our blissful silence will be over until naptime."

"How many hours do I have to wait until naptime?"

"A lot." She laughs, digging her elbow into me. "You're greedy."

"I haven't touched you in two months. I have a lot to catch up on."

"But this is nice, too," Jessa murmurs, inside my embrace.

I let out a sigh, staring at the window, trying to piece together the dream I had last night of my father. This time, there was no screaming or body bag. My father appeared almost angelic with his bright blond hair and deep blue eyes. His skin wasn't pale or sickly, and Uncle Lex was dressed in some jersey as the two of them laughed. My mom joined them as the three of them just sat on the beach staring into the horizon.

It was peaceful and content, then my father waves with a smile on his face before walking away.

Unlike all my other dreams, I woke up without the usual heaviness inside my chest, feeling rested and rejuvenated. I'll never truly understand the reason behind them but won't dismiss the connection to my waking life.

I'm finally able to spend the rest of my life with the woman I've always loved, and with this comes contentment.

So, perhaps, my father only wanted me to find my own destiny even though people would think it's crazy. Luckily, I don't give a fuck what anyone else thinks besides the woman inside my arms.

And his lesson in all of this is life is too short. At any moment, it can all be taken away. So, while we have the gift of life, we must live it with the ones we love and make memories to last a lifetime.

"Are you okay?" Jessa asks with a relaxed voice.

My lips fall upon her shoulder to place a soft kiss. "Perfect."

She turns around only for Bentley to call out 'Mama.'

We both put our clothes on, then Jessa brings Bentley into the room. The kid is excited to see me, calling out my name and demanding I hold him. We sit in bed as Bentley sits between us until he gets restless and needs breakfast.

"So, I was thinking," Jessa begins while slicing up some toast for Bentley. "I know I showed you my journal, but there's something else I need to do."

"Like what?"

"We'll need to get dressed in very warm clothes."

"I'm not liking this already," I warn her.

"Just get dressed. We're heading out."

We take turns showering while taking care of Bentley, then leave the apartment dressed in our winter gear as Jessa leads us to the park across the street. There are only a few people around, mainly joggers on their morning run.

I see her take a deep breath. Then she suggests we walk to the lake. The suggestion is out of character, given her fear of lake animals, and there's one black swan lurking in the water already.

"I need to conquer my fears," she states.

"Oh, c'mon, Jessa. We all have fears, don't do it."

"Why?"

"Because you'll freak out, and I'll have to deal with you all night when all I want to do is be inside you."

She folds her arms beneath her chest, tilting her head to the side while raising her brows. "So, you don't want me to face my fears of swans so you can fuck me like crazy tonight?"

"Exactly."

"What if I face my fear, and it's the most thrilling experience, and tonight, when we're alone, the adrenaline runs through me, and all I want to do are dirty things to you. Things you never imagined possible."

I release a huff, then purse my lips. "Fine. Go hang out with the swan."

"I wasn't going to hang out with it." She rolls her eyes with a sigh. "Just hover near it with caution."

Jessa takes a deep breath as I push Bentley along. We move toward the lake, where the swan swims gracefully while minding its own business.

"Bird-ee," Bentley calls.

I bend down to his level. "It's a swan, Bentley, and Mama is trying to prove she's Wonder Woman, but we both know she'll need a Xanax this afternoon."

Jessa turns to me with an annoyed expression. "You're not helping."

"I'm sorry." I grin, then tug on her jacket. "Carry on."

I hear her chant as the swan swims closer. *"You can do this Jessa, just breathe."*

"Are you okay?"

"It's... it's getting closer," she panics. "Wh... why are the eyes red? Oh God, is it from the blood of humans it consumes?"

I grab her hand, holding it tight. "You're going to be okay."

"How do you know?"

I lean over and kiss the top of her head. "Because I'll never leave your side."

The swan moves closer, but Jessa stills her breathing to turn to me with a smile as I take Bentley out of his stroller and carry him in my arms.

"The both of you. It's a package deal, right? Buy one, get the kid free?" I joke.

Jessa stands on her tiptoes to place a kiss on my lips. Her lips are warm despite the cold, but she looks more beautiful than ever.

"This is how the ending goes, Andy."

"Your journal," I breathe.

"You read all my thoughts, fears, and desires," she says with her gaze fixated on me. "You sure you still want us?"

Snow begins to fall from the sky, delicate with its entrance but perfect with its timing.

The beginning of a new season.

"More than anything else in the world," I tell her, then tilt my head to focus on Bentley. "What about you? Are you okay with me being around?"

Bentley touches my cheek with his chubby palm, then places his mouth on my nose to kiss it with his mouth entirely open.

"And-ee..." he says again. "Dada And-ee."

And in the eyes of a toddler, my entire life changed.

An instant family, a son, and a new destiny.

All because of Jessa.

My best friend, always and forever.

# EPILOGUE

## JESSA

"We're going to be late," I say as Andy buries his head into my neck. "Didn't you say dinner reservations were at six?"

"Seven," he states.

"You said six."

"Sometimes I say things, so you'll be ready on time."

I smack his chest. "So, are you saying we have some spare time?"

My hands wander to his pants to undo his belt. At the same time, Bentley lets out a cry. Letting out a huff, I shake my head. "This kid is a cockblocker."

"He ain't so bad," Andy says with a grin, disappearing to Bentley's room and bringing him out moments later. "Where's Mama, Bentley?"

Bentley points to me but doesn't reach out because it's all about Andy. With his pacifier in his mouth, he rests his head on Andy, still tired from his nap. I grab Bentley's bag, packing his things for his weekend stay with Benedict.

Since Rosemarie's death and our separation, things changed with Benedict. While our marriage was beyond repairable, we were able to come to an agreement regarding custody of Bentley. He wanted to continue seeing his son regularly, so after I moved out of the house, Andy and I lived in Dad and Kate's flat while looking for something more permanent.

I counted my blessings, though I never took for granted Benedict's patience with Andy being in Bentley's life permanently. Co-parenting can go two ways, but thankfully, I'd learned a lot from my own experiences with Dad, Mom, and Kate. I didn't push Benedict to spend time with Andy but encouraged him to be open-minded about giving our son the best possible childhood, which involves all of us being amicable.

As much as I wanted to move back home, Bentley's best interest was to stay close to Benedict. On alternate weeks, Bentley stayed with Benedict with the help of Eliza. While my suspicions at the time were only preliminary, her request to move in permanently made no sense since Bentley wasn't always around. However, it wasn't my place to get involved in my ex-husband's personal life.

But the good news came when Benedict informed me of his desire to move to Manhattan. It'd been a long-time dream of his to expand his family's company, and with Rosemarie gone, he finally decided the time was right. His mother detested anything American, including me, of course.

Even though Manhattan wasn't home or where our family lived, it's closer than London. So, the move began. Andy still had his apartment, though it was too small for the three of us. The bachelor pad was exactly that—a pad for one person and the occasional overnight visitor.

Once again, it all worked out. Nash sublet the apartment from Andy, and I sold my apartment on the East Coast. We purchased a brownstone in Tribeca, a compromise to a somewhat bigger home with a small yard for Bentley to play in.

"Bags are packed. I don't think I've forgotten anything," I say out loud, rubbing my chin.

"Will you relax?" Andy tells me while changing Bentley's diaper. "Benedict has everything."

"You know, you look sexy wearing a suit while changing a diaper," I tell him.

With a smirk playing on his lips, he grabs a banana and hands it to Bentley to eat.

"I'm not telling you where we're going."

"Why?" I stomp my foot, crossing my arms. "You know I hate surprises."

"Some things never change with you."

Heading out the door with Bentley is always a mission—the stroller, his bag, and my own bag. When we finally have everything, we head into a cab to Benedict's penthouse.

Eliza opens the door, welcoming Bentley in her arms. I'm glad out of everyone Benedict could've chosen to have a relationship with, it's Bentley's nanny.

"There's my boy," Benedict smiles while taking Bentley from Eliza. Something passes between them until Benedict grabs an envelope from the table and hands it to me.

"What's this?"

"Our divorce papers. Official as of today."

My first reaction is to laugh, relieved this is all over. But not wanting to hurt Benedict's feelings, I try my best to hide my smile.

"It's okay." Benedict grins. "You can be happy."

I turn to look at Andy standing behind me with a smirk on his lips.

"I, uh, I'm not sure how you're supposed to react appropriately in these situations."

Benedict chuckles softly. "Have a drink tonight to celebrate."

I smile back at him and Eliza. "You too."

After leaving Benedict's, we sit in the cab as I reflect quietly.

"Are you okay?" Andy asks, placing his hand on mine.

"I'm relieved, but I guess I haven't thought about it. We've just been so busy, and it feels like a lifetime ago I was married to Benedict."

"Time is moving fast," Andy concurs. "But hopefully, you can relax and enjoy dinner tonight."

The surprise comes at the restaurant, with all my cousins and their husbands in attendance. Apparently, the kids are being babysat by their parents here in Manhattan tonight.

My brother, Nash, and sister, Sienna, and Andy's sisters are also here .

While things were tense between Luna and us, we managed to reconcile once Andy and I made our relationship official. As much as her actions did hurt Andy, she apologized profusely, and we forgave her in a heartbeat. No matter what troubles we may encounter at times, family is still family.

"Bitches, I'm back!"

Eric enters wearing an extravagant green suit. Far from me to say he looks like a Christmas tree, a very expensive one at that since he just mouthed the brand *Versace* at Ava.

"Eric." Millie scowls. "You look like a Christmas tree."

"Thank you," I agree. "But a pretty tree like the one at Rockefeller Center."

Eric kisses both my cheeks. "Thank you, darling. Now, enough about how beautiful I look, and let's celebrate you!"

It's been one week since my book was officially published and hit the top ten in the charts as a debut author—a book that my journal inspired.

I've been blown away by the response, especially since the sequel is up for pre-order and set to exceed the results of book one.

"I can't believe my darling, Jessa, the innocent one, is now a full-time romance author."

"The innocent one." Andy snorts as I dig my elbow into him with a grin. "Sure."

Eric purses his lips. "Would you like to elaborate, Mr. Evans-Baker? Are we talking browning the sausage?"

I shake my head with disgust, suddenly losing my appetite.

"That's just... too far, Eric," Will complains.

Eric winces. "Swedish bike ride?"

Austin bites down, trying not to laugh. "That's a new way to describe it."

"How about up the chocolate highway?"

Ava places her spoon down. "And we're done with chocolate mousse."

Letting out a huff, Austin rubs her back with a chuckle. It was only a few months ago we saw them when we flew to LA after the birth of their second daughter, River.

As for Will and Millie, they welcomed another son just before Austin and Ava. Another boy named Axel. Both my cousins have been very vocal about these babies being the last, which I don't blame them. Bentley is a handful, and he's only one child.

My cousin, Addy, is sitting across from me, but she's been awfully quiet. Just when I'm about to say something, I notice a stolen glance across the table to Masen Cooper, Andy's male best friend since they were kids.

The memories I have of Masen aren't exactly pleasant. He was always trying to cause mischief when we were kids, pushing the boundaries to get us into trouble. When we were teenagers, he was the first one to sneak alcohol into every party, and boy did he like his women.

With us living back here in the States, Masen comes over to see Andy quite a lot. Though, some things never change.

He's still a womanizer, but according to Andy, he's been quiet lately.

"Okay, listen, everyone." Nash stands up, raising a glass as everyone follows. "A cheer to my talented sister. Even though I'll never read romance, I'm grateful for the smut you put out in the world, which makes women horny and want to fuck guys like me. Cheers!"

We all fall into a fit of laughter, not surprised by Nash's toast. If Rocky were here, he would've cried at that speech. Proud one of us is carrying his legacy.

As the night goes on, we laugh, drink, enjoy each other's company before parting ways. Not for long, though, since we decided to fly to LA next week to spend time with our parents. Bentley loves his cousins, plus they spoil him for attention.

"There's one more stop I want to make before home," Andy says just outside the restaurant.

"Ice cream?"

"You just ate some," he reminds me.

"So, I can go again?"

As we walk along the street, Andy holds my hand amongst the crowds walking.

"Did you think Addy was acting weird tonight?" I ask, the thought only coming to mind as we cross the street.

"She's a psych major. They're a different species."

"That's a mean thing to say about our cousin," I scold him.

"It's not mean. Psychologists seek to understand emotions. Their technique is to observe behavior. Addy isn't like Millie and Ava."

"Is something going on between her and Masen?" I blurt out.

Andy stops mid-step. "Are you kidding? No way. Her best friend is Cruz, Masen's younger brother. Can you seriously imagine how messy of a love triangle that would be?"

I nod, knowing just how fucked up and messy that would be, which makes it all the more forbidden and just confirms what I saw tonight.

*Something is definitely going on.*

"You're right. I'm crazy," I brush it off.

"Okay, we're here." Andy stops outside of an unfamiliar building. "I'm going to cover your eyes for your surprise."

"Really?" I laugh.

"Yes, really," he replies with sarcasm. "Come here."

We enter the building as I stand with Andy's hands covering my eyes. Impatiently, I wait with bated breath.

"Are you ready?" Andy whispers behind me.

He removes his hands as I open my eyes. The building is an art gallery which looks familiar. Then it comes to me, this is where Andy's first portfolio was showcased. The walls are covered with pictures of me, reflecting from a projector.

I gaze in awe at all the photographs, some from when I was young and others from when I was in my teens. Many of the photos were taken when Andy begged me to be his guinea pig when he first received an expensive camera.

I'm mesmerized by all the photos, which onsets nostalgia as the memories of my childhood bring happiness and fill my heart with joy. I only hope Bentley will have a life as wonderful as mine.

As I turn around to express my gratitude, Andy is kneeling on one knee with a box in his hand.

"Andy," I croak as my chest rises and falls at the sight of him gazing at me lovingly. "What are you doing?"

"I'm asking my best friend to marry me."

I move toward him and fall to my knees with tears streaming down my cheeks. My hands move to his face, bringing his lips closer so I can kiss them.

Slowly, I pull away as he grins. "I have a whole speech ready."

My hands wrap around his neck. "Yes! A thousand times over, yes!"

"Are you sure? I've got this whole anecdote which I'm certain you'll enjoy."

Laughter escapes me, unable to hide just how happy he makes me.

"The trouble with me is that I'm the most impatient woman you've ever met."

Andy brushes his lips against mine. "I better get this ring on your finger then, huh?"

I stick out my hand with a squeal. "I'm ready to become Mrs. Evans-Baker."

Carefully, Andy removes the beautiful canary diamond ring and slides it on my finger. He presses his lips against the ring, kissing my finger as I stare in awe at the most exquisite piece of jewelry I've ever seen.

I throw my hands back around Andy's neck while grinning. "We need to celebrate tonight."

"Swedish bike ride?" he teases.

My head shakes as laughter escapes me. "Your wish is my command, baby."

COMING UP NEXT...

**The Trouble With Fate: A Best Friends Brother
Romance
The Forbidden Love Series Book 5**

I am nothing like my sisters.
The Edwards' daughters have a reputation for falling in love
under forbidden circumstances.
Not me, though.
I'm the calm, collected one and Daddy's new favorite since I
cause the least trouble.

This is all thanks to my long-time best friend, Cruz Cooper.
He's every bit the crazy person I'm not and keeps me
grounded with college despite his wild ways. We have all
these plans to live off-campus, then start our careers without
wasting our best years caught up in toxic relationships.

Until the night we had dinner with his parents.
And his older brother walked in... Masen Cooper.

He looked nothing like I remembered. Tall, muscular—sexy in ways I prefer not to think about. Yet five minutes spent with him, and he is clearly still the arrogant jerk who would taunt me as a kid.

Now, he has his eyes on me once again.
But this time, he wants to play a different type of game.
One which will force me to choose between two *brothers*...

ALSO BY KAT T. MASEN

**The Dark Love Series**

Featuring Lex & Charlie

Chasing Love: A Billionaire Love Triangle

Chasing Us: A Second Chance Love Triangle

Chasing Her: A Stalker Romance

Chasing Him: A Forbidden Second Chance Romance

Chasing Fate: An Enemies-to-Lovers Romance

Chasing Heartbreak: A Friends-to-Lovers Romance

Lex: A Companion Novella

Charlotte: A Companion Novella

**The Forbidden Love Series**

(The Dark Love Series Second Generation)

Featuring Amelia Edwards

The Trouble With Love: An Age Gap Romance

The Trouble With Us: A Second Chance Love Triangle

The Trouble With Him: A Secret Pregnancy Romance

The Trouble With Her: A Friends-to-Lovers Romance

The Trouble With Fate: An Enemies-to-Lovers Romance

**The Secret Love Series**

(The Dark Love Series Second Generation)

Featuring Alexandra Edwards

Craving Love: An Age Gap Romance

Craving Us: A Second Chance Romance

Craving Her: A Friends-to-Lovers Romance

## Also by Kat T. Masen

The Pucking Arrangement: A Stepbrother Romance

The Office Rival: An Enemies-to-Lovers Romance

The Marriage Rival: An Office Romance

Bad Boy Player: A Brother's Best Friend Romance

Roomie Wars Box Set (Books 1 to 3): Friends-to-Lovers Series

# ABOUT THE AUTHOR

**Kat T. Masen** is a USA Today Bestselling Author from Sydney, Australia. Her passion is writing angsty love triangles involving forbidden men like besties older brother.

She is also the founder of the Books Ever After store, Books By The Bridge Author Events, and spends way too much time on Tik Tok creating videos for her #1 Amazon bestseller Chasing Love.

Oh ... and she's a total boy mom.
1 husband, 4 boys, and a needy pug.

Purchase signed paperbacks & bookish merchandise.
Visit: **www.kattmasen.com**

Made in the USA
Monee, IL
12 November 2023

46359125R00178